"The Twisted Mind"

"The Twisted Mind"

Madness in Herman Melville's Fiction

BY PAUL MCCARTHY

University of Iowa Press   Iowa City

University of Iowa Press, Iowa City 52242

Copyright © 1990 by the University of Iowa

All rights reserved

Printed in the United States of America

First edition, 1990

Design by Richard Hendel

Printed on acid-free paper

Several passages of Chapters 2 and 4 appeared in an essay in *Studies
in the Novel* 16 (1984), and part of Chapter 5 appeared in an essay in
Colby Library Quarterly 23 (1987).

Library of Congress Cataloging-in-Publication Data

McCarthy, Paul, 1921–

"The twisted mind": madness in Herman Melville's fiction/by Paul
McCarthy.—1st ed.

p. cm.

Includes bibliographical references.

ISBN 0-87745-284-9 (alk. paper)

1. Melville, Herman, 1819–1891—Characters—Mentally ill.
2. Melville, Herman, 1819–1891—Knowledge—
Psychology. 3. Mental
illness in literature. 4. Mentally ill in literature. I. Title.

PS2388.M45M38 1990   90-10754

813'.3—dc20   CIP

To Phyllis

CONTENTS

Acknowledgments   ix

Introduction   xi

Chapter One. Family and Sea Experiences   1

Chapter Two. Scientific Background   11

Chapter Three. Beginnings: *Typee*, *Omoo*, and *Mardi*   17

Chapter Four. Insane Figures in *Redburn* and *White-Jacket*   32

Chapter Five. The World Is Mad: *Moby-Dick*   50

Chapter Six. The Mad Family: *Pierre*   74

Chapter Seven. City and Sea Madness: Stories   94

Chapter Eight. Insanity out West: *The Confidence-Man*   109

Chapter Nine. "Who . . . can draw the line?": *Billy Budd, Sailor*   122

Conclusion   136

Notes   143

Bibliography   157

Index   167

ACKNOWLEDGMENTS

In writing this book, I have been constantly aware of my indebtedness to Leon Howard and Jay Leyda, whose works on Melville have provided guiding ideas and valuable material. I did much of my research in Howard's *Herman Melville: A Biography* and Leyda's monumental *The Melville Log: A Documentary Life of Herman Melville 1819–1891*. I am indebted also to works by Henry Nash Smith, Harrison Hayford, Merton M. Sealts, Jr., and many others as well. This book has benefited also from the advice and encouragement of several scholars who were kind enough to read the manuscript and offer suggestions. I wish to thank Allan Emery and T. Walter Herbert, Jr., who pointed out glaring faults in the first draft, and my friend and colleague Kenneth G. Johnston, who provided welcome insights in his reading of a late draft. William B. Dillingham, whom I have never met, graciously read the first and last drafts, pointed out weaknesses in both, and offered encouragement and suggestions at other stages. Readers for the University of Iowa Press have made many useful recommendations for improving the manuscript, the shortcomings of which reflect my own.

I wish to thank also various individuals at Kansas State University for their interest and assistance: William L. Stamey, former dean of the College of Arts and Sciences, and Henry J. Donaghy, former Head of the English Department, for a sabbatical leave during which I wrote the first draft; Robert F. Kruh, former dean of the Graduate College and the Bureau of General Research, for travel grants; and the librarians in Farrell Library, particularly Katherine Coleman and Cynthia Logan of the interlibrary loan department, for much-needed assistance in obtaining copies of rare mid-nineteenth-century works. I am grateful also for the assistance of librarians in the New York Public Library, Houghton and Widener libraries at Harvard, New-York Historical Society, National Archives, Massachusetts Historical Society, Municipal Archives, New York City, Library, New York Academy of Medicine, Berkshire Anthenaeum, Pennsylvania State Archives, Princeton University Library, Albany Public Library, Medical Archives, the New York

Hospital, Galena Public Library, and Lansingburgh Historical Society.

My biggest debt is to my wife, Phyllis, who patiently listened to my frequent comments on this project, readily and skillfully typed and re-typed countless pages and drafts, including the final one, and still managed to keep me and our children in reasonably good spirits.

INTRODUCTION

Writing to the editor of the *Literary World* on 5 April 1849, Herman Melville elaborated on his personal reactions to news that his friend Charles Fenno Hoffman, writer and fellow contributor to the magazine, had become insane: "Poor Hoffman—I remember the shock I had when I first saw the mention of his madness.—But he was just the man to go mad—imaginative, voluptuously inclined, poor, unemployed, in the race of life distancd [*sic*] by his inferiors, unmarried. . . . This going mad of a friend or acquaintance comes straight home to every man who feels his soul in him,—which but few men do. . . . He who has never felt, momentarily, what madness is has but a mouthful of brains."[1] Melville knew what he was writing about. His father and brother, shortly before their deaths, had apparently shown signs of madness. Other relatives had been afflicted as had men he encountered in almost four years as a sailor in the Atlantic and Pacific oceans. The novels written in the 1840s and later contain many characters testifying to Melville's understanding of the nature and forms of insanity. These include Ahab, Pierre, Bartleby, Babo, Claggart, and a host of minor and unidentified figures appearing throughout the novels and in several stories.

Customarily, studies of insanity in Melville's fiction have focused on a few major characters and various literary, biographical, and psychological factors and influences. Ahab and Pierre are often examined in terms of modern depth psychology. Bartleby's paranoid condition and Billy Budd's "hysterical neurosis" are received interpretations based on painstaking, instructive Freudian analyses. Scholars have shown that these and other characters were shaped in part by Melville's readings in English and Continental drama, fiction, and essays. Biographical studies link Melville's family life and experiences with a number of characters, situations, and plot developments. More specialized studies have considered the relationship of Pierre and Mrs. Glendinning or Bartleby's quandary in light of Melville's own psychological development as viewed in modern terms.[2] All such studies are valuable.

This study will not focus on literary influences or on twentieth-century interpretations of Melville and his works but on the effects of personal experiences on his understanding and portrayal of madness or mental abnormality. Although materials and ideas from works by Shakespeare, Carlyle, Milton, Coleridge, and others enriched Melville's understanding, actual experiences during three periods of his life provided the basis for much of what Melville would come to understand about insanity. The main periods are the family years, 1819 to 1840, and the sea years, primarily 1841 to 1844. The greatest impact on Melville occurred during the family years, when his father and a brother succumbed to what appeared to be mental illness and his mother suffered from a nervous condition and periods of depression. The sea years broadened Melville's experiences and no doubt introduced him to people with a variety of mental disturbances. A third period, 1845 to 1856, principally in New York City and Pittsfield, was less formative, for by 1845 Melville was writing fiction, but during these years, friends who had suffered from mental illness or were knowledgeable about it added to his understanding. Other sources of information during these years and later included magazines, newspapers, possibly lectures, and, most important, books like the *Penny Cyclopaedia* that contained technical information on insanity. The writer's first three novels reveal a few of these influences. Beginning with *Redburn* (1849), treatments of insanity become increasingly evident, pragmatic, and straightforward. Insights into abnormal behavior and characters in this novel and later works often disclose scientific soundness and accuracy.

Experiences and attitudes at the time of writing will also be considered because these helped determine Melville's portrayals of insanity. In 1845 and 1846, while writing *Typee* and *Omoo*, Melville lived at home in Lansingburgh or with his brothers in New York City, and things went generally well. Insanity, a secondary matter then, was treated matter of factly. Years later, burdened with family and economic problems and angered by poor reviews of *Moby-Dick*, Melville focused relentlessly on insanity in *Pierre*. In other works, the writer's situation and circumstances would be influential.

A central theme of this study is that a general correspondence exists between Melville's assessments of experience, himself, and insanity, on the one hand, and the stability or instability of each fictional world, on the other. In *Typee* and *Omoo*, relying essentially on personal experiences, Melville created fictional worlds that, despite disorder and violence, are essentially sane. Insanity in *Mardi* takes a bizarre, allegoric turn, but the writer's interests in the pragmatic and rational are evident. Melville created in *Redburn* and *White-Jacket* grim, pragmatic worlds which, despite injustice and oppression, remain sane. Reflecting Melville's troubles and failures, *Moby-Dick* presents a world in which insanity is commonplace and life itself is often mad or irrational. Turning to more personal experiences and perhaps retreating himself, Melville returns to origins in *Pierre*, to the insane family and city. In the universe of *The Confidence-Man* (1857), reflecting Melville's sense of failure and doom, madness and evil are joined. Over twenty years later, an acceptive Melville created in *Billy Budd* a monomaniac evil in Claggart and a temporarily disturbed father figure in Vere.

The first two chapters of this study will clarify Melville's major experiences at home and sea and the nature of his scientific knowledge. The experiences in particular provide the basis for what Leon Howard describes as evident in Melville's work on *Mardi* in 1848: "the maturing of penetrating intelligence and a sharply realistic mind."[3] That maturation, which may have been evident before 1848, becomes a hallmark after that date of the writer's treatment of insanity.

"THE TWISTED MIND"

CHAPTER ONE. FAMILY AND SEA

EXPERIENCES

In New York City in the 1820s, Allan and Maria Melvill had hopes of the good life: a happy family, a fine home with servants and a carriage, a fashionable neighborhood, excellent schools, and other marks of social and financial success. As the parents were upper middle class, intelligent, and well educated, they regarded their goals and hopes as reasonable and therefore attainable. Whether they were or not, the Melvills fell short. Complications appeared. Allan was an importer in a highly competitive business. He worked twelve-hour days in his store on Pearl Street close to the wharves and came home at night to a woman equally dedicated to responsibilities as a wife, mother, and matron. As a new baby was added to the family every two years, Allan had to provide for bigger and better homes and increased expenses for care of the children and for schools and servants. For a while in the 1820s, life for the Melvills went well. But even during good periods there were problems or complications: rivalries among the children, with Gansevoort, the oldest son, as the pride and joy; frequent illnesses; many visits to in-laws; threats of cholera or other diseases in the hot months; and escapes of the family to Boston, except for Allan, who remained behind to work. The Melvills were a close family but not a secure or peaceful one. As Leon

Howard explains, Herman Melville grew up "in an atmosphere of constant strain."[1]

The main problems were economic. Allan Melvill liked the challenges and rewards of importing and selling fine clothing for men, women, and children. He had visited France several times and chosen his business outlets and purchases with care. He was a competent businessman, personable and alert, but not a shrewd one. In the late 1820s, borrowing large sums of money, he made unsound and perhaps unethical investments. Allan lost heavily and declared bankruptcy in 1830. The family moved to Albany, where he briefly recovered financially before failing again. After an unsuccessful and wearying trip to New York City to borrow money, Allan returned home in December 1831. Shortly thereafter he became ill and died on 28 January 1832. Herman was twelve.

The father's illness and death all but devastated the Melvill family and changed Herman's life. In his last three weeks, Allan was incoherent and raving. According to teachings of the family's Dutch Reform church, a person true to church beliefs should have no fear of death. Only someone with little or no faith, a sinner, would fear death, knowing that sinners could expect hell and damnation for eternity.[2] Maria Melvill was raised in that faith, the father readily accepted it, and the children were thoroughly indoctrinated by church services twice on Sunday and scripture readings at each evening meal. In the final weeks in the two-story house in Albany, everyone could hear the father's utterances and cries. Family members and others were sometimes kept away from the father's room, but if accounts in *Pierre* are reliable, Herman at age twelve managed to enter his father's room unattended.[3] What his reactions were can only be imagined.

There is no hard evidence that Allan Melvill was insane in the final month of his life. One family belief was that the cause of death was pneumonia.[4] In a major 1949 study, Murray explains that Melvill died from lumbar pneumonia and in the final weeks suffered from what is regarded today as "temporary toxic psychosis."[5] According to a 1986 study, Allan Melvill in the final three weeks of life "developed a severely altered mental state, characterized by increasing hyperexcitability, insomnia, confusion, and finally death." The illness causing these symptoms "was biological and directly related to dysfunction of the central nervous system rather than to a manifestation of psychiatric disorder." The study concludes that although Allan Melvill "did die a bankrupt, he did not die a maniac. He died of an organic illness while in the prime of his life."[6] This medical diagnosis appears sound, but it is based necessarily on an examination of family letters and other secondary materials and not on medical reports of the time, let alone on an examination of the man himself. The findings and diagnosis are relevant, but they would seem to be far less relevant than the opinions and comments of relatives and friends who had actually observed the dying man.

On 10 January 1832, some eighteen days before Allan Melvill's death in Albany, brother-in-law Peter Gansevoort, a prominent businessman, visited Allan and then wrote Allan's brother Tom that he believed Allan had worked too hard and lost much sleep. "The excitement however could not be allayed and yesterday he occasionally manifested an alienation of Mind. Last night he became much worse—and to day he presents the melancholly spectacle of a deranged man—I hope it may be in your power to visit Albany *immediately.*"[7]

After a bedside visit, Thomas Melvill wrote on 11 January to Lemuel Shaw, Melville's future father-in-law and a close friend of Allan and the family, "I found him *very sick*—induced by a variety of causes—under great mental excitement—at times fierce, even *maniacal.*" On 15 January he wrote again to Shaw, "Hope, is no longer permitted of his recovery, in the opinion of the attending Physicians and indeed,—oh, how hard for a brother to say!—I *ought not* to hope it.—for,—in all human probability—he would live, *a Maniac!*" (JL 1:51, 52). After brother-in-law Herman Gansevoort visited Allan a few days later, he concluded that "his case [was] hopeless."[8] On 5 January, some three weeks after arriving home half frozen and weary from the New York trip, the ailing father marked in the family Bible two verses from Psalm 55: "4 My heart is sore pained within me: and the terrors of death are fallen upon me. 5 Fearfulness and trembling are come upon me and horror hath overwhelmed me." In the margin of the Bible Maria later commented, "This Chapter was mark'd a few days before my dear *Allan* by reason of severe suffering was deprive'd of his Intellect. God moves in a misterious way" (JL 1:51).

In 1849, more than fifteen years after his father's death, Melville wrote in *Redburn* of the delightful days before the narrator's father died a bankrupt and "we removed from the city; for when I think of those days, something rises up in my throat and almost strangles me." In 1852, about twenty years after the death, Melville wrote of Pierre,

"His father had died of a fever . . . toward his end, he at intervals lowly wandered in his mind."[9] Authors of the 1986 study, Weiner and Weiner, refer to this passage from *Pierre* and add, "Melville fictionally represents the father as physically suffering from a fever and understands his mental wanderings as the effects *of delirium rather than insanity*" (italics mine). The study states also that "there are no psychiatric illnesses which result in delirium, confusion, and death over a three-week time course."[10] This statement, too, likely represents a standard medical evaluation of the 1980s of accounts of a dying man's condition in the 1830s.

However, medical evaluations or other opinions in 1832 of Allan Melvill's condition might well present a somewhat different interpretation. For example, in mid-nineteenth-century America the word *delirium* could refer to insanity. In *Psychiatric Dictionary* (1981), Campbell explains, "Delirium at one time was used in a general way to indicate insanity, psychopathy, and almost any psychopathologic manifestation; now obsolete, such usage explains such appellations as depressive delirium (melancholia), persecutory delirium (paranoia)."[11] In a major 1838 study of insanity, the American Isaac Ray anticipated the Weiner and Weiner medical opinion that one cause of Allan Melvill's condition was "viral encephalitis" by explaining that "acute inflammation of [the brain's] membranes" can lead to delirium.[12] Yet as Campbell indicates, delirium and insanity were at one time related. Ray in 1838 explains that to a casual observer delirium closely resembles mania, an important nineteenth-century classification of insanity to be defined in Chapter 2. Furthermore, in his fiction Melville sometimes relates delirium and insanity, describing Ahab as possessing a mad delirium and Gabriel as showing even when calm a "deep, settled, fanatic delirium . . . in his eyes."[13]

Although relatives and friends observing Allan Melvill in the final weeks of his life were unaware of likely causes of his raving and incoherence, their views of his behavior as abnormal were the prevailing ones and consistent with the evidence.

Fortunately for surviving members of the Allan Melvill family, nothing comparable in drama and significance occurred in the life of the mother, Maria, who, after Allan's bankruptcy and death, managed to take care of eight children and keep the family going. Maria, apparently stronger than her husband, was quietly aggressive and purposeful. Yet in her own way and over the years she seemed to have contributed to family tensions and difficulties. Raised in a patrician family in Albany, Maria expected to advance socially in New York City and eventually become a member of what she regarded as the "fashion-ables." Despite occasional family successes through the years, Maria never realized her ambition. Her disappointments must have been felt and shared by all others in the family. As a mother, Maria was devoted and caring, but she was also strict and sometimes coercive, as shown in her requirement that the children sit quietly around her bed during her afternoon naps. As the maid could have cared for the children during those periods, the practice appears inconsiderate and selfish. After her first two deliveries, Maria began experiencing fainting spells during pregnancy. During the 1820s when the family was growing in size every other year she became susceptible to the nervousness she described as "my great weakness." Relatives seemed to agree with her opinion (JL 1:21, 22). During family crises Maria became prone to periods of depression, which would affect the children. As regular summer retreats to Albany suggest, Maria was overly dependent upon Albany relatives. Allan occasionally pointed out, perhaps with some justification, that his wife loved her brother, businessman Peter Gansevoort, more than she loved him.

After Allan's death in 1832, Maria exerted a firm hand in the family. She sent Gansevoort and Herman out to work, boarded Allan in Albany, kept the girls and others at home, and insisted that the family receive economic benefits above those of what had now become their lower-middle-class station. During the difficult mid-1830s, she sold some of her family lands to supplement infrequent small loans from her brother Peter. Although not constantly economical, she did what she could and placated creditors as long as possible. In managing the family, Maria served as both mother and father and in the process may have loved some children too much and others too little.

Another noteworthy family member, Gansevoort, the oldest of the eight Melvill children, overshadowed everyone else in the family. He was a perennial winner of classroom firsts and scholarship prizes and the idol of his parents. Herman, four years younger, naturally felt inferior and resentful. Gansevoort had his weaknesses, however. After his fur business collapsed in 1837, Gansevoort, twenty-two years old, suffered a minor ankle injury. He was to spend some twelve to fifteen months in bed, recovering from what Miller regards as "a complete physical and emotional collapse." Miller adds that Gansevoort's symp-

toms described by the mother "were not unlike her own 'nervous' at-
tacks in the New York years."[14] While Herman was at sea in the early
1840s, Gansevoort became widely known for his Democratic oratory in
behalf of Tammany Hall candidates in New York City and presidential
candidate James K. Polk. But some regarded Gansevoort as too aggressive or prone to make extravagant claims. As secretary of the
American legation in London in 1845, he became known in inner
circles for excess zeal and occasional displays of poor judgment.

During the spring of 1846 in London, Gansevoort, now thirty-one,
began experiencing periods of lassitude, headaches, and eye strain. In
a 3 April 1846 letter to Herman from London, he expressed concern
with things at home and added, "I sometimes fear I am gradually breaking up. . . . I think I am growing phlegmatic and cold. Man stirs me not,
nor woman either. My circulation is languid. My brain is dull. . . . A
degree of insensibility has been long stealing over me, & now seems
permanently established, which, to my understanding is more akin to
death than life." Enclosed with the letter was a quoted passage from
Measure for Measure describing thoughts of death (JL 1:208–9). In the
ensuing weeks Gansevoort began to suffer from impaired vision and
other defects. He was examined by several physicians. In the words of
the American ambassador McLane, one physician in mid-April found
Gansevoort in a state of "nervous derangement" and stated that the impaired vision "proceeded from no defect in the eye, but from other
causes." Some time later another physician expressed the opinion, in
the words of Ambassador McLane, that Gansevoort was "suffering
from a functional affection of the brain indicated by some confusion of
the intellect and sudden loss of sight . . . [and] considerable loss of
power." There were days of stability and calmness, with physicians now
concerned with the abdominal area. While Gansevoort's recovery was
still to be hoped for, McLane wrote a confidential letter on 4 May to the
secretary of state expressing criticism of Gansevoort's appointment, of
his "rhetorical extravagance of speech & manner, and truthlessness the
most extraordinary" (JL 1:213). Gansevoort's physical condition deteriorated in the last week or two of life. He died on 12 May 1846, the
postmortem revealing that death had been caused by diseased conditions of heart, liver, and kidneys. Gansevoort was calm and rational in
the final days.[15]

By the time of his brother's death, Melville had no doubt realized
that mental instability of some kind was to be expected in the family.

Although his father had been dead for fourteen years, the spectacle of his derangement in 1832 was likely vivid. That it was is indicated in remarks or thoughts of protagonists in *Redburn* and *Pierre* published many years afterward. Certainly, too, the loss of his father left Herman with a sense of rejection and loneliness he would never get over. The gap left by the death would be rarely filled except by someone like Nathaniel Hawthorne, who, by leaving Lenox in 1851, seemed to have been deserting Melville just as his father had done. The psychological legacy left by his mother might be just as important but likely more difficult to determine. Devoted to her children, she sought to raise them properly. But as she was constantly with the family, her "nervousness" and periods of depression would be felt intensely by each child. In his middle teens Melville grew restive around the house, and his later rebelliousness and impatience stemmed at least in part from his mother's strictures and moralizing.

News of Gansevoort's mental upset and then of his death might have left Melville wondering if he would be next in the family to show symptoms of insanity. There had already been his father and brother and also his paternal grandmother, Mrs. Priscilla Melvill, who appeared unstable in 1833 as she lay bedridden in Boston after the death of the family patriarch, Maj. Thomas Melvill, the previous September. The son Allan Melvill had died in January. On 20 February 1833 Lemuel Shaw wrote to Maria describing the grandmother's condition: "Mrs. [Priscilla] Melvill had been confined to her chamber for several weeks. Her mind & especially her memory have been extremely impaired, so much so as at times to render it painful to converse with her."[16] Other Melvills had difficulties of various kinds. Henry Melvill, a cousin seven years younger, was retarded and regarded by some as "insane." Maria Gansevoort, the mother of cousin Stanwix, the model of Glen Stanly in *Pierre*, had several memory lapses and suffered from mental illness before her death in 1851.[17] Melville's niece Lucy, brother Allan Melville's daughter, was committed to Bloomingdale asylum in the 1870s and died there in 1885.

Jay Leyda referred in 1949 to "Melville's greatest fears—the twisted mind and the threatening backdrop of evil."[18] The greatest fear may have been of the "twisted mind," a fear that began and grew in the years immediately following his father's death in 1832. The fear of the twisted mind or of inherited insanity might lie behind the writer's compelling interest in insanity, his apparent compulsion to learn about the disease, to observe its effects on the individual and on others, to write about it repeatedly in his fiction, and to dread its appearance in himself.

Melville's experiences outside the family were obviously important in the formation of his character and outlook. He was still a member of the family when he worked in the mid-1830s at an Albany bank, his uncle's farm, and his brother's fur store. During these years, unlike most youths his age, he was usually not in school. Melville ironically taught school briefly in 1837, partly to add something to the family's finances and partly to get away. He was becoming restless. As the times were hard, he received almost nothing for teaching. In an effort to obtain work, possibly on the Erie Canal project, Melville took a surveying and engineering course in the Lansingburgh Academy in the fall of 1838 but discovered after finishing that work was not available. In 1839, not quite twenty years of age, Melville left home temporarily to ship aboard a "regular trader" bound for Liverpool and back. In May 1840, after another brief teaching stint, he journeyed with his friend Eli James Murdock Fly to Galena, Illinois, to visit uncle Thomas Melvill and look for work, but jobs in that part of the country were scarce, too. That fall in New York City with Fly he tried again until January, when he solved his unemployment problem by signing seaman's papers and shipping out on a Nantucket whaler.

Such experiences proved invaluable some years later when Melville turned to writing fiction. All contributed to his maturation, to a toughening of character and mind. Despite his patrician background and Maria Melvill's attempts to raise her children in a genteel manner, Herman apparently absorbed a great deal of practical, down-to-earth experience, especially outside the family. Sea journeys introduced him to a life that made no allowances for an attentive upbringing, love of good books, or fine relatives. He had to learn to climb a ship's rigging; spend many hours aloft, sometimes in bad weather; scrub decks; risk his life chasing whales; eat scrabbly food; sleep in a dank, crowded forecastle. On this level of daily reality he learned about sailors—the disgruntled, confident, ineffectual, and adaptable—by living and working with them.

Melville's first ship, the *St. Lawrence*, a fairly new and fast-moving trader, carried an interesting crew but no one like the mad Jackson of the *Highlander* in *Redburn*. The ship docked in Liverpool for six weeks, allowing Melville ample time in which to explore the docks, stretching for more than two miles, and the general vicinity. Newspaper accounts then make clear that the densely populated area contained excessive poverty, hardship, and crime. Melville's interest in people and activities there, including the bestial and abnormal, is illustrated in *Redburn* by accounts of men and women who scrounge along the docks for garbage and dead bodies and of others seldom seen in daytime or in normal pursuits.[19] A few years later as an ordinary seaman aboard the Fairhaven whaler *Acushnet*, Melville encountered Captain Pease, who within a year or so became so difficult to live with that the crew became discontented, and four men, including Melville and Toby Greene, deserted in the Pacific. After a month on Nukuheva Island, Melville was picked up by an Australian whaler, *Lucy Ann*, on which conditions were much worse: an incompetent captain, an alcoholic first mate, and rebellious crew members. Under the circumstances it would not be surprising if one or two men aboard ship were unstable or abnormal. The records of his next whaler, the *Charles and Henry*, indicate nothing pertinent, except that the ship left Melville in Hawaii, where in August 1843 he signed aboard an American frigate.

Records of Melville's fourteen months aboard the *United States*, a sister ship to the *Constitution*, have survived, but none, according to Howard P. Vincent, provides evidence of possible models for two marvelously insane characters, Master-at-Arms Bland and Surgeon Cuticle, who, Vincent explains, were actually modeled on characters in other books.[20] Such matters will be considered in Chapter 4, along with discussions of other insane figures aboard the *Neversink*. In imaginative accounts of the ship's crew, Melville at least implies that some aboard the large *Neversink* are not mentally sound. Described as the "children of calamity" and the "offspring of sin," the crew includes "bankrupt brokers," "blacklegs," "castaway tinkers," and other possible suspects.[21] Some of the five hundred men and officers aboard the *United States* likely suffered from bouts of depression, suspiciousness, fear, and hostility and possibly from forms of moral insanity or monomania, major classifications of insanity in mid-century. The medical and surgical journal of the frigate *United States* for the period Melville was aboard ship—9 August 1843 to 9 October 1844—does not list or describe obvious or clearly identifiable cases of abnormal or insane behavior. The journal does list eight cases of "debility," a condition generally defined as a "state or quality of being weak." This word is usually accompanied

in the journal with a clarifying phrase or term, as in "debility with nervous irritability" or "debility and nervous excitement."[22] In modern
psychiatry, the term for debility is *asthenia*, one form of which can be
regarded as a kind of anxiety neurosis. The journal lists also at least two
cases of epilepsy, which at that time was regarded as related in some
way to mental disease. Severe epileptic convulsions could result in
symptoms of mania or monomania. The sailor admitted to the sick
bay for "debility with nervous irritability" suffered from "a chronic
affection of the brain, accompanied with violent epileptic fits." The
journal also lists numerous cases of sailors suffering from "debauch,"
hardly a mental condition, but typical records of such cases list also
such complaints as sleeplessness, tremors, nervous irritability, and
the like.[23]

Crews of America's best warships—the *Constitution*, *President*, and
United States—were a cut above the average naval crew. But as various
chapters, characterizations, and passages in *White-Jacket* make clear, a
distinct minority of the five hundred men and officers aboard the
United States may have been poorly equipped psychologically for the
regimented, sometimes difficult life aboard a crowded ship.

An experienced sailor when he boarded the frigate, Melville probably coped with the demands of that life as well as most. Family experiences and difficulties which may have weakened him in some respects
left him with a number of sturdy qualities. His education, formal and
informal, was a factor in his ability to regard the years at sea with more
than average discernment and objectivity. Other effects of that education will be examined in Chapter 2.

Chapter Two. Scientific Background

Although Herman Melville's formal education was severely interrupted by consequences of his father's death in 1832 and bankruptcy and by a national depression, he possessed at eighteen a fairly adequate background for that time in humanities and sciences. His love of reading probably originated in the family parlor in New York City, which contained travel books purchased overseas by Allan Melvill and some of the father's school books on astronomy, mineralogy, and botany. In the New York City and Albany schools, Melville and his classmates received at least some instruction in chemistry, astronomy, "natural science" or biology, mathematics, and perhaps laboratory work. In Albany in the 1830s he borrowed books from his uncle Peter Gansevoort's library, the city library, and the library of the Young Men's Association, which he joined at age fifteen in 1835. Melville's most concentrated study of science occurred in the winter of 1838, when he enrolled in the Lansingburgh Academy and received four months of mathematics, possibly chemistry, and basic engineering and surveying. At the academy, Gilman explains, "Melville may have extended the scientific knowledge that was the main object of his studies and laid the foundation for his mature interest in natural sciences."[1]

The sailing years, 1841 to 1844, likely provided little opportunity for reading because Melville was usually at sea or on land where books were unavailable or of limited interest. Although whaling ships seldom carried more than a few books or other reading materials, a crewmate might have a few readable items in his trunk in the forecastle. Dr. Long Ghost in *Omoo* owns books described as "sadly worn and battered" and as "invaluable resources" of information, including one identified as "a learned treatise on the yellow fever."[2] If the original had been available aboard the *Lucy Ann*, Melville probably read portions of it. In *Redburn* the narrator refers to several books aboard the *St. Lawrence*, including the Newgate Calendar, an old book on the lives of criminals, and a "large black volume, with *Delirium Tremens* in great gilt letters on the back."[3] There is no record of books aboard Melville's first whaler, *Acushnet*, when he was a crew member or of Melville's reading aboard that ship, but his last whaler, *Charles and Henry*, as Wilson Heflin discovered, carried a library of thirty-seven books and several magazines, including histories and biographies but seemingly no scientific works, although four selections from the "Family Library" listed by Heflin have not been identified.[4]

The writer's education in humanities and sciences continued in the fourteen months aboard the *United States*, which had an enlisted men's library of over one hundred volumes.[5] In Chapter 41 of *White-Jacket*, the narrator describes a number of these books: "Locke's Essays," "Plutarch's Lives," plays by Marlowe and Jonson, and a scientific work, "Mason Good's *Book of Nature*—a very good book, to be sure, but not precisely adapted to tarry tastes."[6] Melville's references to this book indicate familiarity with its contents and possibly with discussions of human understanding, tripartite divisions of the mind, phrenology, melancholy, and physiognomy. Hillway believes that Melville "knew and probably consulted" Good's book and that "conceivably" it was included in the ship's library. He adds that Good's ideas were largely derivative and the book was a popularization.[7] Although this may be so, Melville customarily made excellent use of books he read and consulted. Sometime in the 1840s, presumably by 1848, Melville consulted works by Gall and Spurzheim for information included in *Mardi*.

A much more significant and important work was also available in the enlisted men's library aboard ship. This was Thomas Upham's *Outlines of Imperfect and Disordered Mental Action* (1840), a copy of which was available in the New York Society Library, which Melville was to visit in the late 1840s. Written by Hawthorne's psychology instructor at Bowdoin College, the book was designed for the Harper's Family Library as a popular text on insanity.[8] Although there is no hard evidence that

Melville was familiar with the book, he seems to have been. The book contains valuable information on the faculties of the mind and on kinds of insanity, or what Upham describes as "disordered mental actions." Of people with disordered judgment, he writes, "They seize upon a particular opinion, or, perhaps the minute fragment of an opinion; and they hold it with a tenacity which neither life nor death can separate."[9] Although the word *monomania* does not appear in the book, the idea is evident. Upham explains that such people give themselves up to their object "for better or worse," not temporarily but, as it were, through all time. The book includes discussions also of "insanity of the affections" and of the "moral sensibilities," which suggest another form of mental illness, moral insanity—the term is not used.[10] As the Harper's Family Library (1847) series of 187 volumes included a number of other works on psychology, including several on insanity and phrenology, a few may have been included in the ship's allotment of seventy-two volumes from it.

In New York City in 1845, Melville found suitable information for *Typee* in several libraries. After moving to the city with his new bride, Elizabeth, in September 1847, he made frequent use of Evert Duyckinck's large private library, his father-in-law's library in Boston, and also the New York Society Library, a large private institution located within walking distance of the Melville home on 103 Fourth Street, where he lived with Elizabeth and the other Melvilles. As it was Melville's practice to walk downtown daily and stop at an "unnamed 'reading room,'" a reasonable assumption is that he visited one of two reading rooms in the library on 12th and University Place. Sealts has discovered that Melville was a member of the library from "17 January–11 September 1848 and 17 April–October 1850," or during the time he was working on *Mardi* and writing a version or part of a version of *Moby-Dick*.[11] As a member Melville borrowed only two books, including David Hartley's *Observations on Man*,[12] a materialistic eighteenth-century study of man's constitution which apparently had little influence on alienists or psychiatrists then. Possibly influences of Hartley's ideas appear in *Mardi*, as will be noted. As library facilities were available to nonmembers upon payment of a fee, Melville may have taken advantage of that provision to read in the library or check out books. It is possible that he may have begun visiting there in late 1847.

During these years Melville became a habitual and skillful user of dictionaries and encyclopedias, which provided in compact form reliable facts and information on almost any topic. A favorite source was the twenty-seven-volume *Penny Cyclopaedia*,[13] an English work which provided the writer with material for accounts of a house and the Indian tree, the sagoon, in *Redburn*; bullet wounds, surgical techniques, and human physiology in *White-Jacket*; whales in *Moby-Dick*; and a few Scottish coastal scenes in *Israel Potter*.[14] A set of the *Cyclopaedia* was available in the Society Library.

It is quite possible that in the course of writing *Redburn* and *White-Jacket* in 1849 or possibly by 1848, Melville turned to the *Cyclopaedia* for technical information on insanity. Given his familiarity with the *Cyclopaedia* and interest in insanity and scientific explanations, he may well have checked the Volume 12 article on insanity, with its detailed exposition of the nature, forms, causes, and treatments of the disease—as understood at mid-century. The article presents an apparently reliable overall view of insanity because much of it duplicates passages and interpretations in pages of a major contemporary study, *A Treatise on Insanity and Other Disorders Affecting the Mind* (1835), by eminent English scientist James C. Prichard.[15] The article contains also references to medical opinions and findings of such other contemporary authorities as French scientists Ph. Pinel and E. Esquirol, English scientist James Conolly, American W. C. Burroughs, German scientist Johann Heinroth, and others. Prichard is the most frequently cited authority. In looking for pertinent information on a topic, Melville sometimes consulted authorities cited in *Cyclopaedia* articles. He may have done so in treatments of insanity.[16]

As later chapters should make clear, Melville, beginning most significantly in *Redburn*, created characters that exhibited symptoms and behavioral patterns of insanity described briefly in the *Cyclopaedia* article and at length in books by James Prichard, Amariah Brigham, and Isaac Ray, perhaps at mid-century America's leading authority on insanity. Melville's later works, particularly *Moby-Dick* and *Pierre*, show in addition insights into other areas of insanity that appear comparable in quality and significance to interpretations expressed in the article and book-length studies. The article may have proven especially helpful to Melville for its clear specific explanations, as in the following enumeration of forms of insanity: "The variety of the forms of insanity is almost endless, but they may conveniently for the purpose of description be collected under the following heads:—1. Disorders of the feelings and propensities. 2. Delusions or hallucinations. 3. General derangement of the reasoning faculties. 4. Mixed forms, in which two or more of the preceding are combined; and 5. the state of imbecility or fatuity in which other kinds of mental disorder frequently terminate."[17]

Each of the five forms is explained and illustrated at some length in the article. Whether Melville's sources of knowledge were the *Cyclopaedia* article, books, and/or his own wide experiences, his fiction reveals a familiarity with each of the five forms. In this study, these will be important: "disorders of the feelings and propensities," or, to use the contemporary medical terms, moral insanity; "delusions or hallucinations," or monomania; and "mixed forms," or a combination of moral insanity and monomania, or of one or both with a form of deterioration. Mania as a form of general derangement often involving violent behavior is sometimes considered. The two main forms in the mid-1800s and in Melville's fiction are moral insanity and monomania.

The most interesting and significant mental disease is moral insanity, a classification originating with Pinel, who described the condition in 1801 as "emportement maniaque sans délire." James Prichard, who provided the most precise definition, gave the disease the English name of moral insanity.[18] The description of moral insanity in the *Cyclopaedia* article begins with an almost exact duplication of Prichard's definition from *A Treatise*: The disease consists of a "morbid perversion of the feelings, affections, and active powers, without any illusion or erroneous conviction impressed upon the understanding; sometimes co-existing with an apparently unimpaired state of the intellectual faculties." Henry Nash Smith, author of an important study of Ahab's madness and Melville's knowledge of contemporary scientific definitions of insanity, rightly points out that a literal interpretation then of this disease as "manie sans délire" ruled out delusion even though cognitive failure likely existed.[19] The article clarifies the accepted view of Prichard, Isaac Ray, and others: "Though we have thus described disordered states of some of the feelings and propensities as varieties of 'moral insanity', it must be remembered that generally the prevalence of any of these feelings in a morbid state is attended with some delusion or disorder of the intellectual faculties."[20] However, as Prichard and Ray also explain, the disease can occur without impairment or cognitive failure.[21]

In general terms, moral insanity is a mental disease which affects primarily the emotions and may affect the cognitive faculties. The symptoms are many, ranging from an absence or diminution of feelings to pronounced displays of hatred, fear, or melancholy. Viewed in mid-century as controversial by some scientists, moral insanity was regarded as a sound concept by leading psychiatrists. The general validity of the classification and in particular the idea of the "uncontrollable impulse" were demonstrated during the well-known insanity trial of Abner Rogers in 1844 (to be discussed in Chapter 5). That idea, related aspects of the disease, and evidences of monomania were regarded by the presiding judge, Lemuel Shaw, Melville's future father-in-law, and physicians for the defendant as providing sufficient evidence for a determination of insanity. Various forms of moral insanity are illustrated in Melville's fiction.[22]

Like moral insanity, monomania is a complex disease, different forms of which are illustrated by Melville's Dr. Cuticle in *White-Jacket* and Gabriel and Ahab in *Moby-Dick*. In his travels Melville probably encountered a number of monomaniacs; they appear frequently in his fiction. The *Cyclopaedia* article provides this brief and comparatively simple introduction to the disease: "The term monomania has been proposed by M. Esquirol, and adopted by most writers on mental disorders, to designate those cases of insanity in which the mind is occupied by some illusion or erroneous conviction, the individual still retaining the power of reasoning correctly on matters unconnected with the subject of his delusion."[23] The article amplifies this introduction, distinguishing between monomania and melancholia, which is usually gloomy in nature, and describing kinds of delusion in monomania. The important point is made that whatever the form of monomania or the nature of the delusion, some deterioration of the cognitive faculty is to be expected. "Monomania in the pure form, a mental delusion without further disorder of the intellect, is very rare."[24] Ahab may illustrate the rare form of monomania. The studies of Esquirol, Ray, Prichard, and others provide comparatively thorough explanations of the nature of the disease, its causes and forms; they make clear, for example, that the delusion may be simple or complex, one or several, and difficult to determine. Melville had a remarkable understanding of the disease. He was also aware of similarities between conditions of moral insanity and monomania and of the possibility that moral insanity might develop into monomania, something examined at some length by Ray and Prichard.

The first portrayals in Melville's fiction of simpler kinds of the two principal forms of insanity in mid-nineteenth-century America will be examined in Chapter 3.

Chapter Three. Beginnings

Typee, Omoo, and *Mardi*

Shortly after the frigate *United States* dropped anchor in Boston harbor on 3 October 1844, Melville was discharged from the navy with fourteen months of service. Having put in four years since 1839 as a sailor, he was ready to leave the sea. Melville was twenty-five years old, an experienced traveler, realistic and somewhat disillusioned. But he was glad to be back in the United States, and his family in Lansingburgh, New York, was delighted to have him. Herman fell quickly into old family routines, and in no time at all he was telling everyone about his adventures on Pacific islands, New England whalers, and an American warship.

Not only family members but neighbors and friends were enthralled by the dramatic accounts of his experiences, including the weeks with reputed cannibals on Nukuheva. Melville had abundant time to tell such stories, think about his traveling life, and take it easy, for jobs were not available in Lansingburgh. Although Melville had his sea wages, he needed work to consume his energies. With time available and relatives and friends urging him to write of his adventures, Melville likely began *Typee* in the winter of 1844–45 and completed the manuscript in New York City the next summer.

Melville's most secure and happiest years as a writer and perhaps as an adult likely occurred between late fall 1844, when he began *Typee*, and early 1849, when he finished *Mardi*. In 1845 and 1846 he was single and had little to do but write. The environment in Lansingburgh was familiar and usually reassuring: he began *Typee* at home with his family and completed it in New York City with his two brothers. Their apartment provided adequate room for writing, relative quiet, and access to libraries. The apartment was also located in the midst of big-city scenes and activities. A library was essential, however. After the Harpers rejected the *Typee* manuscript because it lacked authenticity, Melville turned to reference books for information on natives and their lives and customs, which appeared mainly in added Chapters 20, 21, and 27. The English publisher had objections also to infelicities of prose style, which were fine-tuned by a professional writer. Such problems were manageable.[1]

Other problems that later proved difficult to manage were not evident at this time. Melville's large family was very supportive. Family members and relatives encouraged Melville in his writing, and his sisters painstakingly copied the final drafts of early novels for the publisher. Money was not a problem. Sea wages paid for a six-month stay in New York City and brisk sales of *Typee* covered expenses as he wrote *Omoo* and gave him confidence as a writer. The future looked promising. Although the protagonist of *Typee* is prone to depression, fears, and anxieties, Melville apparently had his feelings and psyche under control; as he wrote *Typee* Melville was most likely recalling his emotional state at the time and dramatizing but not reliving it.[2]

As a beginning writer with an excellent subject, Melville likely described most Pacific adventures as he remembered them. He would stick fairly close to the "unvarnished truth" claimed in the preface. At the same time, however, as a natural storyteller he would to some extent unconsciously combine facts and fancy and dramatize them. But Melville was also shrewd enough to recognize his professional limitations and the obvious attractions of his subject; he would not in all likelihood stray far from recollection of experiences and people.

Accordingly, the fictional world of *Typee* is essentially sane and stable. Activities aboard the whaler *Dolly* resemble generally life aboard the whaler *Acushnet* in 1842. On this point, Leon Howard wrote, "The weight of evidence indicates that *Typee* was a mixture of fact and fiction. . . . The adventure was real, even if fictionally extended and dramatized; and the observations were as accurate as memory and research could make them. Melville himself could not always have told where his memory faded and his imagination took over" (p. 292). Shipboard life under Captain Pease in 1842 was often difficult, food and living quarters were often poor, and the work was usually hard, monotonous, and sometimes dangerous. But the experiences make sense, as do those in the novel. The island life in *Typee* was patterned fairly closely on the writer's four weeks on Nukuheva, although Melville lengthened the stay to four months and increased the ferocity and threat of the natives. Cannibalism in *Typee* is an inhuman practice, and the civilized world the narrator recalls is often unstable and unjust. But Tommo sees little evidence of cannibalism and he has no doubts about his desires to return to civilization. Despite shortcomings and failures, life on the island and aboard the whaler is generally worth the effort.

Melville's first novel contains a variety of characters, including several who are insane or close to the thin red line separating the sane from the insane. These characters represent a distinct minority and not the large group found in the later novels. In *Typee*, Melville does not distinguish between the sane and the insane as he does in novels beginning with *Redburn* and including such figures as Jackson, Surgeon Cuticle, Bland, Ahab, and Pierre, who are not only prominent but distinctively set off by reason of their abnormalities. In *Typee* and *Omoo* sane and insane figures alike are interesting because of the writer's fascination with the unusual: the bold, outcast, devious, eccentric, rebellious, heroic. In *Typee* the insane or severely troubled include Captain Vangs, the harbor pilot, Jimmy, Karky, and Mow-Mow.

Portrayals of these and other figures in *Typee* and *Omoo* were likely based on the writer's experiences in the Pacific in 1842 and on an understanding of abnormal behavior gained over many years. There may have been other influences, however. The Upham book on insanity aboard the *United States* could have provided Melville with information on obsession, disordered intellect, and indications of monomania, which was fairly well known in the 1840s. In 1845 and 1846 occasional articles on monomania and other mental diseases appeared in newspapers. During his months in New York City writing *Typee*, Melville was not likely the practiced reader of newspapers he was to become, but he probably kept abreast of the news. Of the metropolitan newspapers, he apparently preferred the *New York Herald* with its columns of maritime information. The *Herald* in January 1845 announced a Clinton Hall lecture on phrenology, not generally regarded then as a pseudoscience. On 23, 24, and 25 May the newspaper described the murder trial of one Andrew Kleim, regarded by fellow workers as "queer" and "strange" and by three doctors testifying at the trial as suffering from a form of monomania. A sensational trial in Kentucky that July involved a physician charged with murder and described by his brother, also a physician, as a "monomaniac." The *Herald* carried accounts in September and October of the consequences of the trial.[3]

Melville may have attended lectures that spring at the New-York Historical Society by a Professor Edward Robinson, who discussed biographical writers, including a William L. Stone, whose *Matthias and His Impostures* "establishes beyond contradiction that insanity, or at least monomania, if not a contagious disease, may become an epidemic." Robinson's comment on Stone and his book, however, comprised only one small paragraph in the 1 April lecture. There is no evidence that Melville heard the lecture or read the book. In an 1851 letter to Evert Duyckinck, he indicated that he owned or had borrowed another book by Stone.[4]

While writing *Omoo* in Lansingburgh in March 1846, Melville may have read in the *Albany Argus* or *New York Herald* of a murder trial before the Supreme Judical Court in Boston of an Albert J. Tirrell, who obtained his freedom with a defense of somnambulism, which Judge Dewey ruled was a "species of derangement"; the defendant was therefore "not responsible for his act." Public reactions in the mid-1840s to defense pleas of insanity were often unfavorable. The *Albany Argus* in July 1846 expressed criticism of a protracted Auburn, New York, trial involving murder and a defense plea of "advanced stage of dementia."[5] Such matters were in the news during Melville's first years of writing.

Melville's writing during these years was probably better than he realized. He had written teenage compositions in the late 1830s, including several lengthy letters that appeared in the *Albany Microscope* in 1838 and two imaginative pieces published in May 1839 in the *Lansingburgh Democratic Press*, but these reveal little evidence of remarkable talent. In his first novel, however, Melville came of literary age, for *Typee* discloses the imaginative and verbal powers that were to become familiar to readers and in addition skillful techniques for a beginning writer. The prose style is natural and flexible, capable of figurative accounts and concrete, precise descriptions. In later novels, it shows a greater firmness, versatility, and richness of language. Comments in this study on the first-person narration will concentrate on the narrator as a nar-

rator or as a character. The lack of biographical evidence and the critical hazards involved preclude more than general comment on the difficult relationship of author and narrator or character. Melville's lifelong
interest in factual information and "truth" and curiosity about things
and people account in part for another technique: the emphasis in
most of his fiction on exposition. A special form of exposition for development of character is what Berthoff describes as a "life-history."[6]
Another technique is a reliance in characterization on qualities and behavior of real people. The extent to which Melville uses this technique
varies from novel to novel.

Of the five characters in *Typee* showing some degree of emotional
upset or mental instability, the native chief Mow-Mow appears to be
the least afflicted. His only noticeable problem is a disposition toward
violence. When he sees Tommo making his escape, he is described as
enraged. After being struck in the throat by the boat hook, Mow-Mow
rises to the surface with a "ferocious expression" (p. 252). Karky, the
village tattooer, is a very excitable native with noticeable emotional
swings. Upon first seeing Tommo, he seizes him in "a paroxysm of de-
light" because he will have a white face to work on. But when Tommo
makes clear that he wants none of it, "nothing could exceed [Karky's]
grief and disappointment" (p. 218). But soon he is jumping around,
flourishing his instruments in Tommo's face. After Tommo gets away,
the native is "overwhelmed with sorrow" (p. 219). In the remaining
weeks of Tommo's captivity, Karky does not let up. Other natives take
up his cause. "Doubtless he had plotted a conspiracy against me and
my countenance" (p. 219). In later encounters, Karky chases after
Tommo, again waving his tattooing instruments, but in vain. The native's excitability and obsession with disfiguring Tommo's face indicate
the possibility of a form of monomania.

Driven and troubled like most of Melville's sea captains, Vangs is one
of the first characterizations based on an actual figure: in this instance,
Captain Pease of the *Acushnet*, who, after a season of hardship and
poor whaling in 1842, suffered from ill health and a quarrelsome,
tyrannical disposition, which Melville seems to have exaggerated in
Typee. Captain Vangs "inhumanly" neglects the sick, provides only
"scanty" food, and responds to complaints with "the butt end of a
handspike" (p. 21). Although a stereotyped ship's tyrant, Vangs is nonetheless a convincing case of an emotionally disturbed man. He is for
the most part a realistic figure, with possible evidences of monomania.

The most distinctively portrayed figures are the English harbor pilot and Jimmy. Each is fairly complex and each illustrates the use of a life history that provides "factual" and biographical information about the character. In later novels such histories reflect the writer's developing techniques for creating irony and symbol. In *Typee* the biographical material is relatively straightforward and realistic. The English pilot is the first of Melville's many excessive drinkers. He is an intelligent alcoholic whose efforts to pilot the *Dolly* into the harbor are inept, voluble, and ridiculous. The pilot is nonetheless "a most extraordinary individual, a genuine South-Sea vagabond" with an illuminating history. He was formerly an English naval lieutenant who "disgraced his flag by some criminal conduct" and then deserted (p. 13). He drifted around the Pacific for years until he arrived at Nukuheva, where he was appointed pilot of the harbor by the new French authorities. Friendly and with a sense of humor, he may not be insane. But years of wandering, a history of drinking, burdens of guilt, and a loss of contact with white society indicate some form of psychological trouble. His impulsiveness, eccentric behavior, and deterioration of sensibilities suggest the inroads of moral insanity.

The beachcomber, Jimmy, who misleads both Toby and the narrator, is another character based on an actual figure. Leon Howard describes an "Irish Jimmy" Fitch, a "tabooed beachcomber," who tricked the original Toby to sign aboard another whaler but did nothing to help Melville until approached by him.[7] The fictional version shows at least some of Fitch's likely qualities. It shows also Melville's reliance in the first two novels upon a prose style that effectively combines realistic and romantic words and phrases. The result is the most complex characterization in *Typee,* with the exception of Tommo. Jimmy's history shows him as shrewd, opportunistic, and manipulative. He convinces sailors to buy native fruit and believe his stories and deserters to sign aboard ships. More than the English harbor pilot, Jimmy shows effects of defection from civilization. He is dishonest, irresponsible, and indifferent to sailors he has helped shanghai or in other ways misled. Outward displays of friendliness and helpfulness are only covers for what James Prichard in his 1835 study of insanity described as a "decay of social affections," a major symptom of moral insanity.[8]

Tommo is the first of the narrator-characters appearing in Melville's works through *Moby-Dick.* Tommo will be regarded here as the character involved in actions on Nukuheva. Like later such characters, he is to some extent vulnerable to the emotional and mental stresses of the adventure. Unlike his friend Toby, he does not adjust readily to what he encounters. At first Toby does not either, for aboard ship he is described as "a strange, wayward being, moody, fitful, and melancholy—at times almost morose" (p. 32). But on the island, Toby becomes realistic and tough, meeting all difficulties and threats with "fearless confidence." He does not flinch before native chiefs. Tommo, however, "absolutely quailed" before them. The contrasts between the two men are contrasts between the aggressive or hardy and the sensitive or touchy. After the first day among the natives, Toby sleeps heartily, but Tommo worries through most of the night. While Toby is gone in search of help, Tommo broods and develops an ailing leg. His fears and worries lead to despair and melancholy. After Toby's second departure and Tommo's realization that he is a prisoner, he sinks "insensibly into that kind of apathy which ensues after some violent outbreak of despair" (p. 123). When he accepts his condition, he regains peace of mind. After Marnoo arrives in the native village and discourages Tommo's ideas about escaping, another reversal occurs. When the pattern is repeated, Tommo decides to act as though all is well so that the natives will not guess his plans to escape. A period of relative calm ensues until Karky's frantic demands and other disturbances upset the prisoner. Later, nursing his ailing leg, Tommo finds courage to make his way toward the beach and possible freedom, carrying with him tendencies toward depression, an overly active imagination, and assorted fears.[9] Having survived his experiences on the whaler and on Nukuheva, the narrator has gained some understanding of them and of himself and the men he knew.

The fictional world of *Omoo* appears somewhat more precarious than that of *Typee*. The Sydney whaler *Julia* carries not only an incompetent captain and an unruly crew but ingredients for an attempted scuttling of the ship and mutinous outbreaks. Life on the islands appears attractive. In the Calabooza Beretanee on Tahiti the narrator and his friend Dr. Long Ghost live without a thought in the world; after leaving the Calabooza they wander aimlessly from village to village on Imeeo. But such peacefulness and indulgence seem meaningless and may even threaten mental stability and growth. Yet neither the narrator nor Dr. Long Ghost views the life with full seriousness. Shipboard life and island activities have their lighter moments. The respective dangers and indulgences can be kept in place if those involved are discerning. If the overall life is unsettling, it is also sane.

Materials in *Omoo* appear to be more closely related to the writer's experiences than is the case with *Typee*. It may be that there is more evidence of such a relationship in *Omoo*. About half the characterizations are apparently based on men Melville sailed with or met after he left Nukuheva in August 1842. According to Howard, Roper, and Hayford, the original crew of the *Lucy Ann* included deserters, men ill with venereal infections, and assorted incompetents. Of the original crew, one-third had deserted, and "more than half of the seamen remaining were more or less unwell from a long sojourn in a dissipated port; some of them wholly unfit for duty; one or two dangerously ill."[10] The crew in *Omoo* resembles in general quality and deportment the actual crew.

Perhaps because of autobiographical elements in *Omoo*, the novel contains a greater number and variety of insane or possibly insane characters. Most are members of the *Julia* crew, and many appear as irresponsible and incompetent, as members of the actual crew may have been. The fictional characters are not necessarily insane, but they appear near the thin red line separating the sane from the insane, if they are not over it. They are alike in possessing unsocial qualities, a tendency toward rages, and a drinking or venereal problem. Sometimes rage explodes into violence. Salem knocks Bungs down in the deck scene and soon thereafter threatens Wilson with a knife. The frequently surly Chips instigates a brawl with Jermin, a capable officer whose sudden rages, pugnacity, and determined drinking habits indicate instability. When he is drunk, his rages are uncontrollable. Except for his volatility, Jermin anticipates another tough, strongly driven officer, Mad-Jack of the *Neversink*. Two sailors on the *Julia*, dying from effects of syphilis, exhibit seemingly abnormal qualities. One man, bunking in the forecastle next to the narrator, "was often delirious, starting up and glaring around him, and sometimes wildly tossing his arms" (p. 44). Soon after his death and burial, another man is found "dying on a chest. He had fallen out of his hammock in a fit, and was insensible. The eyes were open and fixed, and his breath coming and going convulsively" (p. 45). Two other crewmen will be duly noted.

Several island characters illustrate the scope if not the depth of Melville's treatment of insanity in *Omoo*. Varvy, the old hermit visited by the narrator and Dr. Long Ghost, creates strange potions in his freakish still. During their visit, he makes "a variety of uncouth gestures" and humorous, obscure signs. If not insane or deteriorated, he is close to the thin red line. Another old man who pursues Typee and the doctor on Tamai may be more suspect. He has a "most hideous aspect" and makes "frightful signs for us to go along with him some-where, and see something." He appears to be simple-minded and pos-sibly obsessed with the value of an old pair of sailor's pants hidden in a calabash in his "wretched hut" (pp. 243, 244). He, too, may be suffer-ing from a form of deterioration. The narrator's humor is evident in many characterizations, including those of Queen Pomaree and her husband, Tanee, both of whom are immature, arrogant, and quick to physically abuse each other. The emotional failures indicate the possi-bility of a form of moral insanity.

Three characters in *Omoo* appear comparable to the English harbor pilot and Jimmy in *Typee* in that they are more completely developed. Rope Yarn, or Ropey, is the ship's steward. Hayford finds no evidence of such a man on the original crew list, although he refers to a descrip-tion in *Israel Potter* perhaps based on accounts of Ropey and to the pos-sibility that both come from a common source.[11] Whatever his origin, Ropey is both a type and a credible character. He is a "landlubber . . . a pusillanimous, lazy, good-for-nothing" (p. 52), a sailor usually moody and prone to personal uncleanliness, qualities noted of the marine Scriggs in *White-Jacket*. As a character, Ropey is the "most miserable" of landlubbers because he is not only inept and weak but easily fooled and misled by shipmates. His life history is one of bad luck and bad advice. A journeyman-baker in London, he accepted bad advice and went to Australia, where he did all right in Sydney until he married and his wife ran off with the bakery foreman and Ropey's money, at which point Ropey "got fuddled; and over his fifth pot meditated suicide—an in-tention carried out; for the next day he shipped . . . aboard the *Julia*" (p. 54). Ropey later becomes sick and dies in a hospital on shore. "No one knew his complaint; he must have died of hard times" (p. 14). The character's moody qualities, personal uncleanliness, and apparent sui-cidal tendencies are largely emotional failures indicative of a form of moral insanity. In later fictions references to actual or figurative suicide usually suggest some kind of psychological disturbance. That seems to be the case here as well.

The first important monomaniac in Melville's fiction is Bembo, the second mate on the *Julia*. Bembo is evidently based on a man described by Leon Howard as a "reckless Maori," a boat steerer on the Australian whaler *Lucy Ann*. Hayford believes that the original man may have been a native but points out that "nothing in the Revolt Documents in-dicates that he was the semi-savage Maori that Melville makes 'Bembo' out."[12] Melville's portrayal is itself a firm, realistic picture of an experienced native sailor usually portrayed as moody or scowling. As Bembo keeps to himself, crewmen avoid him out of dislike or fear. Bembo is a strong man with resentments and hatreds that can quickly erupt into physical action. Enraged by his inability to harpoon a whale, he jumps on the whale's back to finish the job. Unable to beat Sydney Ben in a fight, Bembo grabs him by the throat and will not let go until he is hit repeatedly on the head. Then his rage "was . . . absolutely demoniac; he lay glaring, and writhing on the deck" (p. 88). That evening while most aboard ship were asleep, the revengeful Bembo attempts to scuttle the ship. "The furious Mowree" is jumped at the helm and pulled away as saner hands save the ship. A short time later, attacked by others, he stands with his knife ready. Bembo's rages and combativeness indicate an obsessive need to destroy or harm whatever opposes him: crewmen, ship regulations, or beasts.

Captain Crash is not evidently based on someone Melville knew or read about.[13] Like the English harbor pilot in *Typee,* Crash is an ex–naval officer who has gone wrong. Crash, however, is treated in essentially serious terms. He admits to the loss of "a colonial armed brig on the coast of New Zealand" (pp. 298–99), but his rambling accounts disclose little information about the loss. When Dr. Long Ghost asks him why he did not return to England to report his loss, the captain gives "incomprehensible reasons for not doing so" (p. 299). Crash is initially described as "a decayed naval officer" (p. 298). That he appears to be, for signs of moral deterioration are evident. Described also as "this extremely suspicious character" (p. 299), Crash becomes involved in several activities signifying a decline or loss of moral standards. He engages in "the illicit trade in French wines and brandies" (p. 299), setting up a place in a grove where he can sell drinks to an occasional native and spend his afternoons in idleness or wait for a whaling crew to come in for festivities. One day the *Leviathan* crew arrives in the grove, carries on too boisterously, and is carted off with the captain to a native tribunal. Only the captain, regarded as the instigator of the trouble, is not released. Various charges are made against him. The main one involves a native girl of fourteen who was "aided and abetted . . . in her naughtiness" (p. 298) by the captain. Found guilty of "manifold offenses," the captain is regarded as "incorrigible" and "sentenced to eternal banishment from the island" (p. 300). The captain's nonchalant, secretive manner and habitual indifference to moral standards and his harmful effects on others are signs that he has crossed the thin red line.

Although the respective narrators of *Typee* and *Omoo* are identified as the same individual, it is not entirely clear why the second narrator as character appears comparatively confident and flexible. He is of course free of Nukuheva and no longer confronted by threats of cannibalism, facial disfigurement, or long imprisonment. He appears a little moody at first because he will never see Fayaway or friendly natives like Kory-Kory again. But aboard the *Julia* he must from the first toe the mark: many crew members are mean and shiftless and the captain is not reliable. He cannot indulge in introspection because things happen rapidly and sometimes unpredictably. The friendship with Dr. Long Ghost is reassuring, however, and often involves Typee in the action. The character gradually becomes more pragmatic and confident as the action unfolds. The narrator, having learned from the past, describes the sane and insane with compassion, common sense, and objectivity.

After finishing with the proof sheets of *Omoo* in January 1847, Melville began *Mardi*, which, like *Typee*, opens with a sailor narrator and a friend who soon desert the whaler. But that spring the direction and nature of the work changed as Melville, immersing himself in great books of literature, history, philosophy, and even science, began to write an involved work of satire, romance, and allegory. Foster describes the two years of work on *Mardi* as "the most astonishing and the most accelerated in . . . [Melville's] life."[14] The two years may have also been among the most secure because *Typee* and *Omoo* were selling well, the reviews were generally favorable, and the marriage in 1847 to Elizabeth Shaw appeared happy. In a confident, experimental frame of mind, Melville incorporated into his accounts of Taji and friends ideas from Plato, Shakespeare, Rabelais, and others, not to mention material from the political and cultural scenes in America in the 1840s. In doing so, he turned away from autobiography and realism to the fanciful and imaginative.

Nonetheless, *Mardi* contributed at least indirectly to the development of Melville's essentially reality-based and partly scientific approach to and portrayal of insanity. The novel contains a number of passages on states of mind and emotions that although normal rather than abnormal are indicative of Melville's interest in the human consciousness. Such passages may anticipate considerations of states of mind in *Redburn* and later works. In Chapter 1 of *Mardi* the narrator describes the effect of a calm on a "landsman," the narrator himself; it can disturb the consciousness and "[unsettle] his mind." During a calm a person may "purposely delude himself into a crazy fancy, that he is merely at leisure" (pp. 9, 10). Melville's accounts reveal probable influences of *Observations on Man* by David Hartley, an eighteenth-century materialist and pragmatist who advocated a vibration theory to explain the essence of body and soul. Melville borrowed the book from the New York Society Library from 17 January to 22 February 1848.[15] In Chapter 2 of *Mardi* the narrator explains that a person feels "a sort of involuntary interior humming. . . . His cranium is a dome full of reverberations" (p. 10).

The passage is clearly satiric and comic. Other passages satirizing scientific knowledge of the brain show paradoxically a serious interest in the brain and in insanity. Samoa's tale in Chapter 98 of an operation to repair injured parts of a human brain by substituting parts of a pig brain refers to details of the operation: the brain cavity, the trepan itself, the securing of the scalp. Another passage satirizes a mechanical explanation of the relationship of body and brain, an approach that was under fire in some quarters then. The relationship would be a factor in considerations of insanity. The individual in the Chapter 98 passage survived for over a year, becoming "perverse" and "piggish" and finally "going mad, and dying in his delirium" (p. 299). The combination of delirium and death becomes a refrain in Melville's fiction.

The treatment in *Mardi* of phrenology and physiognomy is related to later treatments of insanity. Hillway explains that Melville had probably been aware of phrenology since boyhood inasmuch as it was a popular topic among the educated at mid-century in America. Melville's brother-in-law John Hoadley had a phrenological reading in 1845 of his "character and talents." A number of American and English scientists supported aspects of phrenology, for it related the physical brain and the immaterial mind, an important relationship in newer views of insanity; and it emphasized the importance of localization of the brain, a concept endorsed by Isaac Ray, Earle, Brigham, and S. B. Woodward, all prominent American psychiatrists. Yet phrenology was ironically criticized by Ray and others for providing simplistic explanations of insanity which were likely due to an "imbalance of faculties"; the origin of moral insanity, for example, would lie in undeveloped moral faculties in the brain.[16] Melville generally criticizes such simplifications and misdirections. He was familiar also with principles of physiognomy. During the 1849 trip to Europe, he purchased a copy of

Lavater's classic *Essays on Physiognomy*, which he later read. His treatment of aspects of physiognomy is satiric in *Mardi*. It is somewhat serious in *Pierre*: the youth's father, who owned a "wonderful work on Physiognomy," would not permit a painting of himself because "the strangest and shadowiest rules were laid down for detecting people's innermost secrets by studying their faces."[17] The father's mental breakdown may have been caused in part by such a secret.

The first extended treatment in Melville's fiction of a mental disease appears in *Mardi*. The disease is monomania, a few symptoms of which are portrayed in *Typee* and *Omoo*, but the condition is not illustrated or examined at length. In *Mardi* the condition is important and the word *monomania* is used for the first time.[18] Soon after Taji and Jarl desert the *Arcturion*, they naturally keep close track of the water supply in the boat. "[As] our voyage lengthened . . . the idea of being deprived of the precious fluid grew into something little short of a monomania; especially with Jarl" (p. 44).

Monomania serves in *Mardi* to satirize ideas and attitudes, or misuses or misconceptions of them. Monomania is a natural condition in the Mardian world, for it is full of champions or advocates of one idea or another. These are not mild-mannered, back-in-the-shadows monomaniacs like a few in later fiction, but relentless, arrogant, and sometimes outrageous figures symbolizing cultural values of all kinds or distortions or absences of such values.

An exception to the array of monomaniac figures is the narrator, Taji, who initially appears relatively normal. He is an intelligent, experienced sailor willing to gamble on deserting the whaler *Arcturion* and going it alone with Jarl in a small whaling boat. In the passing days the narrator shows that he is practical, observant, and somewhat of a dreamer. But, after falling in love with Yillah, he becomes obsessed with love. After Yillah disappears, Taji becomes obsessed with the goal of finding her. In a sense, Taji is the ideal monomaniac, totally committed but capable of philosophic discussions of death, time, or other topics. Taji's psychology is romantically conceived: his guilty thoughts over killing Aleema or Jarl's death; ruminations on time expressed in terms of soul, not mind; the mind as vast, expansive, even palpable. Sometimes the radically transformed narrator becomes enamored of other things, of learning and great men, as in Chapter 119, "Dreams." Not until near the end of *Mardi* does the narrator's madness become more recognizable. In the final chapter, as Media plans to return to his kingdom and others to stop at Serenia, Taji is described as a madman.

One companion cries out to him, "Nay, madman. Serenia is our haven." Taji, like Ahab and Pierre, is defiant, rebellious, and ultimately suicidal. In romantic terms, he is insane, separated from society by reason of his madness.

Although philosopher Babbalanja becomes obsessed with one idea or another, he usually keeps his wits, equanimity, and receptiveness. Sometimes his intense involvements draw criticism and even charges of insanity, which are delivered with derisive overtones by Mohi or Media, who do not understand Babbalanja's views or stances. Azzageddi, the spirit within Babbalanja, may be regarded figuratively as a character speaking for truth and freedom. Because he speaks so abstractly about will, independence, reason, or botanical laws, Azzageddi is sometimes described by befuddled listeners as a "lunatic" or as "mad." When Babbalanja agrees too vehemently with Azzageddi's views, he, too, is regarded as "mad." Azzageddi illustrates a fairly typical romantic conception of insanity or the insane spirit as free, mysterious, and truth-speaking.

Other satirized monomaniacs include many mad wise men or savants. Oh Oh is "famous as a venerable antiquarian . . . a cognoscenti, and dilettante in things old and marvelous." As an allegoric figure Oh Oh possesses a large nose and deformed body. He possesses also all kinds of artifacts and things of nature, including "the jaw-bones of Tooroorooloo, a great orator in the days of Unja," "a mermaid's comb for the toilet" (pp. 378–80), and many manuscripts, poetical, metaphysical, popular. Most of his prized possessions are worthless. Oh Oh is harmless but suffers from the delusion that such possessions and knowledge are invaluable and represent high truths.

Doxodox, an old reputed wise man on one island, is renowned for command of ideas and words. Babbalanja is beside himself with admiration for this thinker, who "nightly . . . bathes his soul in archangelical circumlucencies" (p. 563) and possesses a mastery of "Tetrads; Pentads; Hexads" as well as "Quadammodotatives." He is certainly Azzageddi's match for profundity. Yet his philosophic logic proves unequal to Babbalanja's "shark-syllogism" (pp. 563, 564). Doxodox is another deluded figure, separated from society but ever ready to profess his genius. He is not too far a cry from Surgeon of the Fleet Cuticle in *White-Jacket*, an actual madman whose misconceptions destroy lives. Hivohitee, the pontiff of Maramma, a harmful figure descended from 1847 Hivohitees, is a spiritual and all but unapproachable religious leader who destroys the spirit of his followers. His physical appearance suggests his inhumanity, aloofness, and seemingly a form of mono-mania: "an old, old man; with steel-gray eyes, hair and beard, and a horrible necklace of jaw-bones" (p. 360).

Overtones of moral insanity may appear in the comic and satiric por-trayal of young King Peepi, who is the inheritor of many images—the courage, physical ability, firmness, and other such qualities of former kings. The king's chief shortcomings are that he is "most unreliable" and that he has no conscience. As the ten-year-old monarch is the in-heritor also of "numerous anonymous souls," he is hardly his own mas-ter (pp. 203, 202). Peepi is subject therefore to impulses he cannot control.

Ranging from the realistic to the satiric and romantic, the treatment of insanity in *Typee, Omoo,* and *Mardi* illustrates a sound understanding of essentials of mental disease. Melville's interest in insanity, though, appears no greater in these novels than his interest in authority figures, native customs, or normal sailors. In *Redburn* and *White-Jacket,* dis-cussed in Chapter 4, troubled or abnormal characters are treated with greater interest, focus, and understanding. One result is the appear-ance of Melville's first major insane characters and an unusual array of minor or background figures.

CHAPTER FOUR. INSANE FIGURES IN

REDBURN AND *WHITE-JACKET*

Melville's sense of intellectual adventure and exploration continued past the completion of *Mardi* in January 1849. Herman and Elizabeth were at her parents' home in Boston waiting the birth of their first child in February. Melville had time to renew old friendships, meet new people, attend lectures in places like the Boston Anthenaeum, and devote many hours to reading. He was fascinated with Shakespeare's plays and lamented the fact that he had never studied them before. At this time Melville was thinking of a new book that would go beyond *Mardi*, perhaps in depth if not in scope. After Elizabeth completely recovered from a difficult delivery on 16 February, the family returned to New York City on 11 April.

Even while still in Boston, however, Melville began to have second thoughts about the quality of *Mardi* and his plans for another such venture. Newspaper reviews of *Mardi* first appeared in March and April. While some favorable ones referred to Melville's brilliant talents or genius and excellent accounts of adventure in the first part, many reviews, American as well as English, criticized *Mardi* as a blatant indulgence in flighty philosophizing, extravagant writing, and boring imitations of Sterne, Rabelais, Browne, and others. The most hostile English reviews condemned the entire work, and one regarded *Mardi* as "a rubbishing rhapsody," as "trash."[1] On 23 April, Melville wrote his father-in-law a rather bitter letter denouncing the tone and unfairness of reviews. It appears evident now that Melville was making too much of unfavorable reviews, too little of favorable ones. A much more disturbing fact was that sales of the novel were poor. With a new baby to take care of and medical and other bills to pay, Melville had to face the facts of life. He would have to forgo the pleasure and opportunity of writing the kind of novel he wanted to and write one instead for money. "Within a week or two of the time he wrote Shaw, Melville evidently decided that his obligations to his family transcended his obligations to himself as an artist."[2]

Melville began writing what was to become *Redburn* in late April or early May and finished the work in about ten weeks, or by early July, under difficult circumstances. Eleven or twelve people were living in the house at 103 Fourth Street: Elizabeth, Herman, and the new baby, Malcolm; Allan, his wife, and their new baby born two days after Malcolm; Melville's mother, Maria, now in her middle fifties; four unmarried sisters, and possibly a maid. The Melvilles were closely knit and got along well, but on occasion the house must have seemed too crowded or noisy to a sensitive writer beginning to hit his stride. During the warm months beginning in May, Melville worked at first on *Redburn* and then on *White-Jacket*, which was finished by early September in a hot room on the top floor adjoining a room with one of the teething babies. Beginning in May the city was stirred by threats of cholera, which materialized the next month. People were warned not to eat fish, fruit, or vegetables and many were reluctant to leave their homes. Many with the means for fleeing the city did so. By late July the daily death toll from the disease had reached three hundred. In a normal year Melville would have taken his annual vacation in August, but in 1849, working under pressure to finish the novels and read the galley proofs, he remained at his desk until late September. The four to five months of concentrated writing paid off in generally good reviews and much-needed additions to the family finances.

What Melville's day-to-day feelings were during these difficult months is likely beyond knowing. Most family correspondence of this time has not survived. Melville's surviving letters are few and give only an occasional glimpse of attitude or mood. In writing to the English publisher Bentley about *Redburn* on 5 June, Melville was admirably objective in describing the book as "a plain, straightforward, amusing narrative of personal experience . . . no metaphysics, no conic-sections" (p. 318). As

Parker points out, it was to Melville's advantage to appear practical in the letter. During his European trip in 1849, Melville wrote in December to Evert Duyckinck, "*Redburn* . . . to my surprise (somewhat) seems to have been favorably received. I am glad of it—for it puts money into an empty purse. But I hope I shall never write such a book again— Tho' when a poor devil writes with duns all round him & looking over the back of his chair—& perching on his pen & diving in his inkstand . . . what can you expect of that poor devil? . . . but a beggarly 'Redburn'" (p. 322). But as readers have shown since then, *Redburn* has proved itself to be a much better work than the author originally realized.

Melville belittled the book because he regarded it as only a little "nursery tale," something "to buy tobacco with." Economics played a role in the selection of the topic, for Melville needed something that could be written rapidly and would likely sell well. Accordingly, the new work should involve no philosophy and no extensive reading or research. As *Typee* and *Omoo* were in part autobiographical, not complex, and sold reasonably well, Melville decided to draw upon other aspects of his experiences. His first sea journey in 1839 was a natural choice.

Writing about experiences that had occurred ten years earlier was complicated by the fact that he was writing about them with family members in the house. *Redburn* begins with a home and family resembling the writer's in Lansingburgh in 1839. In 1849, except for the deceased father and Gansevoort and Tom on a whaling cruise, the family was still intact. With the mother, four sisters, and a brother there and his own finances rather shaky, Melville could naturally think back to the situation ten years before when times and circumstances were even more difficult. Poverty and money become recurrent themes in *Redburn*, reflecting family circumstances back then and perhaps in 1849. Melville's recollections of his father in 1849 must have been strong, for references to him in the novel reveal love and admiration. Nothing is included about the final illness. Writing about a youth's land and sea adventures may have left little room for lengthy accounts of home life. Yet the novel contains many references to insanity and madness: the character's "madness" when he thinks of the glass ship or of the hostile world, Jackson's prominence, the many insane figures in the Liverpool section. These come from past experiences and the present as well. Charles Fenno Hoffman's treatment for insanity, worries about money, and tensions from writing in a crowded, sometimes noisy house could remind Melville of personal vulnerabilities, his own fear of the twisted mind.[3]

The ambitious work Melville had vaguely in mind earlier that year may have been a psychological study or one in which abnormalities play a major role, as they do in *Moby-Dick* and *Pierre*. The abnormalities appear also in *Redburn* and *White-Jacket*, which the writer disparaged as "two *jobs*, which I have done for money."[4]

Redburn is the first American novel, and perhaps the first American fiction of any length, to treat insanity in largely straightforward, realistic terms. Before the novel appeared in 1849, novels by Brown and Cooper and stories by Irving, Poe, and Hawthorne, among others, often provided illuminating insights into the nature of insanity and the behavior of insane characters, but the treatments were mainly romantic or nonrealistic. *Redburn* and *White-Jacket*, both written in 1850 at the height of the romantic movement in this country, are in significant ways romantic, but their portrayals of the abnormal mind, consciousness, and behavior are to a large extent based on pragmatic or scientific assessments and expressed in often realistic terms.

Experiences already described in the 1830s and 1849, people Melville knew or observed during these and other times, and possibly some reading would provide in large measure the realistic base of *Redburn*. While writing the novel, Melville included information from the *Penny Cyclopaedia* on architecture and the Indian tree, the sagoon. With his lively mind, Melville might well have checked a volume of the *Cyclopaedia* for information on aspects of insanity. As explained in Chapter 2, the article in Volume 12 contained scientific definitions of forms and qualities of insanity. Although there is no hard evidence that Melville made use of such information, his portrayals of insanity show sound, concrete knowledge of monomania and moral insanity. The novel also reveals the writer's growing interest in insanity with the inclusion of such words as "insane," "mad," "madness," "melancholy," "monomania," "monomaniac," "delirium tremens," and "delirium." A book referred to in *Redburn* is entitled *Delirium Tremens*; in the mid-nineteenth century delirium tremens was regarded as a form of insanity.

On the practical, everyday level, the world of *Redburn* appears to be dominated by the grim, oppressive, and even unbalanced. The youthful character is threatened by people and activities on land and scorned or belittled aboard ship. The enigmatic Jackson frightens most self-respecting individuals, and Captain Riga, for all his show, cares little for anyone but himself. Both characters appear to be on the far side of the thin red line. The Liverpool dock area, full of crime and poverty, presents the maturing Redburn with unpleasant lessons in causes and forms of abnormality flourishing in the blighted areas. Naive and somewhat arrogant, he develops sympathy for the poor and disenfranchised. By the end of the journey Redburn has gained a more realistic and credible sense of himself and others. In retrospect the mature Redburn reveals an order and stability in the earlier experiences and world where little had seemed to exist.

Wellingborough Redburn is the first Melville narrator vitally concerned with the nature of his own psychology.[5] In the opening chapters of the novel, he describes dreams and fears of boyhood and bitter disappointments of youth. As a boy he loved to stand with his father on the wharf and hear about distant travels. When his father was gone he was lonely. At home after his father died, he dreamed of becoming a traveler himself and of sailing to distant lands. As he grew older the daydreams often centered on the little glass ship and glass sailors in the parlor. Redburn would study it for hours, wondering about its treasure and breaking into the ship to find it. "And often I used to feel a sort of insane desire to be the death of the glass ship." When his mother learned of such a desire, she placed it out of reach "until I should recover my reason" (p. 8). His sense of irrational drives and youthful fantasies may be based on loneliness and dissatisfactions with his bleak home life. When he is ready to leave home, Redburn as character appears fearful, determined, and bitter. "There is no misanthrope like a boy disappointed; and such was I, with the warm soul of me flogged out by adversity" (p. 10). Aboard the Hudson riverboat taking him to New York City, Redburn feels out of place, poor, and finally hostile when informed by the captain's clerk that the price of a ticket has gone up. After paying one dollar but no more, Redburn is aware that other passengers are staring at him. Unable to bear their observations, he stares back at one, then at another, and finally cocks his gun and aims it at one man. People scatter about, "exclaim[ing] that I must be crazy. So I was at that time; for otherwise I know not how to account for my demoniac feelings, of which I was afterwards heartily ashamed, as I ought to have been, indeed; and much more than that" (p. 13).

Although the mature narrator regards such incidents with detachment and a sense of humorous exaggeration, there is an underlying note of seriousness, an indication that the narrator has not forgotten earlier confusions, fears, and hatreds. But he understands them much better now and has come to accept his father's death. The character has not. His father is deeply missed. The youth's confusion, sense of despair and sadness, as well as hatred may be due to his father's absence. Redburn nonetheless possesses gritty qualities that enable him to perform shipboard duties efficiently and to get along fairly well with experienced crewmen, no mean accomplishment. The weeks in Liverpool and on the voyage home add to the toughening process. In the second half of the novel, Redburn gives clear indications of the man he will become: intelligent, sympathetic, and responsible.

As in *Typee* and *Omoo*, character portrayals in *Redburn* are based to some extent on actual individuals. William H. Gilman explains that in writing the novel, Melville "used real people, like the Greenlander, the Irishman, and Jackson, the mates, the cook, and the steward," but, he cautions, "where fact leaves off and invention begins is impossible to say." The original Jackson evidently shared only his name, New York City origin, and approximate age with the fictional Jackson. Robert Jackson was not seemingly insane, and he survived the journey from Liverpool to New York. Although he may have shared qualities with the character, no evidence of that has been discovered. Oliver P. Brown, a Stockholm native and captain of the *St. Lawrence*, provided a few points of background for Captain Riga of the novel, but Riga like Jackson seems to have been shaped largely by Melville's imagination.[6] Yet as critics have pointed out, that imagination worked most productively with recollections and impressions of what had been directly experienced, whether places, things, incidents, people, or books. Jackson and Riga may be derived from several people and places in Melville's experiences, and individual qualities of the two may come from ideas or insights gained from the *Penny Cyclopaedia* article or another source. There is no hard evidence that Liverpool characters in the novel are based on actual people he observed or even talked with in 1839, but it seems likely that the more fully developed ones would have some basis in actuality, as will be claimed shortly.

Most sailors and officers aboard the *Highlander* appear more or less normal, possibly because the crew of the *St. Lawrence* was of above-average quality. At any rate, sailors like the Greenlander and Max the Dutchman possess no more than typical maritime peccadilloes. The Irishman Blunt, with his superstitions and other preoccupations, is nonetheless competent and stable. The mates appear reliable and typical. But a few aboard ship reveal indications of emotional weaknesses.

Appearing before the crew or in a formal situation, Captain Riga would strike onlookers as stable if not approachable or friendly. In the early meeting with Redburn and his brother, Riga appears cheerful, even paternal. Yet beneath the surface lurk less evident and reassuring qualities. After the *Highlander* docks, he spends much of his time drinking and some of it "dead drunk." More revealing, however, is his treatment of crew members, his expression of a "thousand small meannesses." Yet, puzzlingly, on the return journey he shows consideration for the Irish immigrants. The captain's contradictory qualities, his sudden changes in mood, displays of self-hatred, and hatred of others indicate the likelihood of a mental problem, perhaps a form of moral insanity.

An obvious example of abnormality in *Redburn* is exhibited by the sailor brought aboard ship "dead drunk" and left in his bunk. Waking up, "raging mad with delirium tremens," he rushes up on deck, "trembling and shrieking," and, "in a fit of frenzy," commits suicide by jumping overboard (p. 50). Melville's brief account highlights obvious symptoms then and today of delirium tremens. The sailor is "raging mad," irrational, and hallucinating in some way, and he commits suicide. A physical state of intoxication creates an irrational mental state which leads in this instance to self-destruction. Melville's familiarity with delirium tremens likely came from sailing experiences, especially aboard the *United States*, which, during Melville's fourteen months, recorded many cases of drunkenness, although apparently none of delirium tremens. Most of the novels and a few stories include a few characters affected, usually adversely, by alcohol. The most noticeable drinkers include the English pilot in *Typee*; Jermin in *Omoo*; Claret and Mad Jack in *White-Jacket*; Perth, an ex-alcoholic in *Moby-Dick*; and Turkey in "Bartleby the Scrivener." Drinking is a problem on the *Neversink* in *White-Jacket*, but no one has a case of DTs. In these various instances excessive drinking is a contributing factor to an unstable condition. Alcohol makes things seem better for the drinker or exacerbates an unpleasant or painful emotional state. Melville may have obtained technical information on delirium tremens from a volume of *Penny Cyclopaedia* or another printed source. Books by Ray and Amariah Brigham provide discussions of the disease. Ray examines drunkenness, the various symptoms of delirium tremens, the nature of the delirium, and similarities between delirium tremens and moral mania.[7]

Melville's interest in delirium tremens is illustrated further by references in Chapter 18 of *Redburn* to a book owned by Max, a crew mem-

ber. This is "a large black volume, with *Delirium Tremens* in great gilt
letters on the back. This proved to be a popular treatise on the subject
of that disease; and I remembered seeing several copies in the sailor
book-stalls about Fulton Market, and along South-street, in New York"
(p. 86). As *Redburn* and *White-Jacket* indicate, drunkenness and even
delirium tremens can be expected at sea.

Jackson is the first major insane figure in Melville's fiction—whatever
may be his source. Jackson's behavior and opinions mystify many on
the *Highlander*, including the youthful narrator, who, years later, de-
picts him in mainly realistic terms. Although Redburn may have over-
reacted to Jackson, his initial reactions while naive are essentially sound.
"Sometimes I thought he was really crazy; and often felt so frightened
at him, that I thought of going to the captain about it, and telling him
Jackson ought to be confined, lest he should do some terrible thing at
last" (p. 61). Jackson's fairly complex condition appears to be largely
moral insanity. His behavior is unsocial even though it is usually predictable. He shows no concern for or interest in other crewmen or officers, except as objects for criticism or ridicule, and no respect at all for
traditional moral and religious standards. He has only contempt for
such standards and people who uphold them. Highly critical and supercilious, Jackson is sometimes unexpectedly apathetic, "dumb . . .
like a man in the moody madness" (p. 58). His problems are largely
emotional. His main one is a strong hatred pervading and influencing
all apparent attitudes and behavior. This suggests the possibility of
monomania because at times the sailor acts "as if all the world was one
person, and had done him some dreadful harm, that was rankling and
festering in his heart" (p. 61). Yet the sharp focus and concentration of
monomaniac delusion or hatred are not evident. A distinction between
moral insanity and monomania is clarified in Prichard's study: "The
characteristic feature of this malady [moral insanity] . . . is extreme
irascibility. . . . There are other instances in which malignity has a
deeper die. The individual, as if actually possessed by the demon of
evil, is continually indulging enmity and plotting mischief [monoma-
nia]. . . . When the morbid phenomena include merely the expressions
of intense malevolence, without ground or provocation actual or supposed, the case is strictly one of the nature described above [moral
insanity]."[8]

The characterization of Jackson provides a good illustration of Melville's expository and dramatic skills. Chapter 12, "Some Account of
Jackson," presents facts and details about Jackson's life and background

as well as information on his appearance, character, and mannerisms. This example of Melville's life-history approach, with its stress on exposition, illustrates also the writer's technique of buttressing realistic descriptions with romantic phrases and allusions which often enrich the descriptions. Jackson's "infernal gloom" is described as being worthy of "the dark, moody hand of Salvator," and his hidden torments are deepened by references to King Antiochus of Syria, who suffered a terrible death, and to the "diabolical Tiberius," who underwent great tortures (pp. 275, 276). Although somewhat far-fetched, the analogies suggest psychological depths and unfulfilled capacities of the remarkable sailor.

To a noticeable extent, mental abnormality and environment are related in *Redburn*. Places in the novel contribute in some way to the appearance and frequency of insanity. In regarding place as a contributing factor, Melville was hardly original, for Hawthorne and Dickens show the effects of environment on characters, and scientists then were aware of the influence, although they may not have regarded environment in theoretical terms. Ray refers to effects on patients of "accidental, outward events"; Brigham, to money and domestic problems and inadequate education; and Prichard, to "restraints imposed by social order. . . . It is among these circumstances . . . that we are to look for the causes which are most influential in the development of mental diseases."[9]

The chief environments in *Redburn* are the home, ship, and city. The home environment prepares the protagonist for his journey and provides recollections of home and father to sustain him. The dominant places are the ship and city. Even a clean, well-operated four-rigged traveler is not the best place for an emotionally vulnerable youth. During the first few days aboard, Redburn feels "unsettled" and on occasion "melancholy." He is disturbed by the indifference of many sailors and Jackson's contempt. But Redburn manages to buckle down to daily tasks of hard, monotonous work. Before the ship reaches Liverpool, he is not only competent on deck, but agile and sure in the rigging and sails. Shipboard activity strengthens his equilibrium. The close quarters of the ship, however, serve to exacerbate Jackson's suspicions and hatreds and compel Captain Riga to greater self-discipline until the ship reaches port and he can drink away his problems.

In several chapters the relationship between environment, group, and mental state is examined in partly expository terms. In Chapter 29, for example, Melville discusses sailors as individuals and as a group or class with a specific role, function, and reputation. This is in effect a class history. In Chapter 41 appears a comparable treatment of the poor. Environment and poverty combine to affect mentalities of the poor. Instances of mental abnormality seem to go hand in hand with shabby environments and impoverished ways of life. Chapter 41 includes detailed accounts of Redburn's walks around Liverpool in middle-class areas, in "wealthier quarters," and in particular in areas inhabited by the poor:

> In some parts of town, inhabited by laborers, and poor people generally; I used to crowd my way through masses of squalid men, women, and children, who at this evening hour . . . seem to empty themselves into the street, and live there for the time. I had never seen any thing like it in New York. Often I witnessed some curious, and many very sad scenes . . . a pale, ragged man, rushing along frantically, and striving to throw off his wife and children. . . . He seemed bent upon rushing down to the water, and drowning himself, in some despair, and *craziness* of wretchedness. In these haunts, beggary went on before me wherever I walked. . . . Poverty, poverty, poverty, in almost endless vistas: and want and woe staggered arm in arm along these miserable streets. (p. 201, my italics)

Whatever the nature of the man's "craziness," environment and poverty are major external factors. Some scientists of the mid-1800s would regard these as causes.

The same causes appear in the situation of old men and women observed around the Liverpool docks, "searching after bodies" of sailors who had drowned overnight. These people are on the scene early in the morning to get at the "night-harvest" (p. 179) of bodies. Suffering and want have likely affected them mentally and perhaps have affected also the poor involved in crime. Prostitutes and thieves flock the alleys and narrow streets near the docks. Some men and women appear morally as well as mentally deteriorated. Found in the area of "Prince's Dock" are "burkers" who suffocate people for their bodies and "resurrectionists" who dig up bodies for use in medical labs. If some are mental defectives, others have likely stepped over the thin red line separating the sane from the insane. How could Melville think otherwise?

Liverpool beggars in particular gain the writer's attention. "Nor must I omit to make mention of the singular beggary practiced in the streets. . . . Every variety of want and suffering here met the eye, and every vice showed here its victims" (p. 186). Several beggars are described in detail, including "a tall, pallid man, with a white bandage round his brow, and his face cadaverous as a corpse. He . . . said nothing; but with one finger silently pointed down to the square of flagging at his feet" (pp. 186–87). This individual may be perfectly sane. But appearance, manner, and silence indicate otherwise.

Moral insanity and monomania are dominant diseases among the poor and sailoring classes in *Redburn*. Moral insanity, the more complex, can appear in various forms depending on the dominant emotion, which may be love, hate, elation, despondency, or something else. Sometimes the disease can be a crucial factor in cases of suicide or homicide, and, as indicated in Chapter 2, it was regarded by some in mid-century as a precursor to monomania.[10] The disease may not be therefore routinely detectable. "It is often very difficult to pronounce, with certainty, as to the presence or absence of moral insanity, or to determine whether the appearances which are supposed to indicate its presence do not proceed from natural peculiarity or eccentricity of character."[11] In an 1861 article, Ray explained that moral insanity "may be a simple perversion of some sentiment or propensity, or . . . it may be a loss of those fine sensibilities which make the family relations a source of active interest and self-sacrifice." As a scientific classification, moral insanity may not have been based on sufficient and thoroughly examined evidence, and descriptions of the disease lack modern-day precision and exactness. Nonetheless, the classification anticipates modern insights into the nature of insanity; for example, rational thinking may be accompanied by irrational or unpredictable emotions.[12]

One form of moral insanity is represented in *Redburn* by "a little, shabby, old man," a dock-area figure who badgers the narrator to buy a "pure gold" ring. This creature persistently follows Redburn, who rightly regards him as "crazy." He is a strange man with a "mystic and admonitory . . . air." When Redburn politely informs him that he does not want a ring, the man acts insulted, cries, "Don't you? Then take that," and knocks Redburn down (pp. 194, 195). Such behavior shows at least a perversion of feelings—quick anger, complete indifference to Redburn's wants, violence. The man's behavior indicates a noticeable degree of moral and social alienation.

For more complex portrayals, Melville relies to a greater extent on combining expository and dramatic materials in a life history, as in the treatment of the remarkable beggar and sailor–ballad singer Redburn observes, who composes his own songs on the spot and sells copies in the streets. He is not a case study but a credible figure, outgoing and enthusiastic rather than moody and uncommunicative. The enthusiasm and eccentricity indicate the possibility of effects of a form of moral insanity. The man's eccentricity is centered about his singing and a "remarkable" arm, which he swings vertically during the songs. The swinging arm is "naturally unaccountable." A touch of monomania may be evident in the singer's obsession with stories and violent happenings. "He was a monomaniac upon these subjects; he was a Newgate Calendar of the robberies and assassinations of the day, happening in the sailor quarters of the town; and most of his ballads were upon kindred subjects" (p. 190). Although there is no evidence of delusions, there is the likelihood of impairment of the rational faculties and of a form of moral insanity in which "preternatural excitement" of speech and manner is dominant.[13]

White-Jacket was written in the last half of the long, hot summer of 1849, when, if anything, writing conditions at 103 Fourth Street in New York City were worse than they had been in previous months for *Redburn*. Yet despite heat, household interruptions, and worries over bills and the reception of *Redburn*, Melville kept at the book, writing three thousand words daily, and finished it in about ten weeks. The length was 465 pages. Melville may have found *White-Jacket* more manageable than *Redburn* had been, because the pertinent experiences had occurred only five or six years before and they were apparently quite fresh. "Melville's memories of the routine of shipboard life and of several exciting events which took place during his fourteen months . . . were sharp and he was able to use them at will."[14] The naval duty lasted three to four times as long as the *St. Lawrence* experiences in 1839 and occurred on a ship that dwarfed the packet ship or trader and carried five hundred men and officers rather than twenty or so. The impact on Melville was not in proportion, but by the time the *United States* docked in Boston he must have had more than enough of naval routines and duties, of officers and regulations, of ship food, punishments, and monotony. He had made some good friends, met many people, and observed many more. Some reappear in *White-Jacket* because the "models" of more than twenty characters have been identified and others are composites. Some, like Surgeon Cuticle and Master-at-Arms Bland, are based on literary models or inspirations. How many of the five hundred aboard the *United States* revealed instabilities of one kind or another is beyond knowing. But if the surviving medical and surgical journal of the ship and the descriptions and accounts in the novel are at least partly reliable, quite a few aboard ship during Melville's fourteen months experienced psychological problems of some kind.[15]

The world of the *Neversink* is more complex than that of *Redburn* because it is both documentary and symbolic. The many classes of men and officers, the many regulations and functions, reflect the good and bad, the strengths and the weaknesses of naval and Western society. This world contains many conditions and levels, ranging from naval injustices to democratic principles, from ignoble leadership to remarkable achievements, from maturation to frustrating isolation. A general theme here is that sanity and stability weigh more than their opposites. Despite the injustices and stupidities of this world, Jack Chase, Nord, Williams, and even White Jacket will somehow prevail. They must prevail against the pervasive evil influences of Master-at-Arms Bland and Surgeon of the Fleet Cuticle, who are far more threatening and disruptive than Jackson aboard the *Highlander*. For the first time significantly, insanity and evil are linked, especially in the figure of Bland. But Bland's evil, sophisticated insanity is balanced by the humanity of Jack Chase, and the mad hatter qualities of Cuticle are somehow held in check ironically by ship regulations. Flogging through the fleet, the most despicable and inhumane naval punishment, is both evil and mad, but the outrage and common sense of White Jacket and others put it in perspective and anticipate its eventual removal.

White Jacket differs from his counterpart in *Redburn* in several respects. As a character, he is older, more experienced, a better sailor, and more perceptive about himself. Concerned about his relations with others, he does not think about youthful dispositions toward insanity or melancholy. He is more outgoing and involved with other crewmen. However, his jacket marks him as somewhat aloof. As a narrator, White Jacket is more knowledgeable about his past, the ship, crew, officers, ship regulations, and the like. His views of such things show breadth and variety. He can be objective and factual and also satiric, humorous, and ironic. His views of officers and men range from the favorable to the unfavorable. He vigorously defends the rights and dignity of the crew and praises several individual crewmen. But the dominant tone is critical and satiric. In Chapter 18, "A Man-of-war Full as a Nut," appears a survey of vocations and moralities of frigate sailors. This is essentially a class history: "The Navy is the asylum for the perverse, the home of the unfortunate. Here the sons of adversity meet the children of calamity who in turn meet the offspring of sin. Bankrupt brokers, bootblacks, blacklegs, and blacksmiths here assemble together; and cast-away tinkers, watch-makers, quill-drivers, cobblers, doctors, farmers, and lawyers compare past experiences and talk of old times" (p. 74). Accounts throughout the novel illustrate aspects of this pessimistic appraisal. Views of insane figures are similarly critical and convincing. The point to keep in mind is that whatever the apparent mood or attitude of the narrator, portraits of insane figures are based on sound observations and keen insights, as in the following instances.

Scriggs, an old Marine, is an underling of Master-at-Arms Bland. Scriggs serves dutifully but is caught in smuggling operations and slated for punishment. That fact unnerves him. Upon learning that he will be flogged, he cringes in an "agony of fear," a remarkable reaction for a marine. Scriggs is also noteworthy for personal uncleanliness and for indifference to the few luxuries obtainable aboard ship. These failures indicate the likelihood of a form of personal deterioration—perhaps a manifestation of moral insanity. Landless, an ordinary seaman, is ironically cheerful and agreeable. His willingness to oblige others makes him a favorite with officers. But his obedience masks certain lacks: ambition, purpose, or moral direction. His only needs are rum and tobacco. With them, naval life is a lark; without them it is only bearable. And sometime in the past, Landless, like Scriggs, changed, for he has a history of floggings which Melville does not clarify. Presumably, Landless was disobedient or rebellious; perhaps the punishment broke him. Whatever the case, he strikes the observant narrator as someone with an "invincible indifference," "a fellow without shame, without a soul" (p. 384). His cheerful conformism enables him to escape melancholy, protective daydreams, or eccentricity. But his lack of conscience and general indifference suggest a form of regressive moral insanity.

In *White-Jacket*, environment and poverty or its effects are contributing factors in the incidence of insanity. The *Neversink* is the main environment, and a typical sailor, while living a hard life, does not likely live one of poverty. But many aboard ship come apparently from a poor environment, for they are the "unfortunate," the "sons of adversity," the "children of calamity." Doctors, lawyers, and bankers among the crew may have lost their civilian practices and fallen to a low estate. The huge frigate is clearly Melville's main concern and he leaves no doubt that ship conditions contribute to an unstable mental or emotional condition. Although Chapter 12, "The Good or Bad Temper of

. . . men . . . attributable to their . . . Stations and Duties . . ." (p. 44), is largely satiric and humorous, one underlying point is serious: a poor environment makes for poor behavior and attitudes; a corollary: a poor environment can make for insanity. The chapter begins with Quoin, a moody, unpleasant gunner's mate. "As has been seen, Quoin was full of unaccountable whimsies; he was, withal, a very cross, bitter, ill-natured, inflammable little old man. So, too, were all the members of the gunner's gang" (p. 44), who are always grumbling, swearing, and chasing others away from their guns. They are also suspicious and quarrelsome. Under the clever humor lies a set of sailors in the grip of irascible melancholy.

Life aboard ship is so monotonous and restrictive that the daily allowance of one gill, or quarter-pint, of whiskey has almost no palliating effect. Most officers and men wait for a port stop to indulge in drink or they risk drinking spirits smuggled aboard ship. Chapter 43, "Smuggling in a Man-of-war," explains the risks of smuggling whiskey and the dangers of excessive drinking. "Delirium tremens and the mania-a-potu" (p. 176), apparently regarded in mid-century as the same thing, are sometimes consequences of such drinking.[16] Several characters aboard ship show the effects. Scriggs is one. Another is Mad Jack, a highly efficient and brave officer who on one occasion saves the ship from capsizing. But Mad Jack has some bad marks on his record: he has been suspended from duty twice and in one situation almost lost his rank—all because of "frolics" caused by drinking. As he possesses strong opinions and enthusiasms, the combination of drinking, shipboard pressures, high personal expectations, and temper could lead to serious trouble, possibly a bout with delirium tremens or mania-a-potu. Something of the kind may be waiting for Captain Claret, a longtime alcoholic from a family of drinkers, who apparently has a private supply of whiskey. Both officers are vulnerable.

Although the novel was hurriedly written, *White-Jacket* includes two of Melville's most effective characterizations before *Moby-Dick*: Surgeon of the Fleet Cuticle and Master-at-Arms Bland. Both characters illustrate the extent to which the naval society is permeated by strains of mental aberration, and both illustrate Melville's complex portrayals of forms of insanity. The writer's delineation of each character and his background becomes in effect a life history.

Fortunately, no one remotely like Surgeon Cuticle served aboard the *United States* during Melville's tour of duty. Surgeon William Johnson, who served during that tour, is described as having "a distinguished career in the navy." As several have pointed out, Surgeon Cuticle is derived largely not from experience but in part from Smollett's Cadwallader Morgan in *Roderick Random*.[17] Morgan, an assistant of the ship's doctor, observes many botched and inhumane operations and other miscarriages of justice aboard ship.

Cadwallader Cuticle, M.D., is a comic masterpiece. He may be a realistic one as well. Melville effectively combines the two. On at least the realistic level he is clearly a "mental case," if often a humorously and wittily developed one. On that level he is a pompous fool, a deceptively sane medical officer of the highest rank. On that level, too, Cuticle reveals qualities of both moral insanity and monomania, with the latter dominant. His aloofness and indifference are evident during the operation upon the dying sailor and in the earlier remark that "he would rather cut off a man's arm than dismember the wing of the most delicate pheasant" (p. 248). On other occasions Cuticle appears sensible, rational, and charming. Usually, however, he is neither sensible nor rational. Signs of monomania appear in frequent failures of cognition and inflated conceptions of himself and his achievements. Whatever the circumstances, Cuticle always regards himself as *the* surgeon. The delusion is not rigid or grandiose in the sense that Cuticle regards himself as a particular kind of medical genius or as a great surgeon out of the past. He appears quite satisfied with himself as the unexcelled Surgeon of the Fleet Cuticle. That is sufficient eminence, he might explain. The delusions may be characterized by a range of emotions. Cuticle can be gloomy in his cabin, and he has morbid interests in a collection of plaster and wax casts of human malformations. The dominant emotion, however, is "enthusiasm." Among fellow officers, Cuticle is customarily confident, even spirited. As Prichard explains, a common form of monomania is characterized not by melancholy, a former name for monomania, but by elation. "Some patients of this description are proud and elated, and fancy themselves kings or emperors, but on ordinary subjects are capable of talking coherently if not rationally; they appear to be happy in their delusions."[18] Such is the case with Surgeon Cuticle.

Official records indicate that no one like Master-at-Arms Bland was aboard the *United States* during Melville's cruise or any other cruise. Howard P. Vincent asserts that the real model for Bland is a much disliked figure, Sterrit, in McNally's *Some Evils and Abuses in the Naval and Merchant Service Exposed* (1839). The similarities seem to lie in the hatred crewmen had for Sterrit and their attempts to kill him.[19] While

Bland might well be a composite of several sources and influences, the main shaping force would appear to be Melville's compelling imagination, which made Bland's psychology the most complex before Ahab.

Bland's character, more complexly developed than Jackson's, reveals nothing of Jackson's moody misanthropy or of Cuticle's flamboyance. Such words as "mad," "crazy," or "monomaniac" are not applied to him, and he appears to be constantly rational and efficient. Yet this fascinating character is subtly and irredeemably insane. His remarkable control of his emotions is one indication that something is amiss, for he shows no hint of fear or anxiety as he walks stripped of rank among men who would kill him if given the chance. He shows instead "intrepidity, coolness, and wonderful self-possession" (p. 187). The likelihood is that he does not feel the appropriate emotions. A related point is that Bland's hatred is more pervasive and involved than Jackson's. It is expressed through manipulations of others, contempt for people, and illegal shipboard activities. Yet Bland's hatred, like Jackson's, lacks focus. It is not delusory. It seems to be a sophisticated form of misanthropy expressed on the surface by casual indifference toward others and toward naval society. With a natural predilection for wicked deeds, Bland will act for others if that will promote his own ends. He is of course at times charming and is usually sociable. Melville applies a bewildering array of adjectives and phrases to describe intricacies of Bland's character and disposition, which appear to show subtle effects of moral insanity.

While Bland's insanity is more widely and deeply threatening than Jackson's and more elaborate, the portrayal has limitations. Melville is somewhat vague about the scope and depth of Bland's mentality. His unruffled exterior and relentless civility are carefully described, but his thoughts and motivations are left vague. What remains is nonetheless an intriguing, perceptive portrayal of a complex figure outwardly identifiable by symptoms of moral insanity.

Melville's insights into Jackson, Bland, Riga, and others may have come from family experiences, the sailor years, books, or the *Cyclopaedia* article. Whatever the sources, the insights appear relevant and perceptive. Nineteenth-century interpretations of insanity appear dated or simplistic by today's standards, but studies by Esquirol, Conolly, Prichard, and others in France and England and by Ray, Brigham, and others in America have been recognized in this century as important and in some respects modern. The thesis of Ray's 1861 article on moral insanity, which followed principles of his 1838 study, was regarded as "significantly controversial" in 1873 and, according to a modern commentator, is still "with us today, overtly and covertly." Another commentator explains that "the concept of moral insanity proved of great significance in psychiatric history, for it led to the concepts of neurotic character, psychopathic personality and affective disorders; in medical jurisprudence it is still disputed." The studies of Esquirol and Prichard into the causes and nature of monomania anticipated in some respects the modern classifications of paranoia, *manie raisonnante*, and "the compulsive-obsessive syndrome of modern psychiatry." Nineteenth-century thinkers did not arrive of course at exact definitions of moral insanity and monomania. The classifications of that time were too broadly defined or inconclusive.[20] Although Melville was naturally interested in mental diseases, he was not ordinarily concerned with the niceties, exactness, and precision of scientific definitions. He provided his own revealing definitions and analyses in accounts of emotional or mental aberration. In doing so, he was sometimes profound.

The depth of Melville's understanding of mental disease, particularly monomania, and the nature of his literary definitions and analyses, along with related matters, will be examined in the next two chapters, beginning with Chapter 5 and characters in *Moby-Dick*.

CHAPTER FIVE. THE WORLD IS MAD

Moby-Dick

After five strenuous months writing *Redburn* and *White-Jacket* in the crowded house at 103 Fourth Street in New York City, Melville was a tired, somewhat disillusioned man in need of rest and a change of scene. With blessings of his concerned family and others and financial assistance from Judge Shaw, Melville boarded the *Southampton*, a British liner, on 11 October 1849 for an extended trip to England and the Continent. He took along proof sheets of *White-Jacket* with the hope of gaining a better contract in England. The trip proved to be beneficial and eventful. Melville visited a number of noteworthy places, met interesting people, discovered to his surprise that *Redburn* was selling well, and secured a good arrangement for the publication of *White-Jacket*. One passenger on the *Southampton* was George J. Adler, a professor of German and linguistics at New York University, who, like Melville, had just completed exhausting intellectual labors and was going abroad to regain his health. As he confessed to Melville shortly after they met, he "was almost crazy . . . for a time."[1]

The traditional view of the Melville-Adler relationship has been that the learned Adler stimulated Melville's interest in philosophic ideas, including those of Kant and Swedenborg, that were to appear in his writing and thinking for some years. In an excellent 1986 study of the

meeting and relationship, Marovitz explains that Melville's main benefit from the friendship was not philosophic but psychological: Melville
discovered that the other man had tensions and difficulties resembling
his own. "The German philologist simultaneously reflected an image of
Melville's present psychological state and represented to him as well a
portentous confrontation with his own fears and intellectual aspira-
tions." During their many meetings aboard ship Melville's "sublimi-
nal fear" of insanity was usually in his conscious mind. Melville's encounters early in the journey with two crazy male passengers, one of
whom he unsuccessfully attempted to save from drowning, would be a
reminder of his own vulnerability.[2] This appears sound. It is likely
though that such fears were close to the surface before Melville came
aboard ship, for after months of intense writing, some of it on difficult
youthful experiences and scenes of poverty and abnormality, he was
fatigued.

Although there is no evidence that the two friends met again after
parting in Paris, the interest was certainly there. Back in this country,
Melville inquired of Adler in four letters to their mutual friend Evert
Duyckinck, two written in the fall of 1850 and two early in 1851.[3]
In January 1851, Adler sent to Melville in Pittsfield a copy of his recent translation of Goethe's *Iphigenia in Tauris*. Although evidence of
Melville's response has not been found, it is hard to believe that he
would not respond. In 1853, after a violent outbreak of hallucinations
and delusions, perhaps in the form of monomania or agoraphobia,
Adler was committed to the private Bloomingdale asylum in New York
City, from which he wrote to Duyckinck on 10 October 1853, asking for
his assistance and that of "my literary confederates" in obtaining his
freedom. Adler had described his situation and complaints in September letters to the president of New York University and the New York
mayor.[4] There is no known record of responses or replies to Adler's
complaints or to his pleas for support. If Melville had been aware of
Adler's situation, he would undoubtedly have written to his friend.
The hiatus in the Melville-Duyckinck relationship between 1852 and
1856 may possibly account for lack of evidence of Melville's response
to Adler and, conceivably, of his ignorance as well of Adler's stay at
Bloomingdale, but that, too, is difficult to believe, for Melville corre-
sponded with others in New York, especially with his brother Allan,
who as a lawyer and interested bystander might have learned of Adler's
situation and informed Melville. At any rate, Melville did not forget
Adler, for he was among the very few to attend Adler's funeral in 1868.

When Melville left on the *Southampton* for England, he took along a copy of *Old Wine in New Bottles: or, Spare Hours of a Student in Paris* (1848), a collection of letters describing typical Paris scenes and also accounts of insane asylums, patients, prisons, inmates, morgues, and the like.[5] According to his journal, Melville stopped in at least a morgue and an abattoir. He also stayed in a place recommended by the author of the book, Dr. Augustus Kinsley Gardner, a friend and fellow contributor to Duyckinck's *Literary World*. Dr. Gardner was a young physician described by Leon Howard as "perhaps the most stimulating of all the young author's acquaintances at the time; and he, with other literary lights . . . in the Duyckinck circle, kept Melville's mind in a simple state of excitement too strong to be relieved by a simple whaling story."[6] During Melville's productive years he and Dr. Gardner probably talked about one topic of interest to both—the nature and effects of insanity. Although Dr. Gardner's practice was primarily in obstetrics and diseases of women and children, his preference was "in the direction of diseases of the brain." He had received psychiatric training at the Poor House Lunatic Asylum in Boston and for several years was in charge of an asylum near Bloomingdale. After Melville returned to New York City in February 1850, Gardner apparently became the family physician; he was in attendance at the time of Malcolm Melville's suicide in 1867.[7] For someone like Melville, the spirited doctor would seem to be a natural source of information on questions of mental aberration.

Another man indirectly connected with Melville's trip to England and perhaps the individual who most kindled his interest in insanity during these years was his father-in-law, Judge Lemuel Shaw, who was knowledgeable about legal aspects of insanity. Melville was on close terms with Shaw, a family friend for many years and chief justice of the Supreme Judicial Court of Massachusetts. Judge Shaw presided over many important cases, including several involving insanity.

A hallmark case in January 1844 centered on Abner Rogers, an inmate of the Massachusetts State Prison charged with the murder of the asylum warden. Rogers claimed that he had heard voices stating that the warden would kill him. He therefore acted to protect himself. A defense attorney during the 1844 trial in Boston entered a plea of not guilty by reason of insanity. In that day, no single interpretation or definition of insanity prevailed, but the McNaghten decision reached in England in 1843 "supposedly set the pattern in the United States." According to the decision or the rules therein, a person was judged insane if the individual was unable to distinguish right from wrong and suffered from a defect of reason. An insane person would not understand that his or her criminal or illegal act was wrong. The McNaghten rules were applied for the first time in the United States in the Rogers case, but authorities then and now differ as to the extent of Judge Shaw's knowledge of the rules and the extent also of his application of the rules in the trial proceedings. According to a modern legal authority, Leonard W. Levy, Shaw was not only influenced by the McNaghten rules but in effect strengthened them. According to a modern medical authority, Jacques M. Quen, M.D., Shaw was not aware during the trial of the McNaghten rules. Whatever the case, Judge Shaw was apparently influenced by American psychiatrists testifying at the trial, including Isaac Ray, author of a major work on insanity and an asylum director. Ray agreed with the testimony of two other experts that Rogers was insane at the time of the crime because he was suffering from delusions and because, in addition, he was driven to commit the crime by "an uncontrollable impulse to violence" or an "irresistible impulse."[8]

In the formal charge to the jury, and according to one interpretation, Judge Shaw went beyond the interpretations of the McNaghten rules in that he related will or volition, emotions, and mens rea in any assessment of insane or sane behavior. In his charge, Shaw clarified the nature of monomania and the accompanying delusion: "The character of the mental disease relied upon to excuse the accused in this case, is partial insanity, consisting of melancholy, accompanied by delusion. The conduct may be in many respects regular, the mind acute, and the conduct apparently governed by the rules of propriety, and at the same time there may be insane delusion by which the mind is perverted."[9] The most significant statements in the charge clarified a related element of Rogers's insanity: "that the act was the result of the disease, and not of a mind capable of choosing: in short that it was the result of uncontrollable impulse, and not of a person acted upon by motives, and governed by the will."[10]

Though the Rogers trial occurred in January 1844 while Melville was at sea, it received wide attention in both the popular press, especially in Boston and New York, and in professional journals.[11] The crime was violent, Abner Rogers was obviously demented, and the idea of "uncontrollable impulse" and the larger concept of moral insanity were both controversial. It would seem natural that Melville, with his background and curiosity, would talk with Judge Shaw about issues in the trial, including the nature of the two diseases.

Arriving back in this country on 1 February 1850, after sixteen weeks of travel in Europe, an invigorated Melville was soon making progress on his sixth work, which was not to be a book of adventures involving one Israel Potter but a whaling novel that on 1 May, as he informed Richard Henry Dana, Jr., was half finished. To obtain whaling information, he had applied earlier that spring for a new membership in the New York Society Library. However, after working several months in the crowded house at 103 Fourth Street and remembering all too well the previous summer, Melville decided to look elsewhere for a quieter house and area. Elizabeth was in complete agreement. With something different in mind, Melville took his family in mid-July to stay at his cousin Robert Melvill's large farmhouse near Pittsfield, Massachusetts.

A short time later, in early August, occurred the historic picnic in the nearby Berkshires and the unique meeting with Nathaniel Hawthorne, whose stories in *Mosses from an Old Manse* Melville had begun reading only a few weeks before. The meeting proved to be a great one for Melville, who soon became inspired by Hawthorne and his writings. In Robert Melvill's farmhouse a few weeks later, after reviewing stories in *Mosses* and *Twice-Told Tales*, Melville began writing his anonymous "Hawthorne and His Mosses" in which he praised Hawthorne for his great brain and heart, a "touch of Puritanic gloom," awareness of a "blackness, ten times black," and his probings into the "very axis of reality," a depth penetrable for only great writers like Shakespeare and the American Hawthorne.[12]

Only the previous year in Boston and New York City, after finishing *Mardi*, Melville had for the first time read Shakespeare's plays with care. He read several again in 1850, recognizing, perhaps before the fateful meeting with Hawthorne, that the captain of an American whaler need not be an ordinary whaling captain but could be a remarkable one, perhaps a heroic or a tragic figure. Hamlet and King Lear in particular provided Melville with insights into the workings of troubled or abnormal minds of the mighty, of characters who speak "the sane madness of vital truth."[13] Such characters and Coleridge's views of Shakespearean tragic heroes would figure importantly in portrayals of Ahab, the sea captain whose obsessions would in time make monomania a literary as well as psychological byword. Shakespeare's "fool," in Melville's treatment, would influence the behavior of cabin boy Pip, who at sea exchanges his sanity for a divine insanity. From Milton's *Paradise Lost*, the Bible, Carlyle's *Sartor Resartus*, Byron's *Manfred*, and others, including Gothic romances and five books on whaling, Melville drew materials and ideas enabling him to transform experiences chasing whales and living on grubby whaling ships with castoffs and dreamers into high adventure and vigorous art. Of the various influences at work on the writer during this period the most important would be Shakespeare and Hawthorne.

The benefits of Hawthorne's friendship, periods of intense reading and writing, the peaceful farm, and visitors were to some extent countered by the drab realities of house routines, burdens of several kinds, and worries.

The chief burden and worry was likely money. "Dollars damn me," Melville explained to Hawthorne on 1 June 1851, when the big book was almost finished.[14] The complaint had been a familiar one since at least 1847. Only the previous September Melville had borrowed $3,000 from Judge Shaw so that he could make a partial payment of $1,500 on the 160-acre Brewster farm he had named Arrowhead. Only a year or so before, Melville had borrowed money from Judge Shaw for the 1849 trip to Europe, and in 1847 he had paid his share for the house in New York City with a $2,000 loan from Judge Shaw. Even with *Redburn* and *White-Jacket* selling fairly well in 1850, the royalties could hardly cover family expenses, debts, and interest payments the next year on the farm. Before writing to Hawthorne in June, Melville asked the Harpers on 1 April for an advance on the whaling book but was turned down 29 April because he owed the firm $695.65. He was indeed damned. On 1 May he borrowed $2,050 at 9 percent from one "T.D.S."; the amount and terms would come back to haunt him. If Melville had no fear of poverty at this time, the possibility may have made him apprehensive (JL 1:410).

There were other concerns and worries as well. The newly acquired Arrowhead was a source of pride, for it provided a measure of independence and freedom and also the status of ownership. But the farmhouse itself was not sizable. With eight people living there, including Melville's mother and four sisters, the house was crowded. As there was no room to write on the first two floors, Melville wrote in the attic, which would be too hot in the summer, too cold in the winter, and hardly isolated from noises of activities in rooms below. Melville had to ignore the sounds and other distractions and bury himself in his writing. He had to ignore also tensions that would naturally arise in a house with seven adults, at least five of them rather talkative females. The long hours and concentration would wear away at his sensibilities. Some years later in her memoirs Elizabeth described her husband's regimen that year: "Wrote White Whale or Moby Dick under unfavorable circumstances—would sit at his desk all day not eating any thing till four or five oclock—then ride to the village after dark—would be up early and out walking before breakfast—sometimes splitting wood for exercise" (JL 1:412). In the evening, because of eyes weakened by childhood scarlet fever, Melville refrained from writing, but he might skim over a book with large type or spend "the evening 'in a sort of mesmeric state' in his room," thinking about the present work or future projects. Howard points out that the others in the house, "knowing nothing of the normal state of excitement produced by intellectual activity . . . may have begun to fear that winter that Herman—like his father, during the last weeks of life, before him—was 'peculiar.'" [15]

Writing of Ahab, Gabriel, and others, Melville was well aware of peculiarities, including those of the insane. He was well aware also in 1850 and 1851 that some family members and friends regarded him as peculiar or strange. By 1855, several family members were certain that something was wrong with him. During work on *Moby-Dick*, Melville's tendencies toward depression and irascibility may have been less noticeable because of his long hours upstairs writing. When he needed to get away, he could do farm chores, look around the barn, or walk to the village. Hawthorne lived in Lenox, only six miles away. A talk with him would dispel gloom or moodiness. His family was supportive or attempted to cater to his needs when Elizabeth was busy. But sometimes disturbances while he was writing could not be forgotten or simply walked off outside. His mother's habitual moralizing or someone's remarks at the dinner table could bring back recollections of earlier years, of the family house in Albany, of his father and his final illness. Fears of the twisted mind must have been lurking somewhere in Melville's mind as he wrote of Ahab, Elijah, Pip, and Ishmael. There would be other troubling reminders in those months: the 5 October notice in Pittsfield of the sale of the estate of his cousin "Henry D. Melvill, 'an insane person'"; the arrival that fall of a shipmate from the *Acushnet* and their compilation of a list of twenty-two men aboard that ship of whom four "went ashore . . . half dead," one committed suicide, one was killed, and three—not including Melville and Toby Greene—ran away; the arrival in January 1851 of George Adler's translation of Goethe's book—Adler had his own fears of insanity (JL 1:397, 399–400, 403).

In a February 1851 letter to Evert Duyckinck, Melville, in a crotchety mood, rejected Duyckinck's request for a daguerreotype of himself to be used in a new series of biographies in the *Literary World* of "Distinguished American(s) in Public Life." Melville explained that, as "almost everybody is having his 'mug' engraved nowadays," a copy of a portrait is "presumptive evidence that he's a nobody." Perhaps realizing that his explanations may have seemed a little odd, he offered the following comment: "We all are queer customers, Mr. Duycknk [*sic*], you, I, & every body else in the world. So if I here seem queer to you, be sure, I am not alone in my queerness, tho' it present itself at a different port, perhaps, from other people, since every one has his own distinct peculiarity." [16]

All such matters at Arrowhead the first year—recollections of Adler and others, letters, the friendship with Hawthorne, farm work, visits and social activities, the big burdens or concerns like money and family activities, Melville's own problematic stability—provided a background for the writing of *Moby-Dick*. They provide as well clues for the prominence of insanity in the book.

Resembling the white whale in at least one respect, madness is all but ubiquitous in *Moby-Dick*. It can be found in some form almost anywhere—aboard ships, in towns and cities, in the sea. Manhattan itself may not be mad, but conditions in the city appear harassing, even maddening. The city is described in terms of its insularity, its "lanes and alleys, streets and avenues," its Bowery and wharves toward which come thousands on Sunday afternoon to stand and gaze at the water. They are pressured, coerced individuals, "tied to counters, nailed to benches, clinched to desks," [17] seeking freedom as well as answers. Ishmael and others like him want to escape by going to sea. New Bedford, with its "dreary streets! blocks of blackness," provides an escape route. The town may not be the best place to stay for long, however—it has queer qualities and Spouter Inn is described as queer.

The chief places in the novel, and perhaps the most conducive to the growth of insanity, are the ships and the sea itself. The whaling ship, with its irregular, hard life, provides a natural place for abnormality. The *Pequod* is described as a "tranced ship," a "most melancholy ship," a "noble craft but somehow most melancholy," and as the "material counterpart of her monomaniac commander's soul" (p. 423). The whaler is engaged in a journey that is at least questionable and may be mad in view of Ahab's "grand, monomaniac object" (p. 292).

Madness is to be found in *Moby-Dick* in both animals and humans. In

Chapter 1, Ishmael writes, "Why is almost every robust healthy boy with a robust healthy soul in him, at some time or other crazy to go to sea?" (p. 5). The pun may be at least partly serious. As we will see, a number of men aboard the *Pequod* appear disturbed in some manner. Others afflicted are found on ships like the *Jeroboam* or on shore like Elijah after years at sea. Various sea animals are not exempt from the disease. The white whale can be viewed as mad, for it is the "monomaniac incarnation of all those malicious agencies . . . some deep men feel eating in them" (p. 184). During the three-day chase, Moby Dick displays a "demoniac indifference" and is described as "maddened by yesterday's fresh irons" (p. 567). Nor is Moby Dick the only whale afflicted with a form of mammalian insanity. One whale, flaying about with a harpoon embedded in its side, is "tormented to madness," and another, suffering from infection, is driven to madness (p. 389). The sharks gorging themselves on dead whales moored to the *Pequod* are engaged in a wild, mad activity.

The dominant place or environment in the novel is of course the sea, described in various passages as beautiful or beneficial. It contains myriad forms of life, some of which are essential to man. The sea has also its ugly, dangerous side. Storms and typhoons can destroy man or drive him mad. On one occasion, Ahab addresses the sea as "mad," and, in a scene involving Gabriel, "the crazy sea . . . seemed leagued with him" (p. 316). The collective seas provide a natural environment for the mad whale. The mad seas and animals appear indicative of a reality which Ishmael examines in terms of its whiteness. After considering the bewildering range of meanings of whiteness, Ishmael concludes that the universe itself is essentially corruptive, destructive, or meaningless. That is to say, the universe may be without reason, or "mad." If Ishmael's imaginative assessment makes sense, is there any wonder that so many things in the universe or whaling world manifest one degree or another of mental imbalance?

The *Pequod* crew and officers comprise, of course, the main group in the novel. Other groups include natives from the South Seas, town or country people, city folks, and ex-whalers. All are or become landmen. One showing signs of disturbance is Bildad, a former sea captain with the "reputation of . . . incorrigible old hunks . . . a bitter, hard taskmaster." Bildad appears inflexible if not rigid. Ishmael describes him as "the Queerest old Quaker I ever saw" (pp. 74, 75). Bildad's religious and business obsessions are evident in his remarks that Peleg is doomed to hell. Bildad delivers views in a pontifical, righteous manner, another indication that inflexibility is part of a possible mental problem. The old man appears near the thin red line separating the sane from the insane.

During Ishmael's stay in the Try Pots Inn in Nantucket, he learns of the unfortunate Stiggs, a sailor who had stopped at the inn a few years before. After four years at sea, Stiggs returned with his ship to Nantucket and committed suicide at Mrs. Hussey's Try Pots Inn. The facts are few. Presumably, the years at sea and desperately poor results of the whaling effort—three barrels of oil—adversely affected Stiggs and led to his death. His suicide may not be the only one in the novel, for much later at sea aboard the *Pequod* a crewman, perhaps sleepy or careless, falls from the masthead into the sea and is seen no more. Radney, the *Town-Ho* mate, is not a suicide, but he courts death in relations with Steelkit. Ugly, a fanatic worker, and part owner of the ship with worries on that count, Radney hates the handsome, bold, "wild ocean-born" Steelkit. Obsessed with hatred, Radney acts in "a most domineering and outrageous manner" and is described as "doomed and made mad" (pp. 244–45). In his last days, Radney all but loses control in his brutal treatment of Steelkit. Signs of monomania appear evident.

The "tranced" *Pequod* carries a number of quite sane and rational figures and a few like the ship's carpenter with questionable sanity. "No duplicate," the carpenter is clearly different. For an experienced, skillful man who works with others aboard ship, he is surprisingly oblivious to them, isolated as he is by "an all-ramifying heartlessness." Possessing "a certain impersonal stolidity," "a half-horrible stolidity," he tends to regard whalers as things. The carpenter's general attitude suggests possible inroads of a form of moral insanity. Not feeling as others do, he does not relate to them in "normal" ways. He lives "without premeditated reference to this world or the next." The carpenter is accordingly a "pure manipulator," relying not on reason or even instinct but on "a kind of deaf and dumb, spontaneous literal process." Immersed in the inanimate materials of his calling, he is saved from the distractions of moral insanity by a "wheezing humorousness" and a "certain grizzled wittiness" (pp. 467, 468).

Perth, the ship's blacksmith, is another matter. He shows definite signs of monomania. Yet fellow monomaniac Ahab does not regard him as mad, telling him that he should go mad—"Say, why dost thou not go mad?" (p. 487). For once eagle-eyed Ahab does not see clearly. He may not be able to because Perth hides his troubles in his work. "Silent, slow, and solemn; bowing over . . . he toiled away, as if toil were life itself" (p. 484). Perth works to forget alcoholism and deaths caused by it. Such memories cannot be forgotten. Years of alcoholism, hardship, and sorrow have left marks of a profound melancholy: Perth is one of Melville's most deeply sad characters. He is sadness, saddened—to paraphrase the description of Ahab as "madness, maddened" (p. 168). Having punished himself by going to sea (referred to as a form of suicide), he punishes himself further by unmitigated work and separation from others. This "most miserable" character, with no evidences of irrationality, likely suffered earlier from effects of moral insanity. Prichard's 1835 account of aspects of monomania appears noticeably pertinent to the blacksmith's condition and situation: "An individual of melancholic temperament, who has long been under the influence of circumstances calculated to impair his health and call into play the morbid tendencies of his constitution, sustains some unexpected misfortune, or is subjected to causes of anxiety; he becomes dejected in spirits, desponds, broods over his feelings till all the prospects of life appear to him dark and comfortless." [18]

Melville's portrayals in *Moby-Dick* of such figures are clearly superior to earlier ones in his fiction. Qualities of sane and insane figures alike are described with greater precision and relevance. Appearance and mannerisms are more concretely portrayed. Melville's familiar technique of combining realistic and romantic details is shown to excellent advantage in portrayals of the carpenter and others. The blacksmith's skills, habitual drinking, family life, and failures are recorded with an intensity and focus that make for an unforgettable and highly individualized life history.

The writer's superb control and technical skill are evident also in characterizations of three major figures, each illustrating the importance of monomania in the whaling world and each pointing toward the classic monomaniac, Ahab. The three are Elijah, a former whaler now on land in Nantucket; Gabriel, a Shaker from the New York village of "Neskyeuna," and Pip, a young crewman from "Tolland County in Connecticut" (pp. 314, 412).

Elijah first appears in Chapter 19 as a fairly typical, aging, seemingly poor ex-whaler. Initial observations of him emphasize the concrete and ordinary. "He was but shabbily apparelled in faded jacket and patched trowsers; a rag of black handkerchief investing his neck" (p. 91). His speech—to be discussed later—is in some respects routine. Elijah appears, then, despite eccentric mannerisms, to be more or less normal. As Ishmael discovers, however, Elijah's behavior and remarks quickly raise serious doubts as to his stability. Prichard refers to "reputed persons of a singular, wayward, and eccentric character . . . [with] something remarkable in their manners and habits . . . [leaving] doubts as to their entire sanity."[19] Ishmael describes Elijah as "broken loose from somewhere . . . a little damaged in the head . . . this crazy man . . . cracked" (pp. 92, 93, 99). Impatient and suspicious of the other man, Ishmael exaggerates. Elijah's preoccupation with his past, however, makes him indifferent to routine life. The general consequence is a loss of sensibilities noticeable in friendship and social relations, a diminution of normal social emotions. After a time, Elijah's tattered appearance, strange remarks, and pertinacity suggest a form of moral insanity. His obsessive thoughts of Ahab and his expectations that strangers will heed his warnings indicate a possibility of monomania, but in the scientific vocabulary of the time, Elijah is not a monomaniac. Prichard's 1842 study of insanity and jurisprudence makes clear that in monomania the hallucination or obsession centers primarily on the individual's self. "The predominate feeling . . . is always a selfish desire or apprehension, and the illusory ideas relate to the personal state, and circumstances of the individual."[20] This conception applies to Ahab or Gabriel but not to Elijah, whose obsessive concerns are with others but not with himself. He remains a strange, slightly "touched" but pathetic figure, one of the first victims of Ahab's obsession.

The wild Gabriel aboard the *Jeroboam* is not without typical or ordinary qualities if the terms are stretched a little. He is described as "a small, short, youngish man, sprinkled all over his face with freckles, and wearing redundant yellow hair"; he possesses on occasion a plain exterior. But unlike Elijah, Gabriel hides a deep, chronic mental derangement. Even when calm and rational, Gabriel shows "a deep, settled, fanatic delirium . . . in his eyes." He is complex. To get aboard the *Jeroboam*, Gabriel, strengthened by "that cunning peculiar to craziness," "assumed a steady, common sense exterior, and offered himself as a green-hand candidate for the . . . voyage" (pp. 314–15). Once aboard ship, he is sometimes the conventional madman—highly eccentric and potentially violent. Yet his melodramatic actions reveal Melville's sharp, hardheaded insights. Gabriel suffers from a form of complex monomania. Ray explains that in simple monomania the individual focuses on one point. In another class of monomania, an individual may have "a train of morbid ideas."[21] Gabriel is an example. He regards himself as the archangel Gabriel, as the "deliverer of the isle of the sea, and vicar-general of all Oceanica," as the controller of the

Jeroboam itself, and as an archangel at the call of the "Shaker God incar-
nated"; that is, Moby Dick. While the general course of Gabriel's insanity may be predictable, particulars of his monomania are not. He
may be peaceful or violent, humble or arrogant, an archangel or a
crewman. As expected in such a profound monomania, Gabriel's reason
has been affected: flaws of conception and logic are obvious. Causes lie
in large part in his family and religious background. Gabriel was "originally nurtured among the crazy society of Neskyeuna Shakers, where he
had been a great prophet," trained in their "cracked, secret meetings,"
and involved in many cultish practices, including descent "from heaven
by way of a trap-door" and possession of a replica of the seventh vial
(pp. 315, 316, 314).

With the exception of Ahab, Pip is the most strikingly mad figure
aboard the *Pequod*. The young cabin boy is more intricately mad than
Elijah and Gabriel, for he can be profound as well as silly. Likely causes
of his abnormality appeared first in his Connecticut boyhood: the
peaceful village and family life would hardly prepare him for the whaling environment of tough shipmates and dangers. He received little
encouragement from shipmates and little reassurance from memories
of home. He felt lonely, then moody, and as months passed fearful.
Signs of moral insanity likely appeared. Most disturbing of all activities
would be whale lowerings, the worst part of the "panic-striking business in which he had somehow unaccountably become entrapped." In
his first lowering for a whale, Pip evinces "much nervousness." In the
second, he jumps from the whaleboat. In the third lowering, unable to
control fear or imagination, Pip jumps for the last time. The consequences are profound. Left alone "in the middle of such a heartless
immensity," Pip is overwhelmed by a form of monomania. The comparable effects of Pip's abandonment and Ahab's loss of his leg can be expressed in terms of soul. After Ahab's loss of his leg, his body and soul
intermingle, with insanity as a likely consequence. After Pip's submersion, his body remains intact but his soul is drowned. "Not drowned
entirely, though" (pp. 412, 414), Ishmael adds. Thereafter, Pip appears
increasingly eccentric, incomprehensible, or "crazy."

Pip's monomania centers, on the one hand, on his seeming awareness of God. When Pip descends into the ocean, he sees or believes that
he sees "God's foot on the treadle of the loom" and evidence of God's
mighty creations. In the sense that the book is a romantic creation, Pip
does see these unique things. Although he may need to be insane to see
them, he perceives them as entities. On the pragmatic level, Pip is hal-

lucinating. In this sense—the one stressed in this study—Prichard's explanation of a hallucination is pertinent. A hallucination is the consequence of a "very intense . . . morbid reverie . . . [which] produces . . . false impressions . . . [of] unreal objects as actually present."[22] Pip's belief in his own death is hallucinatory. At other times Pip explores profoundly if erratically—perhaps in illustration of Starbuck's explanation in Chapter 110—aspects of resurrection, the ship's fate, and perspective. Profound himself, Ahab is well aware that Pip draws upon deep sources for his "wondrous philosophies" (p. 433). Only Ahab and possibly Ishmael can understand Pip at such times. Unlike Gabriel, Pip is not physically driven to express religious or philosophic truths. His expression and insight are natural and instinctive.

On the other hand, Pip's monomania centers at times on his alleged cowardice and physical absence referred to above. This obsession dwells on self, but, unlike Gabriel's, Pip's obsession is usually self-depreciatory. In wandering about on the *Pequod* deck, he proclaims his cowardice by repeatedly crying out "Shame" and "Coward." This conception of self contrasts most significantly with Ahab's grandiose conception of self. A related obsession is Pip's belief that he is not Pip. Pip has drowned and is therefore dead; or, Pip, a coward, has run away. Yet as the real Pip is aboard ship, he must be someone else: he is, therefore, the bell-boy, the ship's crier who identifies himself with the refrain, "Ding, dong, ding" (p. 522). These views of identity and Pip's jump from the whale boat manifest a profound self-hatred. Not until Pip is befriended by Ahab does he become aware of his own individuality or his need for someone else or of Ahab's need for him. Otherwise, his only positive sense of self comes when, paradoxically, he denies the self in order to express profound truths.

One indicator in *Moby-Dick* of Melville's greater understanding of effects of mental aberration is the treatment of insane speech. The occasional examples of Jackson's dialogue in *Redburn* and of Surgeon Cuticle's ridiculous formalisms in *White-Jacket* provide interesting illustrations of the troubled mind. But the association of speech and mental upset in *Moby-Dick* goes deeper and may represent advances not evident to American scientists then.[23] The carpenter, standing before his bench talking to himself, reveals something of the abstract quality of a form of incipient moral insanity.

More revealing is the speech of major figures, particularly Elijah, Gabriel, and Pip. Ishmael regards Elijah's speech as "ambiguous, half-hinting, half-revealing, shrouded sort of talk." Elijah refers mysteriously to "souls," the signing of articles, and "soul's a sort of fifth wheel to a wagon." Part of Ishmael's confusion about Elijah and his speech is due to his own ignorance. Part may be due to Elijah's obsession with the past. His meandering around in a private world is suggested in the rather puzzling remark, "Well, well, what's signed, is signed; and what's to be, will be; and then again, perhaps it won't be, after all. Any how, it's all fixed and arranged a'ready" (pp. 93, 91, 93).

Gabriel's speech is not as distinctive as it might be had the writer used speech or dialogue more often. When Gabriel's speech is described, the intent and tone come through nonetheless. As he arrives aboard the *Jeroboam* Gabriel no doubt speaks with relative calmness. Later, as his insanity breaks out, he commands the captain to jump overboard and proclaims himself "the deliverer of the isles of the sea and vicar-general of all Oceanica" (p. 315). "The unflinching earnestness with which he declared these things" indicates the depth of his obsessions. After warning Captain Mayhew against attacking the white whale, Gabriel pronounced his truths in "gibbering insanity." Webster defines gibberish as "rapid and inarticulate talk; unintelligible language; unmeaning words."[24] A year or two later, furious that the whale has been attacked, Gabriel from the top mast tosses an "arm in frantic gestures, and hurls forth prophecies of speedy doom" to the attackers. Later, the *Jeroboam* and the *Pequod* cross paths. Because of the epidemic aboard his ship, Captain Mayhew is rowed in a boat alongside the *Pequod* to communicate with Ahab. One of the crewmen in the boat is Gabriel, who believes he controls the epidemic and most everything else. When Ahab shouts down to the captain that he has no fear of the epidemic, Gabriel gets to his feet and shouts, "Think, think of the fevers, yellow and bilious! Beware of the horrible plague" (p. 315). In delivering two other warnings to Ahab and all who can hear him, Gabriel repeats the basic sentence pattern. On the last occasion, "Gabriel once more started to his feet, glaring upon the old man and vehemently explained, with downward-pointed finger—'Think, think of the blasphemer—dead, and down there!—beware of the blasphemer's end!'" (pp. 316, 317).

Of these three monomaniac figures, Pip speaks in the most revealing and distinctive manner. Bright, sensitive, and spirited before the submersion, Pip shows the same qualities after he is struck with insanity. But having witnessed "God's foot on the treadle of the loom," Pip is so upset and confused that he must play games with himself and others and act silly much of the time. Sometimes Pip's riddles and puzzles take on philosophic form, as in the quarterdeck scene in Chapter 99. As Pip and others take turns observing the doubloon nailed to the masthead, Pip points out in professorial manner, "Here's the ship's navel, this doubloon here, and they are all on fire to unscrew it. But, unscrew your navel, and what's the consequence?" The language is suitably concrete and specific, but the meaning is elusive. He expresses other paradoxes. Pip does not often refer to his obsession with God. But as the central one, it shapes his wit. Possessing remarkable insights, Pip shows a breadth of speech unmatched by any other character except Ishmael. He repeats the "I look, you look, he looks" refrain three times with noticeable variations, including references to bats and crows. While the schoolboy recitation includes serious philosophic overtones, it exhibits a bizzare silliness reflective of both instability and wisdom. His disturbing thoughts of self or nonself can be countered by a form of dissemblance as when he creates a silly rhyme or word like "Hish." He can also speak in a bantering way of cowardice, drowning, or running away. As Queequeg lies ill, Pip sings of his own other self, the lost Pip: "Seek out one Pip, who's now been missing long: I think he's in those far Antilles. If ye find him, then comfort him; for he must be very sad; for look! he's left his tambourine behind:—I found it. Rig-a-dig!" (pp. 435, 434, 479). At other times, when he turns to matters of origins, death, and resurrection, the tone becomes speculative and the language serious.

The dominant figures in the *Moby-Dick* society are of course Ishmael and Ahab. Ishmael as narrator no longer feels like following funerals or knocking off people's hats. He has managed to cope with moods and hostilities, although he retains much of his earlier skepticism. As character, Ishmael is pessimistic and discontented. He is noticeably disturbed by city restraints and confinements and critical of the "dreary" New Bedford streets and houses, finds the black church depressing, and at one point regards Queequeg as mad and the Spouter-Inn as "a queer sort of place." In Nantucket, Ishmael is contemptuous of Elijah's mentality and irritated by his incoherence.

The character has obvious problems, for his "hypos" indicate in modern terms a "state of depression somewhat more chronic and morbid than our 'blues.'" That condition may be regarded as a form of hypochondriasis, which may "appear . . . [as] a specific neurosis . . . [or] in association with such disorders as anxiety neurosis, obsessive-

compulsive neurosis, and most often with the initial states of any psychosis."[25] One of the few critics beside Henry Nash Smith to consider
characters in *Moby-Dick* in mid-nineteenth-century terminology, the
German critic Armin Staats places Ishmael and Ahab in a taxonomy
based on James Prichard's *A Treatise*. In this interpretation, according
to Smith's translation, Ishmael is in the first or introductory stage, his
"melancholy" representing a "neurotic" or apparently a moral insanity
stage which leads to Ahab's psychotic or monomaniac stage. Staats explains that in both stages, moral insanity and monomania, disturbances
occur in emotions and in cognition. Explanations in the *Penny Cyclopaedia* article and in Prichard's *Treatise*, however, indicate that theoreti-
cally disturbances in moral insanity occur in only the emotions, not in
cognition; actually, moral insanity may or may not include failures in
cognition.[26] The distinction is important, for although Ishmael can be
suspicious, depressed, and occasionally confused, his mental processes
do not appear to be actually affected.

During the many months at sea, the touchy, imaginative Ishmael
manages to keep his equilibrium. Queequeg is a major factor. The native's friendship and presence diminish Ishmael's sense of alienation.
His example and strong character reinforce Ishmael's faltering sense of
self and enable him to get along better with others. But it is Ishmael's
decisions and actions during the long journey that largely account for a
gradual maturation or for significant changes in attitudes. Ishmael
learns to control his fear when a storm lashes the ship or a whale
plunges alongside a whaling boat. As a crewman he must regularly
climb the rigging, furl canvas, pull an oar in a boat, and scrub decks.
Such duties allow little time for moody introspections.

What Ishmael must finally learn nonetheless is to resist his natural
tendency to daydream or to place too much importance on intangibles.
The narrator tells of a boyhood experience when he was sent to bed by
his stepmother to fall "into a troubled nightmare of a doze" and then
awaken "half steeped in dreams" to feel "a shock running through all
my frame," and then "a supernatural hand seemed placed in mine."
He lies there for some time, "frozen with the most awful fears" (p. 26).
This suggests the possibility of a hypnagogic trance[27] or a cataleptic
condition found in some mental illnesses. This is not to say that
Ishmael was ill at the time but that he may have become somewhat dis-
oriented. Years later aboard the *Pequod*, as a "lad with lean brow and
hollow eye; given to unseasonable meditativeness" (p. 158), Ishmael,

on the masthead, risks losing hold of reality, of deluding himself as to what is real and what is not.

Somewhat later in the remarkable try-pots scene, Ishmael loses contact briefly with reality and almost capsizes the ship. He had been standing for hours at the tiller guiding the *Pequod* and watching the try-pots activity. The nighttime scene—the darting fires, the hissing blubber, the "Tartarean shapes of the pagan harpooners" dancing around—gradually mesmerizes him until the "rushing *Pequod* freighted with savages, and laden with fire . . . seemed the material counterpart of her monomaniac commander's soul." As Ishmael grows drowsy, the Gothic scene before him "at last begat kindred visions in my soul." The visions may be occurring during a hypnagogic trance. During this time of approaching unconsciousness, Ishmael turns around to face the stern. When he awakens, "I was horribly conscious of something wrong" (p. 354). Aware now of only blackness with occasional flashes of red, he is certain that the tiller has been inverted. At the time he is not suffering from an "unnatural hallucination," as the narrator explains, for a hallucination is created by the mind independent of external conditions, but from an illusion or mistaken perception of external conditions. Because the condition is temporary and Ishmael recognizes his failures, he appears to be in modern terms neurotic, not psychotic. In other words, he is suffering from a form of moral insanity. Having been frightened out of his wits, Ishmael will avoid similar circumstances in the future or react differently if he has to confront the nighttime scene again.

In contrast, Ahab at fifty-eight has lived a lifetime of comparable experiences, some overwhelming, and has survived all of them. An account of the experiences is a testament to his courage, adaptability, and integrity. He survived the early loss of both parents, one of them insane. In the tough occupation of whaling, he advanced rapidly, perhaps gaining his own ship before he was thirty, a not unusual feat in the mid-nineteenth century. Knowledgeable and pragmatic, he proved to be an efficient, brave leader. In the course of many years, Ahab survived the attack of a whale, a bolt of lightning, a deadly skirmish with a Spaniard,[28] rebellious sailors, sea storms.

But such an account gives little idea of the price Ahab had to pay; it does not clarify the harmful effects of the life on him mentally and emotionally. Ahab's psychological difficulties began not with his loss of leg to the whale but many years earlier during what the captain de-

scribes as "forty years of privation, and peril" (p. 543). Early in this period appeared the first signs of emotional stress or of moral insanity.
Physical dangers and hardships, monotonous daily routines, almost
endless whale watches, leadership responsibilities, the necessity of privacy and periods of thought and introspection gradually wore down his
emotional strength and reserves, turned him inward; relationships
with others suffered. At forty the captain had become crotchety, aloof,
only occasionally communicative, with deep angers and resentments
directed at owners, crewmen, whales, the weather. Whaling was no
longer challenging or fulfilling.

Ahab's marriage "at past fifty" marks the approximate beginning of a
second stage of mental difficulty identifiable as a settled condition of
moral insanity. Ahab married to forget the hardships and loneliness of
whaling and to find affection and companionship. He lost them the
day after the wedding as he embarked on another long whaling adventure. He missed his wife and son very much. After admitting to Starbuck that in marrying the girl he had widowed her, Ahab immediately
adds, "And then, the madness, the frenzy, the boiling blood and the
smoking brow, with which, for a thousand lowerings old Ahab has
furiously, foamingly chased his prey—more a demon than a human"
(p. 544). The "thousand lowerings" may be a hyperbole for dramatic
effect, a reference to the career of forty years, to the years after he became "old Ahab," to the years since his marriage, or to the few since the
leg mutilation. Whatever the case, Ahab describes no sane man or recent madness. It is likely that the "thousand lowerings" extend over a
period of ten to twenty years. If so, the lowerings cannot refer to a period of monomania, a comparatively recent condition, but to periods of
moody detachment, to strong hatreds and angers, all controlled by a
"broad mentality," a strong, firm intelligence. The condition remains
one of moral insanity.

A third and final stage in Ahab's madness begins with the traumatic
loss of his leg. The most documented and involved, this stage includes
early monomaniac hates and angers precipitated by the great "corporal
animosity" (p. 184) arising from the loss, which, as Smith points out, is
a physical cause or "external shock" contributing to insanity.[29] This
stage includes also months of suffering. The "final monomania" strikes
Ahab as the *Pequod* rounds Cape Horn and his "torn body and gashed
soul [bleed] . . . into one another; and so interfusing [make] . . . him
mad" (p. 185). This conception of the relationship of body and soul was
neither original nor the received view in the mid-1800s, when most

psychiatrists regarded the two, body and mind, as separate. The latter represented the traditional Christian view of the nonmaterial soul or mind as separate from the physical brain. As the soul or mind was regarded as eternal, diseases of brain or body could not affect it. Whether or not he pondered the matter, Ray doubted this immaterialist-materialist dichotomy, explaining that the mind and brain were interdependent and made for a "single, individual man" so that the mind, "which was the mortal brain functioning, would be diseased." This fairly advanced interpretation seems to have expressed Melville's general conception of the "interfusing" of body and soul.[30] In the months following the amputation, Ahab's physical suffering clearly affected his mental faculties.

The "final monomania" in the third stage includes not only physical violence and raving—similar to an acute attack of mania—but a deceptive calmness that misleads the *Pequod* crew into believing that Ahab's delirium has been left behind with the Cape Horn winds. The calmness resembles Gabriel's. In Ahab's case, however, the delirium or "full lunacy" has turned inward and is not ordinarily discernible, certainly not to crew members.

The paragraphs in Chapter 41 on Ahab's monomania and "bodily dismemberment" can be best described as an example of "poetic analysis" because they combine figurative language and precise explanation, poetic imagery and careful analysis. The passages reveal not only Melville's perceptive insights into complexities of monomania but his powerful and dramatic exposition of insights. Concrete, realistic words are combined with figurative words in a dramatic analysis and definition of Ahab's delirium. Melville uses three synonyms for insanity, "lunacy," "madness," and "monomania," combines them with contrasting adjectives, "broad," "full," "narrow," and "special," and proceeds to trace the process of insanity from "broad madness," or moral insanity, through a "full lunacy," or violent monomania, through the "narrow-flowing monomania," or somewhat constricted insanity, to the "special lunacy," or sharply obsessed monomania, which "stormed his general sanity." Referring to "human madness," Ishmael pointedly admits, "When you think it fled, it may have but become transfigured into some still subtler form" (p. 185). The obsessed stage is accelerated by Ahab's second physical injury—the severe groin wound suffered in Nantucket, which constitutes a second physical cause. In his "monomaniac mind" (p. 463), Ahab regards the subsequent torment as supernaturally related to the torment following the leg loss. The groin injury makes him even more determined to exact revenge. Tragic dimensions of the "final monomania" take final shape as Ahab draws upon disappointments of early years, the deepening troubles of middle years, or second stage, to regard the whale at last as "the sum of all the general rage and hate felt by his whole race from Adam down" (p. 184). Conceived in terms of evil, God, a whale, and a whaling captain, Ahab's delusion is created by a mind both coldly sane and furiously mad.

In James Prichard's taxonomy, Ahab's delusions and general illness show symptoms of a grandiose monomania far more conceptualized and focused than Surgeon Cuticle's. Except under the greatest strain, Ahab thinks rationally on any subject, including his own obsession; such a portrayal of monomania ran counter to the received opinion.[31]

Melville's treatment of Ahab's monomania is innovative in another sense. It shows for the first time in Melville's fiction a lengthy, detailed dramatization of unconscious levels of the mind. In this area he advanced beyond the concerns and studies of scientists of the time, specifically Esquirol, Ray, and Prichard, and in depth beyond accounts of Brown, Poe, and Hawthorne as well.[32] The quarterdeck scenes in *Moby-Dick* are notable for dramatic revelations of areas of Ahab's mind. The deepest probings, however, of unconscious areas of his mind appear in expository accounts in Chapters 41 and 44. A passage in Chapter 41 contains a cryptic metaphor suggestive of Ahab's unconscious or his "larger, darker, deeper part" (p. 185). The passage includes the following: "Far beneath the fantastic towers of man's upper earth, his root of grandeur, his whole awful essence sits in bearded state; an antique buried beneath antiquities, and throned on torsoes! . . . He patient sits, upholding on his *frozen* brow the piled entablatures of ages" (p. 185, my italics). Although the metaphor may be literary and political rather than psychological, "his root of grandeur, his whole awful essence" suggest elemental forces in Ahab's unconscious mind, which are suggested also by images of burial and death and by the reference to "frozen brow," a phrase possibly anticipating descriptions of mind in *Pierre*: "Those barbarous hordes which Truth ever nourishes in the loins of her frozen, yet teeming North."[33] Ahab's own "hyperborean regions of the mind" would be implied in this remarkable metaphor. Such images lack the fluidity and brilliance, however, of the "strange shapes of the unwarped primal world . . . glid[ing] to and fro" and awaiting Pip in his own psychological descent into oceans of the mind. Such figures as "joyous, heartless, ever-juvenile eternities" and "God-omnipresent, coral insects," although referring primarily to mun-

dane eternities, convey a sense of the uncharted depths of Pip's mind
(p. 414). In turn, descriptions in the Ahab passage convey a sense of
colossal forces in the mind, not to be understood or eluded, not even by
Ahab. Both sets of descriptions can be regarded as Jungian archetypes
originating in the collective unconscious. Similar ones of Ishmael also
indicate something of the nature of the unconscious.

The boldest explorations of a troubled mind and unconscious appear in Chapter 44 descriptions of Ahab's monomaniac nightmares.
Praised for its brilliance, the last paragraph of the chapter is nonetheless faulted for complex abstractions, reliance on coined terms, and
other devices for creating a model of Ahab's mind.[34] Such terms as "life-
spot," "living principle," "common vitality," and the "spiritual throes"
figure have been regarded as imprecise. These terms and metaphors
nonetheless succeed in creating a sense of Ahab's mental turbulence.
The "intolerably vivid dreams of the night" may refer to monomaniac
nightmares too extreme to be accepted on a cognitive level. They are
evidently too extreme in emotional terms as well, for they occur during
a "clashing of phrensies" and concentrate finally in the "throbbing of
his life-spot." The last phrase may be, as Feidelson asserts, a reference
to the heart.[35] It seems more likely that the phrase refers to the area of
both head and heart, to intense pressures Ahab feels in his head and
chest. A key metaphor in the Chapter 44 passage begins, "These spiritual throes in him heaved his being up from its base, and a chasm
seemed opening in him, from which forked flames and lightnings shot
up, and accursed fiends beckoned him to leap down among them . . .
[into] this hell—yawn[ing] beneath him" (p. 202). Despite the confused
visualization, it effectively dramatizes traumatic effects of Ahab's insane fury. During this period, Ahab's unconscious mind figuratively
opens, releasing into the conscious hitherto hidden forces—raging
guilts, hates, fears—suggested by the flames and lightning and by the
"accursed fiends." Both personal and collective forces of the unconscious are on the verge of overpowering the conscious Ahab, who, in
the search for the whale, has deluded himself into believing that he is
equal to any confrontation on earth, whether it be with man, beast, or a
manifestation of the supernatural.

The portrayal in Chapter 44 of Ahab's mental processes contains a
somewhat cumbersome structure of faculties. This four-part paradigm
follows naturally from the two-part paradigm of body and soul illustrated in Chapter 7, as Ishmael thinks of the soul as eternal and separate, and also from the account in Chapter 41, as he describes the inter-

fusing of body and soul that brings on monomania. Although the soul-mind-will-brain paradigm is mechanical, it clarifies the tortured workings of Ahab's powerful mind. After Ahab bursts from his cabin, his soul in effect flees from his mind. Brodtkorb explains that when the narrator Ishmael realized that the mind and soul could not exist apart he created a grand purpose, a vulturelike creature which drives off the "common vitality," or "soul plus mind." Zoellner keeps the separation of soul and mind intact by positing two Ahabs: a daytime Ahab directed or vitalized by this creature and a nighttime Ahab with a soul.[36] It appears, however, that the description refers not to an actual separation but to a metaphoric one. Ordinarily, the mind is "leagued with the soul"; the soul is an "integral" of the mind. Under the great emotional stress of a monomaniac nightmare, the soul or spiritual elements are subjugated or, in a sense, nullified by the union of mind and will. This union is the "unbidden and unfathered birth" from which the "eternal, living principle," or soul, flees "horror-stricken" (p. 175). This union appears to be the crux of Ahab's "special lunacy," the sharply focused monomania which marks the most radical upset of Ahab's tormented mentality. During this period the soul is present but subjugated or dormant. The paradigm is vitalized by remarkable imagery which organically relates conscious and unconscious forces of Ahab's mind. Despite confusions of language and ideas, the long passage in Chapter 44 provides a more convincing portrayal of deep mental anguish and upset than do case studies of Ray or Prichard dealing with comparable conditions.[37]

Shakespeare's plays and heroes no doubt influenced Melville's conception of Ahab's will, and accounts of religious and dramatic figures by Bayle and Carlyle may have contributed to that conception. The conception may have derived something also from Thomas Upham's scientific *Outlines of Imperfect and Disordered Mental Action*, a copy of which was available in the New York Society Library and also likely available, Wilson Heflin explains, in the enlisted men's library of the *United States* on which Melville sailed in 1843–44.[38] A professor of psychology, Upham regarded the mind as consisting of the intellect, sensibilities, and will. An important aspect of the will is power, which is not a faculty but an attribute suffused throughout the mind and concentrated in the will. Any decision or action of the will is based on power, which becomes a factor therefore in any "disordered action" of the will.[39] A disordered action or "insanity of the will" is more likely to come from insane aspects of other parts of the mind than from internal defect of the will. Upham's simplistic explanations clarify Ishmael's complex accounts.

Ahab's rationality, or mind, driven by monomaniac conceptions of self and power, nullifies the effects of the soul and, in aligning itself with the disordered will, creates the delusions of a global mind. In such a development the will has power and is also powerless. Upham's description of the effects of a "deep-rooted and permanent melancholy" upon the will also clarifies the powerful account of Ahab's midnight upset.[40] Upham's scientific accounts and Melville's dramatic exposition cannot be lengthily compared because of different purposes and audiences. But only Melville's fictional account creates a credible sense of the ineluctable mysteries and complexities of the deeply troubled mind.

Although the portrayal of Ahab's consciousness is a highlight of *Moby-Dick*, Ishmael's psychology and the aberrations of Elijah, Gabriel, Pip, and others are depicted with similar brilliance if with perhaps somewhat less depth. These and other characters illustrate the distance Melville had traveled in trying to understand his own complex mentality and consciousness. What he learned from his introspections no doubt helped clarify dramatic treatments of Ahab and others and indicated possibilities for later psychological explorations. These occurred a short time later as he turned to thoughts about another obsessed character to be discussed in the next chapter.

Chapter Six. The Mad Family

Pierre

Family life at Arrowhead became somewhat more relaxed after the completion of *Moby-Dick* in mid-July 1851. Melville's oldest sisters, Helen and Augusta, had painstakingly completed the fair copy of the manuscript for the publisher, and everyone ceased worrying about Melville's habit of working straight through the day until four or five in the afternoon. The English publishers had agreed to buy the new book, and the Harpers were about ready to sign an agreement. For a few months Melville had little to do except a few farm chores. He could take it easy, admire farmland and crops, walk around the countryside, or talk with friends and visitors. The Shaws visited the farm in August and September, in particular to assist Elizabeth, who was pregnant with her second child and not a good housekeeper even under ordinary circumstances. The Melville sisters were helpful around the house, but Elizabeth was the one in charge.[1] With no work at hand, Melville invited his friends George and Evert Duyckinck for a visit. After they and a few others arrived for an eight-day stay in August, the indefatigable Sarah Morewood appeared on the scene to put Melville's ideas into practice with an elaborate picnic and climbs into the nearby Berkshire hills. Melville participated energetically in all such activities and led one venture up Saddleback mountain. The activities included a visit to Hawthorne at Lenox and excursions to nearby lakes. Socializing gave Melville an opportunity to enjoy himself and his status as a recognized writer, family man, and ex−New Yorker now country square.[2]

The situation that autumn resembled in a way the one in spring 1849 after the completion of *Mardi* when the Melvilles were staying in Boston following Elizabeth's difficult delivery in February. Melville had time then to read and think of great literary works and wonder about his next work. Whatever the book might be, it would go farther than *Mardi*. At Arrowhead in 1851, with visitors appearing frequently and a farm to keep up in early fall, there was little time for reading; but with a new baby in October Melville had to consider prospects for the next work. As the first six novels had covered most of his adventures, Melville decided to turn elsewhere for new materials. A natural subject, as critics have pointed out, would be his youth and family life. "If he were to continue to ground his writings on some sort of autobiographical basis while postponing his experimentation with retelling another person's story, he would have to turn back to his early life."[3]

Nathaniel Hawthorne would be the one to speak with about the next book, but there is no record that Melville did. He admired Hawthorne's stories and the recent *House of the Seven Gables*, which focused on two old New England families and their curses. The friends may have shared Melville's interest in European romances, including *Zanoni*, with its resemblances to *Pierre*.[4] In a letter of November 17 that revealed the intensity of his friendship, Melville referred to Hawthorne's admiration for *Moby-Dick* and his own intention to write another book. In a state of mind to humorously question his own sanity, Melville added, "Lord, when shall we be done growing? As long as we have anything more to do, we have done nothing. So, now, let us add *Moby-Dick* to our blessing, and step from that. Leviathan is not the biggest fish;—I have heard of Krakens."[5] Only a few days later, Hawthorne and his family left Lenox to live in West Newton. Melville's actual reaction to the departure is not known, but the sense of loss must have been powerful. With no one to listen to his ideas and share his feelings, Melville probably turned to his new work with a dedication not evident even during the winter months of writing *Moby-Dick*. Hard, protracted work in the attic would help him forget that Hawthorne was no longer at nearby Lenox.

Higgins and Parker advance the view that although Hawthorne's influence on Melville was fundamental, catalytic in ways, Melville was

most profoundly influenced not by his friendship with Hawthorne or
Shakespeare's plays but by Pittsfield itself.[6] Returning as an adult to the
town, Melville would naturally find in scenes there reminders of the
past—Broadhall, at that time his cousin Robert's house but formerly
his uncle's, would bring back memories of his father, of his father and
uncle Tom Melvill talking in the house, of his long stays on the farm
when he was working for his uncle. During those years, as Higgins and
Parker conjecture, Melville may have learned something of a possible
family secret: the father may have had an affair and an illegitimate
daughter. According to this approach, Melville's searches into the past
and his own psychology would be revealed first in *Redburn*. "In this
view, the innocuous *Redburn* might have laid open the floodgates to the
unconscious, and months may have passed before Melville paid full attention to what was emerging from that wonder world."[7]

While this general view is enlightening, it must remain in part con-
jectural until some kind of confirmation appears. What activity or oc-
currence first compelled Melville to search his unconscious is unknown. He may have begun looking deeply within himself during his
first sea journey in 1839, on the trip west with Eli Fly in 1840, or in
a crow's nest on the *Acushnet* the next year. Thoughts of his father
could have occurred anytime. Thoughts of Albany, the family house,
and scenes there would bring back intense recollections of his father's
death and the unforgettable condition leading to it. There may have
been another family secret, not very well kept if it was a secret—the
incidence of insanity or mental illness among the Melvilles and his own
susceptibility to the disease. Reflections on anything like that—fears of
the "twisted mind"—would open up the floodgates or in rational moments impel him to search for insights into complications of his own
emotions and thinking. Having already portrayed aspects of his thinking about abnormality in *Redburn* and *White-Jacket* and having gone
much farther in dramatizations of the abnormal in *Moby-Dick*, Melville
apparently felt he was ready in the new work to examine complexities
of insanity in a family.

The farmhouse near Pittsfield would be the right place for Melville
to write about such a family. If Pittsfield and the general area were full
of memories for Melville, the farmhouse brought past and present together in other family members, particularly his mother, who, at sixty,
was alert, strong-willed, and as opinionated as ever. Her frequent suggestions for improvements of the farm and household activities irritated Herman. Helen, fourteen when the father died, would have

many memories of him, and Augusta, ten in 1832, would remember, too. As copiers of the new manuscript and adults with strong memories and feelings for their mother, they certainly had reservations about revealing family secrets and experiences to the public. Melville must have felt greater doubts. But as he was attempting to disguise family identities and relationships and was writing, as he informed Sophia Hawthorne, something akin to a "rural bowl of milk," he may have believed that he was writing a domestic romance and not something on the order of a literary "Krakens."[8]

If Melville had been psychologically vulnerable in New York City in 1849, he became more so in Pittsfield in 1851, especially after the second child, Stanwix, was born October 22. Everyone was proud of the new boy and the growing family, but the household had to adjust to the new baby and medical bills and other expenses had to be paid. Sales figures on *Moby-Dick* were not yet available, and Melville still owed the Harpers $400. Early in November Melville began on his new work, settling into routines more severe than those for *Moby-Dick*. Family members were rightly concerned: he permitted only a few interruptions and had resumed his practice of working steadily through the day despite sundry activities in rooms below him. As the winter progressed, Melville took his daily walks in the snow and cold, but female members not disposed to venture outside had to content themselves with the usual indoor routines and polite conversation. Tensions naturally appeared. Sara Morewood, who liked the family, especially Augusta, and who recognized that circumstances at Arrowhead were at times difficult, entertained the family at a Christmas dinner, during which she spoke to Melville about his strict regimen: "I laughed at him somewhat and told him that the recluse life he was leading made his city friends think that he was slightly insane—he replied that long ago he came to the same conclusion himself."[9] Melville's uncle by marriage, Dr. Amos Nourse, aware of family circumstances and Herman's work habits, made a more perceptive assessment: he pointed out that Melville was "devoting himself to writing with an assiduity that will cost him dear by & by" (JL 1:448).

By late November Melville had written 350 pages of manuscript which included the Saddle Meadows part and the first 100 pages on the city part. It is not known if Melville at the time regarded the work as complete. At any rate when he traveled with Elizabeth to New York City in early January he innocently assumed that the new book would noticeably improve his finances. Although Bentley had paid 150 pounds in August for the English publication of *Moby-Dick*, Melville's American publisher informed him in early September that total earnings for the six books were $8,569.34, or about $1,400 a book. The figures could hardly be reassuring. Melville needed strong assurances and some concrete evidence that he could make a living from his writing.[10]

What the writer discovered in New York City that January changed more than the length and tone of the new work. Perhaps for the first time he discovered that many reviews of *Moby-Dick* were unfavorable and some were pointedly critical of bizarre characters like Ahab and Fedallah, unbelievable actions involving a white whale, and tiresome expositions of whaling. Reviewers complained also of artificial dialogue and an extravagant prose style. Although comparable criticisms of *Mardi* had appeared three years before, the circumstances this time were different. Convinced that he had written an original and great work, Melville expected recognition for his achievement. To learn that "*Moby-Dick* had failed with an influential part of the literary establishment" was a traumatic shock to his self-esteem, already vulnerable, and to his conception of himself as a writer. The second discovery was that his longtime American publisher, the Harpers, had lost faith in his writing. New arrangements with the firm reduced his earnings per dollar by more than half, from 50 cents after expenses to 20 cents—a sizable loss in earnings. There was something else Melville would no longer receive: the customary courtesy of free copies for distribution to friends. Such copies he would have to pay for himself. Once again Melville was damned, doubly damned as it must have seemed.[11]

There is no known record of Melville's attitudes as he began in January to expand the manuscript and at the same time renegotiate the contract with the Harpers. Melville's anger and bitterness were apparently expressed in sections added to the manuscript about Pierre as a young author and his relationships with publishers, critics, and readers. Highly charged words and ideas from actual reviews of *Moby-Dick* reappear in passages of the novel. "As he progressed with his expansions, Melville more and more perverted the manuscript into an outlet for his personal anxieties about his career."[12] Working feverishly in New York City and Pittsfield, Melville added 150 pages of insertions and finished the manuscript in mid-February.

Although *Pierre* contains evidences of Melville's reading in Shakespeare's plays, Hawthorne's fiction, Gothic romances, and other works, the chief source of materials and ideas would appear to be personal experiences and recollections of his father's family and to a limited extent the situation at Arrowhead. Murray's notable study of the novel emphasizes the biographical content or close ties between characters and actual figures: Pierre and Melville, Mr. Glendinning and Allan Melvill, Mrs. Glendinning and Maria Melvill, Lucy and Elizabeth Melville, Isabel and Priscilla Melvill, a cousin, and so on.[13] Some critics challenge the biographical faithfulness of the portrayals. Whatever the extent of the resemblances, Melville concentrated on a fictional family, their individual drives and psyches. What he had begun in *Redburn* would be greatly expanded in the new work, which might go beyond *Moby-Dick* in exploring the inner mind and insanity. If there was a psychological Kraken, Melville was determined to explore its unknown ways as he worked steadily at his desk in the attic, mulled over things downstairs at night, or worked on his farm or went for walks. His own fears of inheriting insanity were part and parcel of attempts to understand what had happened to his father, indirectly to his mother, and in a sense to his brother.

Free of the compulsion to write about whales, ships, islands, and men, Melville concentrated largely in *Pierre* on the rise and fall of one family in the country and city. Environment is accordingly limited. In the first part of *Pierre*, peaceful, rural Saddle Meadows provides an appropriate setting for a hereditary, aristocratic family living in a mansion. The mansion, the Misses Pennies' cottage, the red house where Isabel stays, and the houses described in Isabel's story to Pierre are important places affecting the psychological states of the characters. The second part focuses on the generally indifferent or restrictive city environment of endless streets, crowded neighborhoods, and stone buildings.

Although structure and unity in *Pierre* are marred by some lack of proportion and inadequately integrated materials in the city part, the novel possesses a generally sound plot. Perhaps influenced by Hawthorne's novels, popular romances, and European works, Melville adopted a third-person point of view which allowed for greater objectivity than found in a first-person novel and a developed plot that provided scenes and drama for portrayals of the family. The plot, despite flaws, effectively dramatizes the fall of the Glendinning family.

Pierre's search for truth about himself and the family and his gradual loss of sanity are related factors shaping the plot. As the dominant figure, Pierre is involved mainly with his mother, Lucy, and Isabel in the first part and with Lucy and Isabel in the second. In each part, dramatic scenes in which Pierre gains insight are frequently alternated with solitary episodes in which he attempts to understand the insights or related matters. To some extent melodramatic incidents are balanced by clarifying passages or sections. The plot tends toward melodrama because the characters themselves tend to act or think in prescribed ways: the mother can do no wrong and the deceased father always acted nobly; Lucy is the innocent female and Isabel the designing sexual one; Pierre, the high-minded youth, strives to do good by doing bad.

The least afflicted member of the Glendinning family is the father, who died in Pierre's boyhood. Seemingly a good, mature man, Mr. Glendinning was greatly admired by his son. Melville provides little information on the father except what Pierre learns at an early age from his aunt and nurse. The nurse attending the sick man during his delirium cannot understand why "so excellent a gentleman, and so thoroughly good a man, should wander so ambiguously in his mind" (p. 71). She has no knowledge of the father's behavior during the time the premarital portrait was painted and no knowledge of him before then. The aunt informs Pierre that the father was in love with a young French woman. The two "sides" of the father's earlier life are suggested by the youthful portrait and the middle-aged portrait. The flashback involving the aunt and at least one portrait appear to be autobiographical, as perhaps are other elements.[14]

As Mrs. Glendinning is noticeably suspicious of her husband's bachelor past, she hates the youthful portrait, which she believes reveals sinful proclivities. Mr. Glendinning himself could hardly have forgotten the affair, for a child born out of wedlock was a serious sin against family and God. His guilt feelings about the affair and child would be unbearable in the final weeks of his life when he "lowly wandered in his mind." The nurse cannot understand why the father would be incoherent or "dream horrid dreams, and mutter unmentionable thoughts" (pp. 70, 71). The "horrid dreams" would seem to suggest the man's terror at thoughts of an eternity in hell. His behavior resembles Allan Melvill's when he was described by Thomas Melvill as "maniacal." In Pierre's attempts at the Apostles to reconstruct his father's past, he concludes that his father's insanity had been due to a "sin-grief irreparable" (p. 287). In the final days, the father was not only referring incoherently to an unknown daughter but "raving" about "horrid dreams." He had become a "raver" (p. 178). Such details aside, the rather brief account of the father appears intentionally moderate.

"Melville wrote *Pierre* while living with his mother, his wife, his sisters, and his children. The autobiographical elements in his outcry against family suffocation embarrassed his own family."[15] In a general sense, Maria Melvill served her son as the model for Pierre's mother in *Pierre*. The main similarity between the two women would appear to be pride. Mary Glendinning is haughtily certain of her family's prominence and superiority and her own singular position in the family. So much is she taken with herself and the Glendinning family that outsiders are customarily regarded as inferior. Mrs. Glendinning's other notable qualities may or may not resemble Maria Melvill's, but they are important. Her inflexibility follows from her pride. She simply will not change her mind or stance if she does not wish to. Perhaps because of personal insecurities Mrs. Glendinning is adamant in her way of life and choices. When these are threatened, she reacts with bristling defiance. After the first interview with Isabel, Pierre speaks in the breakfast room with his upset mother. After he leaves the room, she impulsively flings her fork at her own portrait, furious that her son has taken up, as she asserts, with a slut.

Anger and hatred are other important features of the fictional mother's character. After Pierre reveals his interest in Isabel and later his marriage to her, Mrs. Glendinning reacts with hatred to anything he does or says. Any alliance other than the approved marriage to Lucy is abominable. Mrs. Glendinning's intense, quick angers, impulsive actions, and rejection of her son are indications of a form of moral insanity. Pierre regards his mother's madness as of two parts, the first appearing before his departure from Saddle Meadows and the second, the "final insanity" (p. 287), leading to her death. The chief cause of her death and insanity is "a hate-grief unrelenting" (p. 287). In the final weeks of her life, Mary Glendinning, like her husband, was very likely overwrought. The condition of moral insanity quickly deteriorated into monomania. Like her husband she dies with her rational faculties clearly disturbed.

Sometimes regarded as a primitive, a symbol of female sexuality, evil, nature, or of Pierre's unconscious, Isabel Banford is at least a psychological portrait. Isabel is apparently modeled on Herman Melville's cousin Priscilla, who stayed at Arrowhead during the winter of 1853–54. Henry A. Murray lists ten parallels between Priscilla and Isabel, including parallels of a French mother, birth, age, and visits by Herman's father. Murray notes also that Priscilla had feelings and thoughts that "were vague and confused, mysteriously dream-like," and describes Isabel as "intellectually retarded" in her childhood.[16] Isabel's two interviews with Pierre do not show her as retarded but as intelligent if at times vaguely oriented. Another possible but unlikely model would be Mrs. A.M.A., the alleged illegitimate daughter of Allan Melvill. Melville likely drew as much from his imagination and the need to create a contrast to Lucy as from actual individuals.

Isabel's past is appropriately mysterious. Nothing is known of her mother, and her father, Mr. Glendinning, appeared only briefly in her life before his death. During the narrative of her life, Isabel appears sad, insecure, and fearful. She admits to Pierre that her awareness of actuality is not strong. "Scarce know I at any time whether I tell you real things, or the unrealest dreams. Always in me, the solidest things melt into dreams, and dreams into solidities. Never have I wholly recovered from the effects of my strange early life" (p. 117). Dreams and fantasies are forms of escape for her.

The story of Isabel's early life is told in terms of four houses in which she lived in France and this country.[17] The first two houses are especially important. The weird circumstances and inhabitants in the French house may account in part for her underlying fears and a sense of insecurity. But it is the second house in this country which most disturbs her. As Isabel describes her experiences in the house, presumably an insane asylum, she asks Pierre, "Do not speak the word to me. . . . The word is wholly unendurable to me" (p. 121).

Isabel's years in the asylum have made her a storehouse of information about forms of insanity and operations of an asylum. With the exception of Ishmael, Isabel is the most informed of Melville's characters about insanity. "During my . . . stay, all things changed to me, because I learned more, though always dimly. Some of its occupants departed; some changed from smiles to tears; some went moping all the day; some grew as savages and outrageous, and were dragged below by dumb-like men into deep places, that I knew nothing of." During the stay "I saw coffins silently at noon-day carried into the house, and in five minutes' time emerge again." Some released inmates left in rags, some were "driven on foot." In her years there, Isabel stayed in several rooms in the house, including a "much larger and very long room" in which many inmates were observed. "They would vacantly roam about, and talk vacant talk to each other. Some would stand in the middle of the room gazing steadily on the floor . . . and never stirred. . . . Some would sit crouching in the corner. . . . Some kept their hands tight on their hearts, and went slowly promenading up and down. . . . But most of them were dumb, and could not, or would not speak, or had forgotten how to speak. . . . Some were always talking about Hell, Eternity, and God. . . . Some harangued the wall; some apostrophized the air; some hissed at the air; some lolled their tongues out at the air; some struck the air" (pp. 119, 120–21).

Isabel speaks with a formal intensity because she is frightened by such recollections and wants to hold them at a distance and because at the same time she is impelled to describe them clearly. The long parallel sentences and phrases provide a careful survey of patients and illnesses: the "strangely demented people," the nonstop talkers, the mute, the flamboyant, "the sluggish persons crouching in corners." These and other patients described by Isabel appear to fall within principal classifications of insanity in this study—monomania, moral insanity, mixed forms, plus those of imbecility and mania.

In a sense, then, Isabel serves as a guide for Pierre in his ventures into regions of insanity. Melville himself needed no such guide because of many experiences with forms of mental abnormality. It is not known if Melville was ever inside an asylum or a similar place, but, in view of his lively imagination, the assumption is that at some time or another he was. In the 1830s when Melville was growing up in Albany, the town had an Alms House Square, a 116-acre tract with a lunatic asylum open to visitors except on Sundays. Although an asylum then could be a frightening place to visit, a teenager like Melville, willing in a few years to face real dangers at sea, would go there if he was really curious about inmates and asylum life. In Lansingburgh, which had no comparable facility, a family customarily took care of its own mentally ill or paid another family to do so. Galena, Illinois, visited in 1840 by Melville and his friend Eli Fly, placed its poor and insane in the county asylum. While staying with his uncle in Pittsfield in the mid-1830s or living later at Arrowhead, Melville might have ventured into a room or hallway of the local "almshouse . . . which provided shelter for paupers and mentally troubled individuals." The writer's New York City addresses—103 Fourth Avenue and 104 East 26th Street—were both within walking distance of Bellevue Hospital, which included a building for the insane. Bloomingdale Asylum, where brother Allan's daughter and George J. Adler lived for many years, was on the edge of Manhattan and within carriage range. There was also the equally well-known McLean Asylum in Boston.[18]

When Pierre is introduced to the women at the Misses Pennies', someone in the room responds with a "sudden, long-drawn, unearthly, girlish shriek." The person is undoubtedly Isabel. Soon thereafter it is explained that the person "had been attacked by a sudden, but fleeting fit, vaguely imputable to some constitutional disorder or other" (p. 45). The fit and disorder are not explained. Isabel's fainting suggests excitability and perhaps instability. When pressures or strains become excessive, she can respond only in an extravagant manner. As Isabel has never learned "normal" responses, she tries to keep her feelings hidden. Her excitability and melancholy suggest a form of moral insanity in which "strongly excited feelings" are a major feature. The suicide attempt during the boat trip to Staten Island indicates a further stage in her condition: she has become as obsessed with Pierre as he is obsessed with her. Just before she attempts to jump into the ocean, she "convulsively grasped" Pierre's arm and "convulsively spoke" of her feelings for Europe. Isabel's obsessions and frustrations indicate that her illness has been complicated by elements of monomania.

In the mid-nineteenth century, most scientists, including Ray, Prichard, and Brigham, regarded worry, grief, alcoholism, poverty, and heredity as among the chief causes of insanity. Such causes are briefly discussed in the *Penny Cyclopaedia* article on insanity. Family difficulties and abnormality were also regarded as predisposing or precipitating causes. Dain explains that a Dr. John Butler, an asylum superintendent, was "unusual in attributing most mental diseases to unhappy childhood: he thought a happy home was crucial to mental health."[19]

Family situation and heredity are clearly important causes of insanity in *Pierre*. The father's moral failures and early death, the mother's pride and inflexibility, and an overly protective family environment adversely affect both mother and son. The absence of a suitable family environment during Isabel's formative years clearly harms her psychological development. The relationships of Pierre and his parents and their hereditary influences on him are clear in an outline or simplistic plot sense. Both parents died of madness; Pierre, next in line, may well succumb to mental disease. Such an outline is amplified by scenes, narrative, and exposition, all of which illustrate the depths to which the writer pursued such matters. In passages describing, for example, Pierre's reactions to the final news of his mother, Melville follows Pierre's tormented thinking as he strives to find order in his mother's melancholy and grief, her insanity and "final insanity," and meaning in her complex feelings toward him. His involuted thinking leads him fi-

nally to the realization that he is doomed, that he has his "own hereditary liability to madness" (p. 287).

The first serious disclosure of Pierre's liability occurs after he has
read Isabel's stunning letter, which would upset a secure, confident
young man. Pierre cannot handle the trauma. One passage reads:
"This amazing letter, deprived Pierre for the time of all lucid and definite thought or feeling. He hung half-lifeless in his chair. . . . The per-
ceptible forms of things; the shapes of thoughts; the pulses of life, but
slowly came back to Pierre" (p. 65).

This scene in effect begins a plot centered on the family's disintegration, Pierre's search for truth and understanding, and his deterministic
movement toward insanity. In broader terms, the plot begins before
the time of the novel, with Pierre's growing up and the father's premarital affair with the French lady. Pierre's life would have continued
serenely if the father had not died and Isabel had not been born. Once
she arrives in Saddle Meadows, action and scene unfold inevitably.

Motivations of characters in *Pierre* are clarified in greater detail than
in the previous works. The novel shows also a greater reliance on poetic analysis, which combines figurative language and some degree of
logical or sequential exposition. The language is not in the ordinary
sense realistic and straightforward but rather formal and somewhat
elaborate. Yet it is sufficiently concrete and specific to create a sense of
aptness and clarity if not of realism. Figures of speech and concrete
details often make for hardheaded observations. Mountain and valley
imagery creates a sense of spatial elements in the mind. Nature imagery can suggest different moods and kinetic images a sense of the flow
of thought. Although the analysis may be more "winding" than sequential, more associative than logical, it is often sharply focused and
persistent. The following passage focuses on the clarifying effects of
distressing news on the mind:

[The clarifying] is not so much accomplished by any covertly in-
ductive reasoning process . . . as it is the magical effect of the ad-
mission into man's inmost spirit of a before unexperienced and
wholly unexplicable element, which like electricity suddenly received into any sultry atmosphere of the dark, in all directions
splits itself into nimble lances of purifying light; which at one and
the same instant discharge all the air of sluggishness and inform it
with an illuminating property; so that objects which before, in the
uncertainty of the dark, assumed shadowy and romantic outlines,

now are lighted up in their substantial realities; so that in these
flashing revelations of grief's wonderful fire, we see things as they
are. (p. 88)

The combination of careful analysis and figurative language is
shown to best advantage in portrayals of Pierre's unconscious mind.
Whether or not Melville probed more deeply into Pierre's mental processes than into Ahab's, he was mining in Pierre materials resembling
his own complex and more resistive state of mind. Henry A. Murray
believes that examinations of mind and psyche in *Pierre* are at such
depth as to anticipate revelations of Freud and Jung. Melville may not
have been alone in this respect, for in *The Scarlet Letter* and *The House of
the Seven Gables* Hawthorne was describing realms of the unconscious
mind. Both writers and Melville in particular were venturing into areas
as yet unexplored by most American scientists of the time. Ray and
Brigham, as well as Englishmen Prichard and Conolly, do not exhibit in
writings I am familiar with evident interest in or study of the human
unconscious as such. Frederich Rauch, author of an 1840 psychology
text, apparently did some advanced work on the relationship of dream
content and the consciousness. Melville's portrayal of the unconscious,
Pierre's in particular, is examined by Higgins and Parker, who consider
as well the treatment of Pierre's general psychology and the novel's
unity. My concern, much more limited, is with a few aspects of Pierre's
unconscious and insanity.[20]

Major scientific investigations of the human unconscious were occurring in mid-nineteenth century in Europe. According to Ellenberger, important work was being done by von Schubert (1780–1860),
Carl Carus (1789–1869), and Schopenhauer (1788–1860), each of
whom contributed significantly to an understanding of the unconscious and anticipated theories and work of Freud and Jung. By the
1870s and 1880s several scientific theories of the nature of the unconscious had appeared. Melville possibly may have been aware of these,
although it is far more likely that he gained insights into the unconscious from works by English romantic poets or Goethe. Although familiar with representative works by these writers, Melville could not
have read works by Carus and von Schubert, which were untranslated
in the nineteenth century, and he did not read Schopenhauer in translation and at length until 1891, although he read short passages on
Schopenhauer in 1871 (JL 2:720–21). At any rate, with his family
background, wide reading, and searching introspection, Melville was

capable of expressing in *Moby-Dick* and *Pierre* conceptions of the unconscious that resembled interpretations of Carus's ideas as explained
by Ellenberger. Carus distinguishes three layers of the unconscious:
"(1) The *general absolute unconscious*, which is totally and permanently
inaccessible to our consciousness. (2) The *partial absolute unconscious* to
which belongs the processes of formation, growth, and activity of the
organs. This part of the unconscious exerts an indirect influence on
our emotional life. . . . (3) The *relative or secondary unconscious* compre-
hending the totality of feelings, perceptions, and representations,
which were ours at one time or other and which have become unconscious." Von Hartmann advanced another three-part structure, the
third level of which was "the relative or psychological unconscious,
which lies at the source of our conscious mental life."[21]

Although Melville's conception of the unconscious may not be as
elaborate or as systematic, it reveals in *Moby-Dick* and *Pierre* an awareness of the general nature of the unconscious, of areas or materials
therein corresponding to Jung's divisions of the unconscious into the
personal and collective, as Murray explains, and of the interrela-
tionships of the conscious and unconscious. Melville's treatment of
such elements appears most concentrated and purposeful in accounts
of Pierre's life. As a young boy standing alone in his father's sickroom,
he hears his father in delirium cry out for his daughter. Shocked and
confused, Pierre is saved from further anguish by the healing work of
the mind. The forbidden words are repressed or buried in unconscious
areas of his mind. "But it belonged to the spheres of the impalpable
ether; and the child soon threw other and sweeter remembrances over
it, and covered it up; and at last, it was blended with all other dim
things, and imaginings of dimness; and so, seemed to survive to no real
life in Pierre. But though through many long years the henbane
showed no leaves in his soul; yet the sunken seed was there: and the
first glimpse of Isabel's letter caused it to spring forth, as by magic"
(p. 71).

Years later, having received the stunning news of Isabel's letter,
Pierre recalls his aunt's explanations of his father's portrait, his friend
Ralph, and the book on physiognomy in his father's room. The aunt
referred to the "very wonderful work on Physiognomy . . . in which the
strangest and shadowiest rules were laid down for detecting people's
innermost secrets by studying their faces" (p. 79). She casually pointed
out that the father did not believe "any such ridiculous ideas" (p. 79).
As an adult the sometimes acute Pierre studies the forbidden portrait

once again for revelations of his father. After a few minutes he slips into a reverie: "Thus sometimes stood Pierre before the portrait . . . unconsciously throwing himself open to all those ineffable hints and ambiguities, and undefined half-suggestions, which now and then people the soul's atmosphere, as thickly as in a soft, steady snow-storm, the snow-flakes people the air. Yet as often starting from these reveries and trances, Pierre would regain the assured element of consciously bidden and self-propelled thought: and then in a moment the air all cleared, not a snow-flake descended" (p. 84). The reverie, leaving no "conscious sediment in his mind, . . . [left] all Pierre's thought-channels as clean and dry as though [no] . . . alluvial stream had rolled there at all" (p. 85). However, what has been hidden or repressed in the unconscious is brought out by the news of Isabel's letter.

The trauma induced by Isabel's letter affects Pierre in several ways: one is that thoughts of anyone other than Isabel, his father, and himself are obliterated. But before the first meeting with Isabel occurs in the red farmhouse, Pierre discovers that he cannot quite forget Lucy. Thinking about Isabel sooner or later revives thoughts of Lucy. Considerations of Isabel's happiness bring to mind Lucy's sorrow. The interplay of conscious and unconscious elements is portrayed in several contiguous passages that appear shortly before the first meeting of Pierre and Isabel. The first passage begins, "But, as yet, he could not bear the thought of Lucy, because the very resolution that promised balm to Isabel obscurely involved the everlasting peace of Lucy. . . . Well for Pierre it was, that the penciling presentiments of his mind concerning Lucy as quickly erased as painted their tormenting images" (pp. 104–5).

Not even the dedicated, introspective Pierre can anticipate or control the deeper regions of his mind. Tormenting images of Lucy soon reappear:

Standing half-befogged upon the mountain of his Fate, all that part of the wide panorama was wrapped in clouds to him; but anon those concealings slid aside, or rather, a quick rent was made in them; disclosing far below, half-vailed in the lower mist, the winding tranquil vale and stream of Lucy's previous happy life; through the swift cloud-rent he caught one glimpse of her expectant and angelic face peeping from the honey-suckled window of her cottage; and the next instant the stormy pinions of the clouds locked themselves over it again. . . . Only by unconscious inspira-

tion, caught from the agencies invisible to man, had he been en-
abled to write that first obscurely announcing note to Lucy;
wherein the collectedness, and the mildness, and the calmness,
were but the natural though insidious precursors of the stunning
bolts on bolts to follow. (p. 105)

In language suggestive of some aspects of Jung's personal unconscious or Carus's "secondary unconsciousness," the third passage dramatizes Pierre's mental upset and his final determination of Lucy's fate.
"Strange wild work, and awfully symmetrical and reciprocal, was that
now going on within the self-apparently chaotic breast of Pierre. As in
his own conscious determination, the mournful Isabel was being snatched
from her captivity . . . so, deeper down in the more secret chambers of
his unsuspecting soul, the smiling Lucy, now as dead and ashy pale, was
being bound a ransom for Isabel's salvation" (pp. 104–5).

In a short time Pierre's condition deteriorates as he becomes further
involved with Isabel and ties to the past. After the first interview with
Isabel, he discovers that he cannot sleep; on the following morning he
has a strained scene with his mother. Shortly thereafter, upset by attempts to understand Isabel's story, his father, and the need to act,
Pierre retreats to the mountain and the Mennon stone, where he "slid
himself straight into the horrible interspace, and lay there as dead"
(p. 134). During the second interview Pierre confesses his love and ac-
claims his devotion to truth. Yet away from Isabel, he is confused by
doubts and hatreds. He acts erratically, disturbs Reverend Falsgrave
with a late call, makes accusations about the treatment of Delly, and
becomes melancholic over the state of the world. That Pierre has already followed his obsessions too far is indicated in a portrayal of what
appears to be the farthest reaches of Pierre's mind, the collective unconscious. Pierre is perilously close to the edge, as this passage suggests: "In those Hyperborean regions, to which enthusiastic Truth, and
Earnestness, and Independence, will invariably lead a mind fitted by
nature for profound and fearless thought, all objects are seen in a dubious, uncertain, and refracting light. Viewed through that rarefied atmosphere the most immemorially admitted maxims of men begin to
slide and fluctuate, and finally become wholly inverted." If the thinking
man goes too far, Melville warns, he may "entirely [lose] the directing
compass of his mind" (p. 165).

As Pierre proceeds on his fanatic way, he destroys his father's portrait, cruelly rejects his mother and Lucy, and in the city publicly insults

his cousin Glen Stanly and criticizes residents of the Apostles. At the Apostles, with Isabel and Delly, Pierre sets himself to write a "comprehensive, compacted work" that will clarify for the world great and unstated truths. Although the talented youth has received earlier recognition for minor literary works, he deludes himself into thinking that he is a genius capable of original thought and of assimilating ideas from books he has read. His misconceptions about himself and truths of great books are clarified in this passage: "He did not see . . . that all the great books in the world are but the mutilated shadowings-forth of invisible and eternally unembodied images in the soul; so that they are but the mirrors, distortedly reflecting to us our own things; and never mind what the mirror may be, if we would see the object, we must look at the object itself, and not at its reflection" (p. 284). Henry A. Murray explains that in the line "all great books . . . are but the mutilated shadowings-forth of invisible and eternally unembodied images in the soul" Melville "vaguely adumbrated some of the central ideas in Jung's philosophy of the unconscious." This area of the unconscious is presumably the collective unconscious in which are to be found archetypes and symbols of basic human truths.[22]

In unconscious areas of the mind, troublesome forces lie in wait to erupt into the conscious levels. If Pierre mulls around too much, hoping for some kind of flashing illumination, he may lose what remains of his sanity. He must be cautious indeed about wandering in "the Switzerland of his soul . . . lest illy prepared for such an encounter, his spirit should sink and perish in the lowermost snows. Only by judicious degrees, appointed of God, does man come at last to gain his Mont Blanc and take an overtopping view of these Alps; and even then, the tithe is not shown; and far over the invisible Atlantic, the Rocky Mountains and the Andes are yet unbeheld." At this point appears a warning to Pierre and other relentless searchers into the depths of the mind: "Appalling is the soul of a man! Better might one be pushed off into the material spaces beyond the uttermost orbit of our sun, than once feel himself fairly afloat in himself!" (p. 284).

At the Apostles, Pierre must not only grind away at his comprehensive work but act as the head of a family, with Isabel as wife, Lucy as sister, and Delly as ward. Although the relationships do not exist in fact, they exist psychologically, particularly in the confused mind of the nominal husband, brother, and protector. The responsibilities are exhausting.

Pierre must occasionally get away. Every night he leaves the Apostles to walk the nearby streets, finding the most desired refuge in rain and storms. After a time he enters "mysterious tap-rooms" where he can protect his eyes and watch "the varied faces of the social castaways" (p. 341). Tiring of these retreats and needing greater isolation, Pierre turns to walking in the "utter night-desolation lanes of the obscurest warehousing." One night "as he paused a moment previous to turning about for home, a sudden unwonted, and all-pervading sensation seized him. He knew not where he was; he did not have any ordinary life-feeling at all. He could not see; though instinctively putting his hand to his eyes, he seemed to feel that the lids were open. Then he was sensible of a combined blindness, and vertigo, and staggering; before his eyes a million green meteors danced; he felt his foot tottering upon the curb, he put out his hands, and knew no more for the time" (p. 341). It almost seems that he had lost himself in the "Switzerland of his soul." Actually, he had fainted.

The fainting spell can be regarded as an attack of syncope, which, in the absence of organic lesion, can be caused by the sight of blood or an injury.[23] Another possible cause is exhaustion. Pierre may have been in the state of mind regarded by Dr. Murray as indicative of the "Hyperborean regions" passage in Book 9, Saddle Meadows. In those regions "the most immemorially admitted maxims of men begin to slide and fluctuate, and finally become wholly inverted." Dr. Murray regards such regions as indicative of abulia, which is "symbolic of the state of emotional exhaustion with paralysis of will (aboulia) which may result from a protracted mental conflict." In modern parlance, abulia is regarded as an absence of willpower or "wish power: the term implies that the individual has a desire to do something but the desire is without power or energy. . . . The more frequent disturbance in the will is a reduction or impairment (hypobulia) rather than a complete absence." Impairment of the will, hypobulia, rather than absence of will appears to be the problem in Pierre's case. The view that hypobulia and the rare abulia are "fundamental symptoms" of schizophrenia[24] underlines the pertinence of the nineteenth-century classification of moral insanity, which identifies disordered or depleted emotions, and perhaps will, and estrangements from others.

The morning after the fainting spell, discovering that he cannot use his eyes, Pierre settles into "a general and nameless torpor." This marks the beginning of the Enceladus incident during which are revealed extreme elements of Pierre's insanity. "During this state of semi-unconsciousness, or rather trance, a remarkable dream or vision came to him. The actual artificial objects around him slid from him, and were replaced by a baseless yet most imposing spectacle of natural scenery" (p. 342). In his 1835 study, Prichard describes a trance as a temporary condition in which an intense daydream and ordinary daily activities are blended. Prichard also regarded something of this kind as an example of "ecstatic affections," during which the nervous system is in a suspended or partly suspended state, the imagination is active, and the individual "fancies himself to exist under different circumstances from those which actually surround him." Prichard apparently regarded this as a form of insanity (unspecified).[25]

Pierre's Enceladus vision is intense and protracted. It presents a detailed picture of the mountainside which Pierre in his trance regards as "phantasmagoria of the Mount of the Titans" (p. 342). As psychological portraiture, the episode is only partly convincing because segments provide little information about Pierre's reactions or particular visions. As the focus or point of view moves closer to the scene, aspects of Pierre's hallucinatory trance become clearer. Pierre's vision of the forest conveys a sense of abnormal anger and hatred. Among the masses of leaves appear "horrible glimpses of dark-dripping rocks, and mysterious mouths of wolfish caves." Passing through the outer edge of the forest, he is confronted by masses of rock covered with moss. "All round and round, the grim scarred rocks rallied and re-rallied themselves; shot up, protruded, stretched, swelled, and eagerly reached forth." Pierre's strange vision ends with the Titans springing up and throwing themselves up the slope. At this time, seeing the giant Titan, Pierre cries out in his sleep, "Enceladus! it is Enceladus." When the phantom faces him, Pierre sees the Titan no more; but he does see upon the giant's chest "his own duplicate face and features." At this point Pierre awakens "from that ideal horror to all his actual grief" (pp. 343, 344, 346).

Although Pierre regains his senses after the "wild" trance has passed, his condition remains unstable. The trance marks an extreme of his sickness, a monomaniac state of a grandiose nature in which Pierre sees himself as of heroic stature, as a champion of Truth among the forces of falsehood and vice. This remarkable conception of self would appear to be an example of Jungian inflation. At any rate, in his conscious state of mind Pierre shows similar signs of monomania. After recovering from the trance, he concentrates on determining what his next action will be. "Concentrating all the remaining stuff in him, he resolved

by an entire and violent change, and by a willful act against his own
most habitual inclinations, to wrestle with the strange malady of his
eyes, this new death-fiend of the trance, and this Inferno of his Titanic
vision" (p. 347). Even in respect to something like his eyes, Pierre's ob-
sessional nature is evident. All the complexities and ambiguities have
faded away, as he now resolves on "entire and violent change." Any
moral compunctions about such actions have long since disappeared.
His obsession has obliterated anything else.

Soon thereafter, the accumulated hatreds and obsessions erupt in
homicidal fury as Pierre shoots Stanly and Fred, killing one and
wounding the other. Thoughts of his family—his father's honor and
his mother's reputation—left him weeks ago. Pierre's general mood in
the cell in the Tombs is of moody defiance. The two girls die with him,
a testimonial to the disintegration of mind and ideals, the final collapse
of the family.

The focus in Chapter 6 has been on the fairly predictable effects of
insanity in a family or family group in a village and the city. The focus
shifts in Chapter 7 to short stories and the often unpredictable outbreaks of insanity among characters largely unknown to each other and
meeting in a variety of places.

CHAPTER SEVEN. CITY AND SEA MADNESS

Stories

After completing *Pierre* in early 1852, Melville worked on his farm near Pittsfield in May and June. As farm work and chores were not to his liking, he hired a boy to help. Mrs. Maria Melvill, who was very much on the scene at Arrowhead, made certain that the boy earned his pay. Their joint efforts must have been productive, for the county assessment that year of the farm buildings and land went up. Later that summer reviews of *Pierre* began to appear. As Melville was to discover, the reviews were almost uniformly unfavorable and many were hostile. The reviewer for the *Boston Post* in July stated that the novel "is, perhaps, the craziest fiction extant. It has scenes and descriptions of unmistakeable power. . . . But the amount of utter trash in the volume is almost infinite."[1] A relatively mild assessment was advanced by the *Albion* in August: The book "must . . . be pronounced a dead failure. . . . *Pierre* is an objectionable tale, clumsily told." In October, *Graham's Magazine* regarded the novel as a "failure. . . . The author has attempted seemingly to combine . . . peculiarities of Poe and Hawthorne, and has succeeded in producing nothing but a powerfully unpleasant caricature of morbid thought and passion." The details of Pierre's "mental malady . . . are almost as disgust-

94

ing as those of physical disease itself." One reviewer, perhaps William Gilmore Simms, stated in the *Southern Quarterly Review* that "Herman Melville has gone 'clean daft,' is very much to be feared; certainly he has given us a very mad book" (JL 1: 458–63). The poor reception of *Pierre* not only hurt sales but damaged Melville's reputation. Sealts regards the novel as "nothing short of disastrous to his prospects as an author."[2]

During the fall and spring of 1853, family members were worried enough about Melville's general situation to make determined efforts to find a suitable consulate position for him in Europe or the Pacific. While Melville was agreeable and recognized the need to find a sensible way to earn a living, he kept busy nonetheless. His excursion with Judge Shaw in July to Nantucket proved enjoyable to both men and seemingly provided materials for another work of fiction. Melville met Shaw in Boston and the two men traveled by rail to New Bedford and then by boat to Nantucket. While in Nantucket, Melville met a lawyer named Clifford who told the story of Agatha Robertson, the wife of a Falmouth whaling captain who deserted her after two years of marriage. At Arrowhead after the excursion, Melville received Clifford's detailed account of the wife, who waited patiently for years for her husband to return.

During the winter and spring, Melville buried himself once again in the farmhouse attic to work full time on a novel, presumably an expanded version of the Agatha story. Melville's characteristic addiction to writing long hours in the attic likely spurred family attempts to find a consular position for the harassed man. What he was actually writing no one knows, for all evidence of his work during these months was destroyed or lost. Melville had tried to interest Hawthorne in writing the Agatha story, but when Hawthorne indicated that Melville was the one to write it he apparently did. On a trip to New York City in April 1853, Melville took a manuscript with him. The assumption is that after the embarrassing failures of *Moby-Dick* and *Pierre* the Harpers had no confidence whatsoever in Melville's writing and rejected the manuscript. Referring to Henry A. Murray's views, Sealts explains, "But 'since no such story was ever published or found in manuscript form, the chances are it was destroyed, probably burnt by Melville himself in a moment of self-negating desperation' after his abortive trip to New York in the following spring."[3]

Any such desperation would have been natural. The rejection of the manuscript must have been a stunning blow. Melville needed the reassurance of a contract, not to mention money for the ever-present bills and debts. Poor reviews of *Pierre* were still appearing and in a short while expenses for the new baby would begin. Writing for Melville was not only burdensome; it simply did not pay. A consular appointment would have been welcome, but none was forthcoming. Nor could he get away from occasional reminders by relatives and friends of his failures as a writer. The situation at Arrowhead did not greatly improve when his sister Kate left in spring 1853 to marry and Helen departed in January for her marriage. Melville's cousin Phyllis from Pittsfield lived at Arrowhead during the winter of 1853, and a servant may have stayed there to help Elizabeth with the children. The house was therefore crowded again. Spring of 1853 was to be especially difficult. Lizzie wrote simply, "We all felt anxious about the strain on his health," and the mother, Maria Melvill, stated that "this constant working of the brain, & excitement of the imagination, is wearing Herman out."[4] The arrival of the new baby in May was a joyful event for all, but it added to household confusion.

Little could be done, however, about arrangements at Arrowhead. The mother and sisters had been part of the family group since Melville's marriage to Elizabeth in 1847. The oldest child, Malcolm, now four, would be manageable at times and could play outdoors, but the baby, Stanwix, followed his own instincts, and his crying would upset the concentration of anyone, especially someone like Melville. The difficulties of writing at Arrowhead, the writer's responsibilities as head of the family, repeated failures as a writer, and the pressing need to write something that would pay some bills, buy a few things, and even prove critically acceptable to reviewers were burdens for a person well aware of psychological vulnerabilities. Overly sensitive to taunts by some reviewers that he had lost his mind or was mentally troubled, well aware of attitudes of some relatives and never far from the harping of his mother, Melville no doubt knew that he was overtaxing himself and that fears and bugaboos were resurfacing. From time to time he may have doubted his own sanity.

Under the circumstances, Melville decided not to risk another novel but to try something different—short stories. *Putnam's* had approached him that spring about the possibility of writing stories for their new magazine that would pay $5 a page, a far more attractive rate than any from a forthcoming novel. Melville understandably made the change.

In three years, he wrote fifteen stories, seven for *Putnam's* and seven for *Harper's Monthly Magazine*, all of which paid quite well and included the lengthy "The Encantadas." He wrote also the serialized *Israel Potter* in 1855.

Even though insanity is not a prominent topic in the stories, it appears in some form in six of the fifteen stories and represents a recurrent concern for the writer in the Arrowhead years. "Bartleby the Scrivener" and "Jimmy Rose" are city stories based on city and family experiences of the past. "Cock-A-Doodle-Doo!" and "The Lightning-Rod Man," based on experiences in the Pittsfield area of the early 1850s, portray rural scenes. To some extent "Benito Cereno" had something to do with his sailing past, and "The Encantadas" comes out of experiences in the Galápagos Islands during his first whaling voyage of 1841–42.

In these writings Melville turned from broad treatments of *Moby-Dick* and *Pierre* to the confinement of a few characters, a small area, and a segment of the past. Melville is not concerned in the stories with portraying a mad world but different worlds in which madness in some form is always present. The abnormality may be a particularly baffling kind as in "Bartleby" and "Benito Cereno" or something relatively routine as in "Jimmy Rose." Some stories indicate a shift in focus from the interior consciousness of characters to the external scene.

Like "Bartleby the Scrivener," "Jimmy Rose" is a big city story, focusing on the business world that Melville was familiar with and on the social scene. Jimmy Rose in his prime was at the top. A bachelor admired for handsome appearance, brilliant manners, and business acumen, Rose was a stunning success in all respects. But suddenly his fortune turned around; he lost his money and that of his friends. Everything changed: "At the first onset of his calamity, when creditors, once fast friends, pursued him as carrion for jails; though then, to avoid their hunt, as well as the human eye, he had gone and denned in the old abandoned house; and there, in his loneliness, had been driven *half-mad*" (my italics).[5] Pressures of the business community became excessive. As his world fell apart, Rose retreated. He saw few people, became bitter and lonely. His "half-mad" condition would seem to suggest a few antisocial signs of moral insanity. But, as Melville writes, "time and tide . . . soothed him down to sanity" (p. 342). With a few friends, one meal daily, and nourishment from frequent visits to social gatherings, Rose manages to get by. His cheeks regain their bloom, and determination and a good disposition save him from the ravages of long-term insanity.

"Cock-A-Doodle-Doo!" and "The Lightning-Rod Man" are puzzling because satire, humor, and allegory noticeably dilute the realism, and the characters themselves are strange. The sexual comedy of the first story is a complex reflection of the narrator's physical and mental complaints, his "dyspepsia." The narrator's melancholy alternates occasionally with lighthearted moods—the other side of his monomania.[6] Nothing diluted appears in the intense confrontation of inflexible figures in "The Lightning-Rod Man." Neither the man of science nor the exponent of religion or independence is normal. The salesman is described as a "lean, gloomy figure" with "sunken pitfalls of eyes . . . ringed by indigo halos" (p. 118). Even though the description is not to be taken literally, it suggests a gloomy, foreboding individual. Yet he is a determined, persistent salesman for his lightning rods and a relentless advocate of proper safeguards against lightning striking buildings. He is, however, easily upset. When the owner becomes argumentative the salesman becomes angry. When the owner insists on an iron bar for a rod, the salesman cries, "Are you mad?" At the end, when the owner insults him, the salesman cries out, "Impious wretch" and foams at the mouth. Nor is the owner calm and reasonable. Irritated that the salesman stopped at the house during a storm, the owner will not allow him the last word on anything. He insists on using an iron bar for a lightning rod, standing by the hearth, disregarding the lightning, and relying on the protection of God, not on that of science. Taunting the salesman with pagan names, he scorns his science. The owner is one of Melville's defiant rebels, determined to do things his own way.[7] When the other man springs on him, with the "tri-forked thing at my heart . . . I seized it; I snapped it; I dashed it; I trod it" (p. 124). Both characters are obsessed: one with views of science, the other with views of independence. Each is maddened by an inability to see himself and his ideas from another perspective. Each becomes unsocial, even hostile.

"Sketch First" of "The Encantadas" contains Melville's introduction to the Galápagos Islands he visited in 1841. "It is to be doubted whether any spot of earth can, in desolateness, furnish a parallel to this group." The islands are unmatched for "solitariness" and for "emphatic uninhabitableness" (p. 126). Consisting mainly of expanses of rocks and ashes and steep, sparsely wooded hills, the enchanted islands are, however, good places for "all sorts of refugees" and "solitaries" of all kinds.

Although descriptions in the ten sketches do not include such words as "mad," "crazy," "insane," or comparable terms, words like "monster," "misshapen," "misanthrope," "rascals," and "tyrants," which appear throughout, indicate the likelihood of at least some instances of abnormal behavior, probably in areas of both moral insanity and monomania. If the islands are good places for outcasts and criminals, they would be seemingly good places for the mad and near-mad. Two prominent outcasts, both leaders, are illustrative.

Deeded Charles Isle for his services to Peru, the Dog-King appears at first to be tough but fair, revengeful but sane and intelligent. But as he recruits an army of castoffs and misfits, he grows ambitious and arrogant. He brings to the island an army of dogs to keep his men under control. When men rebel against his rule, he executes them, disbands the human guards, and relies on the ferocious dogs. Pressures make him crafty. "By insidious arts . . . he . . . cajoles certain sailors to desert their ships." Men become increasingly unruly under his leadership. Finally, they mutiny. In a big battle, many dogs and some men are killed. Afterward, the Dog-King is banished. By this time he is a changed man, cruel and inhuman, showing, it is suspected, deterioration of character and emotion—a likely manifestation of moral insanity.

The most obviously insane figure in "The Encantadas" and the strangest is Oberlus, ruler of Hood's Isle. He is described at first as an allegoric figure who arrived on the island with "qualities more diabolical than are . . . found among any of the surrounding cannibals" (pp. 162–63). A strange man, with a wild, earthy appearance, Oberlus manages to grow potatoes on the island of rocks and ashes. He is also naturally tyrannical and cruel. After he is severely beaten for kidnapping a sailor, he changes for the worse. "Brooding among the ruins of his hut, and the desolate clinkers . . . the insulated misanthrope now meditates a signal revenge upon humanity, but conceals his purposes" (p. 166). The men he manages to lure ashore are subjugated and used. Oberlus's goal is to massacre the crew of a ship and sail the seas, but the opportunity never materializes. Instead on one occasion he persuades sailors to bring four boats ashore. Three boats are destroyed and the fourth is hidden. Later, as Oberlus and his men sail for land on the remaining boat, the others mysteriously disappear. Only Oberlus arrives. In Peru, he becomes the leader of a "mongrel and assassin band." Caught in the act of burning a new vessel, Oberlus is jailed for "a long time," a monomaniac full of hatred of others, a far more dreadful specimen of humanity than any in *Typee* and *Omoo*. He is not, however, an example of misanthropic monomania, which affects those believing themselves to be objects of hatred, plots, and the like.[8]

———————————

Portrayals of insanity in "Bartleby the Scrivener" and "Benito Cereno" appear more pragmatic and complex. Melville's city background figures significantly in the first story. He had stayed in Wall Street with his lawyer brothers Gansevoort and Allan in 1845 when he was writing *Typee,* and in 1847 both Herman and Allan and their respective brides set up housekeeping at 103 Fourth Street. In 1840, after the Galena trip with his boyhood friend Fly, both men attempted to find jobs in Wall Street. Although both failed, Fly stayed on to become a copyist. In Albany, Fly, a friend also of Gansevoort Melville, had been an apprentice lawyer for five years in the offices of Peter Gansevoort. In New York, Fly asked Gansevoort for assistance in securing a position as commissioner of deeds, but Gansevoort responded that Fly should try to do things on his own. When Fly later became an invalid, Melville assisted him in various matters. Rogin believes that "Fly supplies the missing history of *Bartleby.*"[9]

Whether or not Fly is the man behind the mysterious Bartleby, there is no question that New York and Wall Street, or Melville's imaginative portrayals of them, provide the basis for the story's setting. Environment or place helps determine Bartleby's fate and that of others as well; if not a cause of mental upset or abnormality, it is a contributing factor in the development of Bartleby's puzzling behavior and attitude. As the "unambitious lawyer-narrator" does not appear to be involved in courtroom tensions or high finance, the Wall Street environment is not constantly hectic or harassing. Yet descriptions of buildings, streets, and offices make clear that for most people the pursuit of money and success is constant.

The lawyer's office, large and appropriately businesslike, contains mainly plain wooden desks, chairs, and benches. Glass folding doors divide the office into two sizable parts with the narrator situated in one part, the copyists in the other. After Bartleby is hired, his place is with the narrator, who obtains "a high green folding screen, which might entirely isolate Bartleby from my sight" (p. 19). Work and office life are thus compartmentalized. The windows provide no relief from the monotonous locale and office activity because they reveal only another brick building three feet away. Although Bartleby appears oblivious of such buildings, he spends much of his time in one. After the lawyer and others leave for the day or weekend, Bartleby stays in his "hermitage" in the office. He remains in the office building even after the lawyer-narrator, exasperated by Bartleby's polite negativisms, moves his business to another building. Bartleby remains in the old one until he is taken away to the Tombs, a structure as cold and indifferent as a city block of Wall Street office buildings.

Despite his limitations, the lawyer-narrator is an intelligent man, capable of understanding and managing his original office force of two scriveners and an office boy, but not of anticipating or understanding the motives and needs of "Bartleby . . . a scrivener the strangest I ever saw or heard of" (p. 13). That is not to say that Turkey and Nippers, his first-line scriveners, are without their oddities.

Both characters clarify Wall Street values and standards and to some extent the nature of the environment enveloping Bartleby. A familiar interpretation is that Turkey, inefficient and irritable in the afternoon, represents England, a country past its prime, and Nippers, nervous and erratic in the morning, is America, a country on the rise.[10] Another likelihood is that each character shows the harmful effects of living and working in the Wall Street area. In somewhat allegoric terms, each character is generally normal for half the day and somewhat eccentric or possibly abnormal the other half. What could more effectively illustrate the harmful effects of business and commercial practices than the lives and activities of Wall Street employees? Turkey, almost sixty, has been a dedicated, faithful employee for years. But by noontime, the monotony of copying legal documents begins to exact its toll. He becomes overly energetic. "There was a strange, inflamed, flurried, flighty recklessness of activity about him." He blots documents, becomes reckless and noisy, and on occasion can break up his pens and throw "them on the floor in a sudden passion." Although prudent and respectful before noon, Turkey can be "slightly rash with his tongue, in fact, insolent" after noon. No less indicative of instability is Turkey's dress, which the narrator regards as almost beneath reproach. Every day his "clothes were apt to look oily and smell of eating-houses. He wore his pantaloons very loose and baggy in summer. His coats were execrable; his hat not to be handled" (pp. 15, 16, 17). Turkey's clothing may disclose the indifference of an aging man, but it likely discloses as well reservations toward social and business standards, possibly a loss of respect for himself and others. For too long Wall Street pressures have been wearing away Turkey's social amenities. The emotional outbursts and insolent remarks of an older, experienced man indicate frustration, discontent, inability to cope, outrage: they indicate also what appears to be a form of moral insanity.

Nippers, efficient and sensible in the afternoon, is no less victimized by Wall Street life. As the narrator explains, "I always deemed him the victim of two evil powers—ambition and indigestion. The ambition was evinced by a certain impatience of the duties of a mere copyist." Nippers' ambitiousness goes so far as to show "an unwarrantable usurpation of strictly professional affairs, such as the original drawing up of legal documents" (p. 16). The narrator, perhaps not entirely serious, describes Nippers' ambition as "diseased" and regards visits by "certain ambiguous-looking fellows in seedy coats" as evidence of that condition. Nippers, who is "considerable of a ward-politician," may be a part-time bondsman as well. Although such activities do not clearly indicate psychological failures, something is clearly wrong. Nippers' chronic frustrations, discomforts in the office, usurpations with documents, and "nervous testiness and grinning irritability" point to problems not to be resolved or forgotten through outside activities (pp. 17, 16). For a young man, Nippers shows too many strains and irritations, probable signs of an incipient moral insanity.

The man who responds to the narrator's advertisement for a scrivener proceeds to confound all others in the story and modern-day readers and critics as well. Bartleby does not fit clearly into any single niche, whether economic, religious, psychological, philosophic, or something else. Yet certain points about him are clear. The narrator provides a reliable if not very detailed physical picture. Bartleby is a "motionless young man" with calm gray eyes and a quiet voice with a "flute-like tone." The narrator adds, "I can see that figure now—pallidly neat, pitiably respectable, incurably forlorn." For a few days, the impression is favorable. Bartleby is efficient and copies carefully if mechanically. But after a short time, signs of trouble appear. On the third day, when the narrator asks him to read a paper with him, Bartleby states simply, "I would prefer not to." Yet later he responds as expected. "As days passed on, I became considerably reconciled to Bartleby. His steadiness, his freedom from all dissipation, his incessant industry (except when he chose to throw himself into a standing revery behind his screen), his great stillness, his unalterableness of demeanor under all circumstances, made him a valuable acquisition" (pp. 19, 25–26).

However, changes soon appear in his steady, compliant demeanor. On a Sunday morning when the narrator stops by the office before church, Bartleby appears "in his shirt sleeves, and otherwise in a strangely tattered dishabille." Saying that he was busy then, he asks the lawyer to return in a short while. When the narrator returns, Bartleby is gone. The office reveals a way of life: "for an indefinite period Bartleby must have ate, dressed, and slept in my office, and that too without plate, mirror, or bed." Bartleby has been subsisting on "a ricketty old sofa," a blanket which he keeps rolled under his desk, and a "tin basin, with soap and a ragged towel," and, apparently, "ginger-nuts and . . . cheese." The dismayed narrator concludes, "What I saw that morning persuaded me that the scrivener was the victim of innate and incurable disorder." The next morning Bartleby appears increasingly passive and withdrawn. His replies to the narrator's questions and requests are uniformly courteous and negative. He prefers not to do one thing or another. The next day, Bartleby informs the narrator that he would do no more writing. At this time "his eyes look . . . dull and glazed" (pp. 26, 27, 29, 32).

In the final weeks, Bartleby refuses to leave the office, accept money, vacate the building, take another job, or go to the narrator's home. The narrator is well aware that his copyist suffers from a "disorder," but others regard him as a nuisance or as a vagrant. As he is not disorderly, dangerous, or irrational, he is not clearly mad or insane. In 1861, Isaac Ray wrote in the *American Journal of Insanity*, "The existence of insanity in any form is not always proved by the presence of any particular symptom, or even group of symptoms, but rather by changes of mind or character, which can be explained on no other hypothesis than that of disease."[11]

The statement by Ray may appear acceptable or relevant to readers who regard psychological judgments or criteria as valid. The statement may appear unacceptable or irrelevant to those who question such judgments and criteria or who regard them as irrelevant because Bartleby is not insane. He is a sane character victimized by economic, political, or other conditions. The general point is that complexities of language, ideas, narration, and characterization account for different interpretations. Modern psychological interpretations vary because there is no consensus that Bartleby is suffering from a form of schizophrenia. Although nineteenth-century terms and judgments can hardly be more exact or factual than modern ones, they are pertinent and illustrate what Melville was working with. The story contains ordinary contemporary words or phrases describing someone like Bartleby: the narrator describes him as "moon-struck," "the victim of innate and incurable disorder," a "demented man," a "little deranged." Ginger Nut regards him as a "little *luny*" (pp. 20, 29, 31, 44, 22). Melville's knowledge of Burton's *Anatomy of Melancholy* (1621) provides Wright with helpful clues for deciphering mentalities in the story: Turkey and Nippers represent melancholy of the head and Bartleby represents melancholy of the body.[12] In terms of the mid-nineteenth-century emphasis in this study, Bartleby shows a complex of symptoms associated with moral insanity and monomania. As explained earlier, the two diseases possess similarities; symptoms of both may appear in one individual; a condition of moral insanity may develop obscurely into a "full-fledged" case of monomania, as in the instance of Ahab. That is not the case with Bartleby, a mild, passive, and regressive character. Symptoms of moral insanity in Bartleby include a diminution of emotions, melancholy, absence of interest in people, places, or activities, and no apparent impairment of cognitive faculties. Bartleby's reveries, habitual negativisms, and final refusal to eat indicate the likelihood of delusion, a characteristic of monomania. The delusion is that he can lead his own kind of life even though it runs counter to or independent of the social reality of which he is a part. Bartleby, oblivious to whatever is not his self, is concerned with only his body and consciousness. If he cannot live on such terms, he will live on no terms at all.

Most aspects of Melville's "Benito Cereno" appear difficult: plot, characterization, point of view, theme, ideas, symbolism. Thematic considerations may focus on slavery, questions of authority, contrasts of civilizations, relations of whites and blacks, innocence, and evil. Insanity is only one aspect of the story, but it is an important one. Don Benito Cereno is unbalanced, Babo appears monomaniacal, and several of Babo's henchmen, particularly Francesco, Lecbe, and possibly Atuful, are hardly normal. Most of them follow their leader into some form of insanity. Physical conditions aboard the *San Dominick* must appear maddening to enslaved white men aboard, and thematic elements—in particular, slavery, questions of authority, and race relations—can be regarded as reflections of individual, group, and national insanities.

Setting is an important aspect of Melville's portrayal of insanity in "Benito Cereno." The place is located near "a small, desert, uninhabited island toward the southern extremity of the long coast of Chile." Everything in the early morning scene appears to be gray—the low, undulating sea, the hovering fowls, the "troubled gray vapors." These details, which create a sense of "[shadows] present, foreshadowing deeper shadows to come," suggest something of the mysterious, Gothic, and hidden (p. 46).

The ship is obviously of crucial importance in the story. The *San Dominick* is portrayed in part through Delano's perspective; in the early morning mist and at a distance, the ship appears to be at first a "white-washed monastery" with a "ship-load of monks." On a closer approach, again largely from the American's view, the "true character of the vessel was plain—a Spanish merchantman of the first class" (p. 48). It is a fine vessel, or once was, with many decks and cabins and elaborate galleries and balconies. On closer examination, though, the ship appears deteriorated. The elaborate, Gothic prose suggests a long history of "faded grandeur" and many journeys and storms. Boarding such a ship is in some respects like "entering a strange house with strange inmates in a strange land" (p. 50).

In several ways, the Spanish merchantman resembles the American insane asylum described by Isabel in *Pierre*. Both ship and asylum are large, wooden structures with many evidences of age and decay, many hidden rooms and hallways, and many inmates who at first can be seen only dimly along the ship railings or peering through asylum windows. "The ship seems unreal; these strange costumes, gestures, and faces, but a shadowy tableau just emerged from the deep" (p. 50). Isabel reacts to the asylum in somewhat similar terms. Both the asylum and the ship to a lesser extent are havens for the insane.

The point of view is a complex blending of perspectives of Captain Delano, the writer, and a third official perspective evident in the last part of the story.[13] The principal viewpoints are essential in the creation of the intricate labyrinth of actions and reactions of different psychologies of characters aboard the *San Dominick*. Captain Delano's viewpoint is not simple, for it covers much of the pragmatic and factual and includes as well ironic overtones indicative of values and possibilities about which the captain usually has little or no inkling or understanding. Providing the basic ironies and also an overall integrative view is the authorial point of view, which is a corrective of Delano's viewpoint and provides clues as to what is happening or what may happen and fills in gaps in the action and provides pieces of the puzzle Delano remains unaware of. The two points of view provide not only the outlines of abnormalities aboard the ship but something of their substance. The prose style is necessarily subtle, complex, and evocative.

The two sea captains, Delano and Cereno, are clearly opposites. The American, one of the sanest of Melville's important characters, is cer-

tainly the most trustworthy sea captain. He is steady, pragmatic, and
alert, but lacks subtlety or imagination. The Spanish captain is complex, reserved, and sophisticated. He is sophisticated enough to hide
his secrets and fears from Delano. His upset state of mind is a reflection
not only of qualities of character but of recent events. The massacre of
white sailors and officers, the barbaric murder of his friend Alexander
Arana, and the subsequent seventy-three days of terror have seriously
affected Benito. Only Babo's constant presence and watchfulness and
Benito's own fears keep him from falling apart.

For all his confidence, sea experience, and general alertness, Captain
Delano is hardly the individual to understand Benito's condition. Delano lacks a sense of irony or a recognition of his own limitations.
Nonetheless, he makes shrewd assessments of Cereno's condition, although the assessments are colored by his subjectivity and sense of pity.
When Delano first observes the captain, he notes that Cereno bears
"plain traces of recent sleepless nights and disquietudes." Descriptions
of Cereno are often from Delano's perspective but directed by authorial insight. At the beginning he realizes that Cereno lacks the force
to maintain order on the large ship. He notes also a "debility, constitutional or induced by hardships, bodily and mental, the Spanish captain
. . . too obvious to be overlooked" (p. 10). However, unlike the author,
he is likely unaware of the effects of debility, which include, as noted in
Chapter 1 in reference to *Neversink* sailors in sick bay, "nervous irritability" and "nervous excitement." The modern term for debility is asthenia, one form of which is related to anxiety neurosis.[14] Nor is Delano
likely aware of the cause or meaning of his own observation that Cereno at times moves around "like some hypochondriac abbot . . . at
times suddenly pausing, starting, or staring, biting his lip, biting his fin-
ger-nail, flushing, paling, twitching his beard, with other symptoms of
an absent or moody mind" (p. 52). Delano appears unaware that the
behavior is caused by deeper troubles. In modern psychiatry hypochondriasis may be regarded "in association with such disorders as
anxiety neurosis, obsessive-compulsive neurosis, and most often with
the initial states of any psychosis."[15]

Captain Delano often misinterprets evidence of psychological difficulty, disregards it, or fails to pull things together. At times Delano regards Cereno as an imposter of some kind, as someone guilty of "wicked
imposture" in his strange behavior, as acting on the basis of some design. At other times he observes important indicators but does not
understand them, as indicated above in reference to Benito's ner-

vousness. He also does not know what to make of Benito's withdrawal qualities, in a sense the other side of his hypochondria, his "nervousness." Dillingham regards Benito Cereno as a victim of brainwashing as practiced by Nazis and others during World War II. Babo's methods for controlling Benito are "identical with the techniques used in brainwashing—removal of social and perceptual supports, the destruction of self-image by humiliation and revilement." [16] Silence, apathy, withdrawal, and physical submission—consequences apparently of brainwashing—are shown in Benito's behavior. He is described as resembling a "somnambulist" and as exhibiting "sudden, staring, half-lunatic looks" and "then lapsing into his torpor." A torpor, a state of "numbness, stupefaction," would be a manifestation of Benito's withdrawal states. At one point, Benito is described as "more withdrawn than ever" (pp. 59, 63).

The writer's references to somnambulism, torpor, and withdrawal states show at least an awareness of conditions under examination in mid-century by James Prichard. Cereno's passivity and immobility, while only temporary, suggest something also of the immobility of catalepsy, another condition under examination by Prichard. The crux of Melville's portrayal of Benito Cereno, however, would appear to be a form of moral insanity which can "include" elements of hypochondriasis and withdrawal states. [17]

Babo has been regarded by critics as a symbol of evil, Satan, a primitive, a spokesman for the African world, a militant civil rights leader of the late 1700s, and a monomaniac. [18] There are other possibilities as well. In the story, opinions or assessments of Babo are usually expressed through the thoughts and remarks of Captain Delano, who shows far less understanding of Babo than of Benito Cereno. Although he has some doubts of Babo, Delano characteristically assumes that the black is what he appears to be: a devoted servant for Captain Cereno. He accepts Babo's actions and remarks literally so that he confidently believes that Babo in Senegal was a poor slave who now wants to do nothing but serve his master; that Babo has the "contentment of a limited mind" (p. 84); that he accidentally cuts Benito's throat; that Benito's sullen reaction is only an indication of "a sort of love-quarrel" (p. 88); that he would die for his master. Occasionally and accidentally Delano comes close to the truth about Babo—with his "regular European face . . . he is a devil" (p. 89)—but not until Babo leaps into the boat and tries to kill Benito does he finally realize the terrible truth about the loyal servant.

The complete truth about Babo does not come out, for after his capture he ceases to speak. Testimony of Benito and others at the trial reveals Babo's part in the mutiny and slaughter and the new life aboard ship that follows. Something of his life in Senegal is revealed but nothing in detail about his earlier years and family life. There is much more known of his "previous life," however, than of Ahab's or Bartleby's. In general terms slavery and oppression have shaped him into a complex individual who somewhere along the line loses his sanity and balance and becomes a highly complex individual driven by hatred of white men, oppression, desire for revenge, and a goal of freedom. His complexity and intelligence enable him aboard the *San Dominick* to confound Delano with his seeming simplicity and devotion. Delano is informed by Benito that because the officers have been lost, Babo, who was originally "captain of slaves," was also his "constant attendant and companion . . . in all things his confidant" (p. 90). At the trial more revelations of Babo's complexity and intelligence appear as he is shown to have been the "plotter . . . [who] ordered every murder . . . [and was] helm and keel of the revolt" (p. 112).

The years of slavery and of rebellion against slavery have created a totally dedicated and highly efficient leader; they have created as well an obsessed character. He is, as Dillingham explains, a monomaniac.[19] As fanatic as Ahab, Babo possesses greater control of himself and others because his goals are far more limited and his emotions through the years have been harnessed to the task. Unlike Ahab, he does not have monomaniac nightmares. His head, that "hive of subtlety" (p. 116), has taken over. In almost total control of his emotions, he does not reveal strong emotions until he jumps into the lifeboat and is ready to kill Benito Cereno. Then "his countenance [became] . . . lividly vindictive" (p. 99). But apparently that is the last revelation of emotion. After his capture, with his hatred turned inward, Babo settles into passivity and silence, ready to die.

Notable indicators of mental illness in the stories—passivity, violence, deception, and fanaticism—appear in different forms in *The Confidence-Man*, to be discussed in Chapter 8. The *Fidèle* is a natural gathering place for a variety of characters, female and male, sane and insane.

CHAPTER EIGHT. INSANITY OUT WEST

The Confidence-Man

More than any other fiction by Melville, *The Confidence-Man* (1857) reveals the writer's years of preoccupation with the forms and nature of insanity. That preoccupation did not culminate in the deepest portrayals of insanity, which appear in *Moby-Dick* and *Pierre*, but in the most pervasive and constant treatment of mental abnormality in his fiction. Many characters aboard the steamer *Fidèle* on April Fools' Day, or referred to on that day, show signs of abnormality. These include major characters—the man with the weed or Johnny Ringman, Goneril, the Titan, Charlemont, China Aster, and Colonel Moredock—and such other figures as the wooden-legged man, the dried old man, and the crippled soldier. Both characters and author employ words and phrases signifying an awareness of or familiarity with various forms of abnormality. Some words and phrases appear semitechnical or formal: "tic-douloureux," "hypochondriac mania," "calenture," "deep melancholy," "mental derangement," "mental suffering," "neuralgic sorrow," "very melancholic," and "demoniac unfortunate." Other references are common or colloquial terms: "lunatic," "lunacy," "moon-calf," "brain-fever," "out of his mind," "losing your mind," "old crazy man," "crazy beggar," "mad house," "moody madness," "mad man," and "wandering mind."

The society of *The Confidence-Man* consists largely of passengers aboard the *Fidèle*, headed down the Mississippi River on April Fools' Day. The crowded steamer provides a natural environment for the display of Americans and non-Americans of many kinds, backgrounds, and proclivities, as shown in Chapter 2. "There was no lack of variety. Natives of all sorts, and foreigners; men of business and men of pleasure; parlor men and backwoodsmen; farm-hunters and fame-hunters; heiress-hunters . . . truth-hunters, and still keener hunters after all these hunters. Fine ladies in slippers, and moccasined squaws; Northern speculators and Eastern philosophers; English, Irish, German, Scotch, Danes . . . jesters and mourners, teetotalers and convivialists. . . . In short, a piebald parliament, an Anacharsis Cloots congress of all kinds of that multiform pilgrim species, man."[1]

The *Fidèle* society lacks the cohesion and rules evident in the ocean-going societies of the *Neversink* and the *Pequod*. The captain and officers of the steamer remain behind scenes, hidden from view, concerned mainly it seems with mechanical operations of the ship. The few shipboard rules and practices are apparently accepted by the passengers, who both illustrate and help determine the values and practices of the society. Traditional Christian virtues and behavior are represented by the mute who appears at the beginning on the lower deck of the steamer and writes biblical passages from 1 Corinthians 13 on his small slate for everyone to see: "Charity thinketh no evil," "Charity suffereth long, and is kind," "Charity never faileth" (pp. 4, 5). Comparable virtues of honesty and goodness are represented by the gentleman, charitable lady, and a few others who appear later. That these various values may not be widely accepted is suggested in the rough treatment accorded the mute and by later actions. Others in this steamship society have different values. The mute's actions bring out the ship's barber, William Cream, who hangs over his shop door a fancy sign expressing a traditional but hardly reassuring ethical code, "No Trust" (p. 5).

Most passengers aboard the *Fidèle* on April 1 do not live according to Christian virtues or comparable ones. Some professing to be Christians pay only lip service to such values. Their lives are usually selfish, inconsiderate, and essentially uncharitable. Most passengers do not realize that observance of the traditional ethical values customarily makes for sane, sensible lives. Nor do they realize that as they deviate from such standards they lose something of their humanity and in the process something of their mental balance as well. Indifference to moral values or willful misuse of them may well affect both moral character and psychological stability. Melville relates personal ethics and psychology. The least honest and trustworthy of characters would seem to be most vulnerable to psychological weaknesses, including insanity. As the ship is crowded with dishonest, devious, and uncharitable passengers, the society is not only tainted with evil but marred by mental and emotional aberrations. Having gone morally astray, many passengers may be as close to insanity as they are to corruption.

The Confidence-Man was written between May 1855 and September 1856, during which time several stories and *Israel Potter* were published. Although Melville's finances were as stable in March 1855 as they had been in years, personal problems were evident. Melville was not yet thirty-six years old and already his sturdy physique was showing signs of wear and tear. Elizabeth's memoir reads, "In Feb 1855 he had his first attack of severe rheumatism in his back—so that he was helpless."[2] The attack occurred at a bad time because the spring plowing and planting had to be done, and if he was unable to work, there would be little money for bills that would accumulate after the fourth child was born in March. "Benito Cereno" was accepted in April, but the money from *Putnam's* would pay few bills. Leon Howard explains that with such problems facing him "Melville was in a state bordering upon panic."[3] The troubles did not go away, for in June he suffered an attack of sciatica. Melville's neighbor, Dr. Oliver Wendell Holmes, responding to the family's request for assistance, examined Melville's ailing back and also his mental state, about which the family was no less concerned. Dr. Holmes's recommendations, the family's worries, and Melville's continuing troubles led eventually in fall 1856 to the writer's trip to the Middle East in an attempt to regain his equilibrium.

Melville's finances in 1855 did not remain stable for long; the main problem was a sizable debt to a Pittsfield friend named Stewart. Although Melville had paid on the principal each year, he had been unable to make yearly interest payments. "By May 1, 1855, the third time Melville missed the interest payment, the loan had become a serious threat to his security. It threatened through the summer, fall, and winter of 1855–56, during much of which he was writing *The Confidence-Man*."[4] One solution to the problem was the sale of the farm, which Herman and Lizzie seriously considered in the summer of 1855 when a state committee appeared in the area looking for a good site for a third state hospital for the insane. Melville's farm and several other area places were under consideration. When a site elsewhere was selected, Melville was "seriously disappointed." Thoughts of an insane asylum or an asylum did not vanish, however, for several characters in the novel in progress refer to "mad-houses." The following June, Melville sold eighty acres of the farm to pay off the loan and prevent foreclosure on the rest by Stewart. The circumstances of the loan may have influenced the writing of the China Aster story in *The Confidence-Man*.[5]

Although the exact composition of the novel remains a mystery, the idea of a confidence man came from Melville's reading of newspaper accounts of a notorious swindler with several pseudonyms operating in the East, including New York City. Articles on the man had appeared in 1849 and 1855.[6] Ideas for the treatment of insanity in *The Confidence-Man* probably came from personal experiences and recollections, but newspaper articles may have stimulated his interest. Melville was a frequent reader of the local *Pittsfield Sun*, the *Springfield Republican*, and other area newspapers and at least an occasional reader of metropolitan papers, especially the *New York Herald*, to which he subscribed from time to time. The weekly *Pittsfield Sun* in the 1850s carried occasional items of interest involving or pertaining to suicide, delirium tremens, and insanity in general; an annual report on conditions at the state "lunatic" asylums or hospitals (number of patients, the need for "strong rooms for the furiously insane," care of melancholic patients, and similar points); and in 1851 frequent advertisements of patent medicines for treatment of "all nervous diseases," including "Tic Doloreux and Neuralgia." In September 1855 the *New York Herald* contained information on a New Haven murder trial that resulted in an acquittal by reason of insanity.[7]

Earlier periods in Melville's life had a significant impact on the writing of *The Confidence-Man*. Events of the 1820s and early 1830s, with their focus on Herman and his father, would be particularly important; his father's bankruptcy, "maniacal" behavior, and death significantly influenced the new work. "The ur-story underneath *The Confidence-Man* is the bankruptcy, madness, and death of Allan Melvill. He is the missing person behind the novel's confidence games." The father of the protagonist in *Pierre* is described as having a "wandering mind"; a similar phrase appears also in the China Aster chapter of *The Confidence-Man*. Miller, finding further ties between biography and fiction, believes that in the novel Melville was "reliving the pain of parental rejection" and reacting to his Oedipal pattern.[8]

A more concrete influence would be Melville's 1840 journey with Eli James Murdock Fly to Galena, Illinois, to visit his uncle Thomas Melvill and family and also search for work. The two young men likely traveled by steamboat across the Great Lakes and returned by steamboat down the Mississippi River to Cairo and then went up the Ohio River. During the stay in Galena, Melville and Fly probably took a trip by steamboat up the Mississippi River and back. As a gateway to the West, Galena itself was an exciting place with people arriving in town to travel on the river or head west. With scenes of townspeople, merchants, and rough frontier types, the town likely provided Melville with recollections fifteen years later for his novel. Experiences aboard the steamboats would no doubt be put to use later in fiction.

The crowds aboard the *Fidèle* on April 1 represent a largely Western society in which disorder and harassment are indicators of both immorality and psychological aberration. On the lower deck of the *Fidèle*, peddlers and chevaliers are busily hawking all kinds of materials, including money belts and stories of "Meason, the bandit of Ohio, Murrel, the pirate of the Mississippi, and the brothers Harpe" (p. 4). The hawkers, prospective buyers, and the bandits themselves may be free of psychological aberrations, but James Hall, a source for materials in *The Confidence-Man*, describes the Harpe brothers as possessing "a savage thirst for blood—a deep rooted malignity against human nature."[9] Such a malignity, perhaps an extreme form of misanthropy, indicates the likelihood of a form of insanity. As passengers on the forecastle of the steamer examine the sleeping form of the mute, they make many comments, including "Odd fish," "Casper Hauser," and "moon-calf" (p. 7). Odd fish and mooncalf are colloquial terms casting doubts on an individual's mental capacity, appearance, or sanity. Casper Hauser was a strange foundling of the early nineteenth century in Germany who was variously described as "in a state of semi-idiocy" and as a "psychopath."[10] The use of such terms may raise some doubt about the mental balance of the speakers themselves.

Scenes in *The Confidence-Man* usually focus on a mysterious figure who dons one disguise or another in his lengthy exposure of man's lack of charity, trust, or faith. Almost as many scenes reveal that characters lacking significantly in these or comparable virtues will lack also some degree of balance or sanity; characters noticeably uncharitable or untrustworthy will usually show obvious aberrations. Often, in essence, scenes involve confrontations between the seemingly sane and insane. The first such scene appears in Chapter 3 as passengers cluster around the black cripple in "the forward part of the boat" (p. 10).

A loud cynic, the wooden-legged man, stands there, making his views clear. A large Methodist minister walks up and asks if he has no charity. The question begins a heated argument during which the minister loses his temper, picks up the cripple, and shakes him "till his timber-toe clattered on the deck like a nine-pin" (p. 15). The minister will have none of the other, and the bitter wooden-legged man, after walking away, returns part of the way to hear the minister attempt to explain his parting remarks. "'What does all that mean, now?' asked the country merchant, staring. 'Nothing; the foiled wolf's parting howl,' said the Methodist. 'Spleen, much spleen, which is the rickety child of his evil heart of unbelief: it has made him mad.'" The minister adds, "Let us profit by the lesson; and is it not this: that if, next to mistrusting Providence, there be aught that man should pray against, it is against mistrusting his fellow-man." The minister continues, "I have been in mad-houses full of tragic mopers, and seen there the end of suspicion: the cynic, in the moody madness muttering in the corner; for years a barren fixture there; head lopped over, gnawing his own lip, vulture of himself; while, by fits and starts, from the corner opposite came the grimace of the idiot at him" (p. 16). Although works by Milton, Shakespeare, and Cervantes in particular influenced the development of *The Confidence-Man*,[11] this passage and others like it may owe something to Melville's possible knowledge of actual asylums. The consideration in 1855 of his farm as a site for an asylum may have reminded him of a visit or a boyhood inspection, but it is hard to believe that he needed a reminder, for references to asylums, madhouses, inmates, or the equivalent appear in not only *The Confidence-Man* but in *White-Jacket*, *Pierre*, several stories, and *Billy Budd*. Experiences on steamboats, a packet ship, whalers, and a frigate had no doubt familiarized Melville with the antics of loud cynics, combative men like the minister, and prospective inmates of asylums, and with earthy language. The wooden-legged man himself appears more or less sane, but his excessive suspicion and hatred may be early warning signs of "moody madness," monomania, or a crusty case of moral insanity.

The Goneril account is the first of five stories related by a con man in the novel. The story is in fact filtered through three viewpoints with Ringman as the last storyteller. The account is a detailed life history that leaves little doubt of Goneril's complex abnormality. She is an almost attractive woman whose figure is "too straight, indeed, for a woman" and who has "a style of beauty rather peculiar and cactus-like" (p. 60). Her mouth is described as perhaps pretty except for a faint moustache. Her mannerisms and habits are naturally strange. Goneril cares nothing for ordinary fruit or "breast of chicken" but prefers "hard crackers and brawn of ham" and loves to nibble on "little dried sticks of blue clay, secretly carried in her pocket" (p. 61). Clay eaters were regarded then as "listless and stupid" yet with a "very remarkable cunning, in satisfying their depraved appetites."[12] More suggestive of Goneril's complexity is her strange habit of briefly touching people for no known reason and in particular of not speaking to anyone until 3 P.M., "it taking that time to thaw her, by all accounts, into but talking terms with humanity" (p. 61). Two prominent and related qualities of this remarkable character are cold hatred of others and a need to hurt or cause pain. She goes so far as to torment her seven-year-old daughter, of whom she has a "deranged jealousy" (p. 62). To regain custody of her child she had brought suit against her husband, who during the trial put forth "the plea of the mental derangement of Goneril," who in turn tries to have the husband "permanently committed for a lunatic" (p. 63).[13]

Whether Goneril is intended to be a satiric version of Shakespeare's Goneril, the actress Frances Kemble, or someone else,[14] the character is clearly intended to be regarded as insane. Several pointed references including the above support that view. Goneril comes across as a cunning, intelligent female who can feel only hatred, coldness, or jealousy toward others. Her mysterious touching suggests the uncrossable gap between herself and others. In her obsessed hatred she most resembles Jackson of *Redburn*, yet, unlike him and several others aboard the *Fidèle*, she can be devious, even subtle—her insanity is not without its fine-grained features. Even disparate qualities of monomania and moral insanity are carefully interwoven.

Near the end of the first half of *The Confidence-Man* appear two minor episodes that illustrate the lack of trust and sympathy and an accompanying lack of mental balance. In Chapter 17 the herb-doctor is busy in the antecabin of the *Fidèle* selling bottles of his "Samaritan Pain Dissuader . . . Warranted to remove the acutest pain within less than ten minutes" when he calls out that the product is "especially efficacious in heart disease and tic-douloureux" (p. 84). Tic douloureux is not a mental illness but a form of facial neuralgia, a painful condition perhaps caused by a cranial or dental nerve.[15] At one stop, "a kind of invalid Titan" comes aboard. A tall man with a "beard blackly pendant . . . his countenance tawny and shadowy" (p. 85), the giant will have nothing to do with the herb-doctor or his product. While the herb-doctor is hawking his wares, the giant remarks in a deep voice, "You lie!" (p. 87). The doctor, not noticing, continues to sell, explaining that the medicine can be "almost as effective in cases of mental suffering as in cases of physical." All of a sudden while he is selling, "a sudden side-blow all but felled him. It was the giant, who, with a countenance lividly epileptic with hypochondriac mania, exclaimed—'Profane fiddler on heart-strings! Snake!'" (p. 88). Prichard regards an excessive concern with physical ills and conditions, or hypochondria, as an indication of possible monomania or, more likely, the first stage of moral insanity. The disease can evolve into a form of monomania. Hypochondriac mania would combine the main features of the two afflictions, a morbid concern and a raving obsession with bodily ills. Epilepsy was regarded at that time as a form of insanity or as an attendant condition of forms of insanity including mania.[16] Whatever the giant's physical state, his mental condition appears highly unstable. A tough, distrustful man, he has no regard for anyone except his daughter.

A much more vocal exponent of hatred and bitterness is the "soldier of fortune," who is neither soldier nor ex-soldier but a man crippled by imprisonment as a murder trial witness in the New York Tombs. His singular appearance and manner are described in precise, stark words. In his bitter social views and disgruntled independence, the cripple resembles the wooden-legged man. He illustrates a frequent Melville point that poverty and misery sometimes lead to mental imbalance or failing. The herb-doctor, to whom he tells his sad tale, regards him as "a demoniac unfortunate" (p. 94). His actions have a nervous, erratic quality; he shows a "half moody, half surly sort of air" (p. 93); and his frequent "strangely startling laughter" appears unexpected, inappropriate.[17] He appears obsessive in his melancholic expectation of the worst. Unlike other harassed figures, the cripple is not dangerous or mean. However, his moodiness, suffering, and antisocial qualities are of long duration and indicate that he is a likely victim of moral insanity.

Whether normal or abnormal, moral or immoral, passengers and their behavior become more complicated in the last half of *The Confidence-Man*. The relationship between psychology and ethics appears more involved. The Missouri bachelor, Charles Noble, the cosmopolitan, Winsome, and others are knowledgeable and perceptive. The sophisticated cosmopolitan may bring out the best or the worst in his riverboat adversaries. A witness to the talk of the cosmopolitan and Missouri bachelor, Charles Noble tells the story of Colonel Moredock, who, in his opinion, resembles the bachelor but is a better man. Noble claims that Moredock was entitled to his suspicions of Indians. The colonel appears to be normal: he is an excellent soldier and frontiersman, a good husband, and a capable government official. Yet as an Indian hater, even as a diluted one, he is something more. His obsession with hating and killing Indians has pushed him across the thin red line into the general area of insanity. His Indian hating began in childhood and in frontier school, where he showed little ear except for "histories of Indian lying, Indian theft, Indian double-dealing, Indian fraud and perfidy . . . Indian blood-thirstiness. . . . In these Indian narratives and traditions the lad is thoroughly grounded" (p. 146). A more important cause of his Indian hating is the Indian massacre of his family. Moredock's mother, "thrice widowed by a tomahawk" (p. 152), is ambushed with most of her family as they move west. Moredock, at the time some distance away, survives. His reaction when he hears the terrible news is remarkably controlled. From that day, he dedicates himself to killing Indians in groups or alone. Thereafter, control and discipline are marks of his character and behavior.

Because of Moredock's discipline and Melville's scanty details, there is little hard evidence that Moredock suffers from a form of monomania, but that appears to be the case. Although Moredock's chronic hatred of Indians has not noticeably affected his thinking, it is unlikely that he can think objectively about Indians, except of ways to harm them, or can conceive of a good or harmless Indian. His thinking at least in respect to Indians appears logical but faulty. Although Moredock's emotions are not examined by the writer, they have likely lost much of their original naturalness and warmth. The more humane feelings in particular have been in effect flattened or distorted by chronic obsessions so that Moredock can seldom respond with ordinary intensity. The result is a lack of emotional balance and depth that seriously affects his overall sensibility. The lack also affects his morality, for with Indians at least he has no sympathy, let alone charity or goodwill.

The emphasis in the second half of *The Confidence-Man* on sophisticated encounters is noticeable in chapters involving the cosmopolitan and Winsome, an intellectual and aloof figure. As Winsome informs the fascinated cosmopolitan, "I like lucidity, of all things" (p. 194). He prefers abstractions to people, likes cold water, thinks everyone should learn something about mummies, and has no faith in people and their abilities. Winsome is satirized for supercilious attitudes and almost total commitment to transcendental ideas. The commitment has resulted in a diminution of normal emotions of sympathy, love, sorrow. Although Winsome is not insane, his aloof relations with others and flattened emotions have placed him on the edge of an incipient moral insanity.

Winsome's extreme distrust of others is evident in reactions to a "crazy beggar, although ragged and uncouth . . . not frightening or vulgar." Hayford explains that the characterization satirizes Poe.[18] More pertinent is the view that the character's mental condition may be regarded as genuine or as feigned madness. Winsome considers him a scoundrel, explaining to the cosmopolitan, "I detected in him, sir, a damning peep of sense—damning, I say; for sense in a seeming madman is scoundrelism. I take him for a cunning vagabond, who picks up a vagabond living by adroitly playing the madman. Did you not remark how he flinched under my eye?" The cosmopolitan does not agree that the beggar is mad. Hayford explains that in Poe's lifetime many regarded him as mad. "Poor Poe's erratic behavior from 1845 on, in New York, whatever its causes, certainly justified the label of madness which many applied to it in his last two or three years."[19] The beggar's singular appearance supports the view that a measure of mental imbalance is present. His shabby dress, description of him as a "shatterbrain," and obsequious bow suggest that he lacks complete control of his rational faculties—there is a reference to "just one glimmering peep of reason." Moments later, about ready to introduce Egbert, Winsome explains that the doctrines he has taught his disciple will "lead him neither to the mad-house nor the poor-house" (pp. 195, 199). But doctrines and especially his lack of trust and inherent suspiciousness detract from Winsome's tight-laced morality.

Two of the most significant stories or encounters in *The Confidence-Man* contain what appear to be disguised references to Allan Melvill's situation near the end of his life: specifically, his bankruptcy and final "maniacal" illness. The Charlemont and China Aster stories are related by the cosmopolitan and Charles Noble, respectively. Charlemont was once a charming man loved by many until something happened and he became morose, regarded people indifferently, or cut them dead. Then he became bankrupt and disappeared. Some months before he declared bankruptcy, a change occurred: "a change of a sort only to be ascribed to a mind suddenly thrown from its balance." The cosmopolitan provides no details about the nature of the imbalance. Some four years later, unexpectedly, Charlemont returns to society, charming once again, personable, and solvent. He tells no one what had happened until one day a close friend asks a crucial question, at which point "[deep] melancholy overspread" Charlemont's face (p. 185). Several days later he provides an answer. It seems that years before his trust and faith in others were destroyed. The trouble lies in part with Charlemont's reactions to the shock of failed confidences and trust. He becomes obsessed with the distrust of others and the need to recoup his financial fortunes. Unlike Melville's father, Charlemont recovers from his financial and emotional problems; yet during the interview with the close friend, he reveals something of his trouble: "some taint of Charlemont's old malady survived, and that it was not well for friends to touch one dangerous string" (p. 186).

Resemblances between fiction and biography appear more significant in the story of China Aster, which may have been written during the Stewart loan difficulties of spring 1856.[20] Like several other characters in *The Confidence-Man*, China Aster possesses too much faith and trust. In this respect he resembles Melville's father, Allan Melvill, who believed God and his own faith and trust would enable him to profit from risky financial arrangements with others. Allan placed much faith on the fact that he was acting for the benefit of his family as well as for his business. In 1827, having entered into a complex secret business arrangement that promised good profits, Allan had to borrow $10,000 from Peter Gansevoort in order to avoid ruin. The ruin came anyway. The business arrangement fell through with a loss of the Gansevoort loan and other loans. Allan Melvill failed not only himself and his family but his friends and relatives as well. Several years later he died bankrupt and apparently mad. Overtones of the father's plight are discernible in *The Confidence-Man*.

Faith, trust, and idealism are misplaced in the novel. China Aster's friend Orchis proves to be his untrusting friend, for he presses Aster to keep up with his payments, pay interest, mortgage his "candlery" (p. 208) until China becomes ill. Orchis's lack of trust and faith and the expectations of society are general causes for China Aster's increasing worries. He can support his wife and children only if his business survives. It fails because Orchis hounds him so ceaselessly that he cannot work. Orchis, a sound businessman, lacks moral sensitivities.

One day the ailing man falls, strikes his head, and is "picked up senseless." He is taken home, "linger[s] a few days with a wandering mind, and kept wandering on, till at last, at dead of night, when nobody was aware, his spirit wandered away into the other world" (p. 218). The reference to the wandering spirit is at least suggestive of the reference in *Pierre* to Mr. Glendinning's wandering mind and to accounts of Allan Melvill's delirium. China Aster, unlike Allan Melvill, a moral man, loses his reason because of worry over money and the distrust and lack of charity of others. He is too good a man for the hard, unsympathetic world.

The writer's preoccupation with the nature and effects of insanity is evident in other characters and situations in *The Confidence-Man*. The novel contains several definitions of insanity or clarifications of its apparent nature. Chapter 8 begins, "If a drunkard in a sober fit is the dullest of mortals, an enthusiast in a reason-fit is not the most lively. And this, without prejudice to his greatly improved understanding; for, if his elation was the height of his madness, his despondency is but the extreme of his sanity" (p. 43). This passage refers to the man in gray. There are other references to mental aberration, real or possible, of a con man or an ordinary passenger. The man with the weed is described as "a little cracked, too." Someone adds, "Misfortune, I fear, has disturbed his brain" (p. 46). The dried old man seeking the herb-doctor is described as "tottering about like one out of his mind" (p. 101). The Missouri bachelor addresses the herb-doctor as "a queer man—a very queer and dubious man . . . about the most so I ever met" (p. 112). Timon is referred to as "that poor old crazy man, Timon" (p. 177). In reacting to Charlie Noble's story of Charlemont, the cosmopolitan says, "Why, Charlie, you are losing your mind" (pp. 187–88). In an atmosphere of suspicion and greed, such remarks are common.

Other indications appear of Melville's wide-ranging interest in mental instability and in different views of the abnormal or normal mind. There are several references to what Melville likely regarded as pseudo-sciences. Ringman informs the naive but arrogant college student that "[phrenologically you] . . . have a well-developed head" (p. 26), and the Chapter 14 satire on judging human nature in terms of fixed principles points to the "ranks of the sciences—palmistry, physiognomy, phrenology, psychology" (p. 71). This novel of talk includes references to a few pertinent books, including "Hume's on Suicide," which is criticized because it encourages solitude. Among the many words and phrases in *The Confidence-Man* signifying mental instability are two deserving comment. Brain fever was a recognized disease and term in the nineteenth century. An account of the term appears in a medical book by John Mason Good briefly mentioned in *White-Jacket*. Symptoms of the disease include fever, restlessness, screaming, forgetfulness, and mental confusion.[21] The country merchant admits to the man with the weed

that he had "a brain fever, losing his mind completely for a considerable interval" (p. 20). Another term is calenture: an Indian hater is described as being seized "with a sort of calenture" (p. 150), a term Melville does not define although the meaning is implied. A calenture
involves "a delirium characterized by delusions." Sailors worn out by
work or heat may hallucinate that the sea is a meadow and risk their
lives soon after.[22]

Although the main directing force in *The Confidence-Man* may be a
form of evil, several characters, including the Missouri bachelor, the
merchant, and the boy as well as the charitable lady and the gentleman
with the gold sleeve buttons, fight bravely against the evil and insane.
The most successful, the Missouri bachelor, described as a "genial misanthrope," manages to hold his own for some time. He maintains his
sanity and a stalwart skepticism. The boy, following suit in the final
scene, keeps both sanity and morality in the confrontation with the cosmopolitan. But in the end the con man or cosmopolitan, the chief actor
in a fallen world, prevails. Depending on the viewpoint, he appears
sane.

After *The Confidence-Man* was published in 1857, almost thirty years
elapsed before Melville returned in the mid-1880s to writing fiction.
During that long period many changes occurred in his family life, relationships with relatives and friends, and attitudes toward writing, himself, and life in general. Some of these changes will be briefly discussed
in Chapter 9, along with Melville's final portrayals of insanity in *Billy
Budd, Sailor*.

Chapter Nine.

"Who ... can draw the line?"

Billy Budd, Sailor

Published in April 1857, *The Confidence-Man* was Melville's last work of fiction to appear during his lifetime. He was thirty-seven years old that April. The years of writing *Pierre* (1852), *Israel Potter* (1855), fifteen stories, including six gathered in *The Piazza Tales* (1856), and *The Confidence-Man* had left him weary and disillusioned. Relatives were convinced that he needed a change to an occupation that would not leave him mentally and physically exhausted and usually in debt. He also needed a vacation. His generous father-in-law Judge Shaw responded characteristically with funds for a long trip that took Melville to England in October 1856, where he saw Hawthorne in Liverpool, and thereafter to several Mediterranean countries, including Egypt, the Holy Land, and Italy, and brought him back somewhat reinvigorated on 20 May 1857 in time to read the first reviews of his new book. Unfortunately, most of the two dozen or so American reviews then and later of *The Confidence-Man* were unfavorable. The longer, more perceptive English reviews tended to be favorable.[1]

The general public reaction, however, seemed to be either indifference or bewilderment; sales were accordingly poor. Because such responses had grown all too familiar since 1851, Melville made his own change: he would cease writing and lecture for a living. That would allow him to select his own topics, describe personal experiences or observations, perhaps capitalize on whatever fame he had as an author, and earn a worthwhile yearly figure. Such hopes did not materialize. Lectures on Roman statuary, classical mythology, and similar topics interested few people, Melville's platform manner was unexciting, and his earnings of $440 the first season and $110 the third and last season could hardly support a family. Having in the meantime turned to writing poetry, Melville circulated a small volume of poetry in the early 1860s, but publishers were unimpressed. In 1863, after selling Arrowhead to his brother Allan, he and his family moved back to New York City, settling at 104 East 26th Street, home for the rest of his life. In 1866, after years of faithful effort by friends and relatives, Melville finally secured a government appointment as district inspector of customs in the massive New York Custom-House at a salary of $4.00 per day, a figure that never increased in nineteen years of efficient, honest service.[2]

Life in New York City began a new era for the writer. Work at the customhouse proved to be "demanding . . . anxiety-producing, humiliating but nevertheless essential to his material well-being and that of his family." As a district inspector Melville was required to supervise loading and unloading activities of all ships at piers under his jurisdiction. He and another inspector shared the responsibilities from sunrise to sunset. Each inspector had several assistants and kept records and journals for each day. Melville's service in good times and bad (corruption in the vast organization was often extensive) was excellent.[3] Although he may have appeared occasionally aloof or preoccupied, Melville apparently got along reasonably well with co-workers and with ship officers and others he met during the long days. At home on East 26th Street, family life had its ups and downs. The customhouse job left him fatigued, and the reception of Battle-Pieces in 1866 was disappointing. Recently discovered correspondence describing views in 1867 of Elizabeth and others of Melville's alleged insanity makes clear that life with Herman was at times almost impossible. The family minister and Sam Shaw, who were privy to Elizabeth's upset over Melville's behavior, sought a way to get her to Boston without arousing his suspicions. Elizabeth seriously considered taking some action, but fortunately for Melville she never did.[4] Only a few months later in September, the oldest child, Malcolm, eighteen years old, died of a gunshot wound. The death devastated Elizabeth and deeply affected Herman, who likely kept his grief to himself. It is quite possible that in time Malcolm's death may have ironically brought the parents closer together.[5] Work at the customhouse and evenings and possibly weekends at home devoted to poetry undoubtedly helped Melville adjust to the loss of his son. In 1870, drawing upon personal experiences, Melville began writing a long narrative poem on travels and searches in the Holy Land. As complex as any previous work by Melville, *Clarel* was to tax the patience and resourcefulness of both Melvilles before its publication in 1876. Peter Gansevoort, Melville's uncle, generously paid for the publication; he died later that year.

Although the 1870s and 1880s were seldom years of contentment and fulfillment, there were satisfying times. Even during the composition of *Clarel*, Melville could impress friends and relatives with his spirit and pleasant manner. The editor Henry Holt in 1871 described Melville as "one of the very most agreeable men I have ever met." Several weeks after Maria Melvill's death in April 1872, Augusta, the daughter, described her brother as "quite like his old natural self, & [he] . . . seems to take an interest in every thing; & it is very pleasant having him here."[6] In 1873 John Hoadley, Melville's brother-in-law, writing to an official, praised Melville's service as a district inspector. Melville's correspondence during these years was almost always accommodating. He would naturally wish to give a good impression in letters to relatives and friends even if he felt tense or moody. Requests for interviews or books usually received terse responses, but letters from informed and sympathetic individuals were answered at length and pleasantly. Melville's "most consecutive correspondence . . . with an admirer," James Billson, English lawyer and editor, began in 1884, continued for some years, and included a number of gifts from Billson. Another English correspondent was the distinguished sea novelist W. Clark Russell, whose article on sea writers in *The Contemporary Review* in 1884 placed Melville at the top. An occasional newspaper or magazine article praised Melville's genius and contributions. An English critic, H. S. Salt, in 1889 wrote a biographical sketch of Melville and commented on *Typee*, *Omoo*, and *White-Jacket*. In December Salt proposed to Melville a new edition of *Typee*. One volume in a new 1889 edition of American literature included "The Bell-Tower" and several poems from *Battle-Pieces*.

In 1882 Melville accepted an invitation to be founder of an authors' club in New York City, but after some thought he wrote to explain that "his nerves could no longer stand large gatherings and begged to rescind his acceptance" (JL 1:xxiii; 2:761–65, 785–86, 816–19). In the late 1870s, family finances were strengthened by Melville's steady work in the customhouse and by monies received from others. In 1878 Elizabeth's aunt left her $10,000 and $3,000 to $4,000 for the children. A year later the niece, Mrs. Gifford, left $10,000 for Elizabeth, $8,000 for Herman, and smaller amounts for the children; a codicil added $5,000 for Elizabeth. The economic burdens Melville had labored under for decades were being lifted at last, ironically long after he most sorely needed financial assistance and independence (JL 2:769, 773).

During the New York years, there were of course family concerns and problems. The younger son Stanwix, born in 1851, experienced difficulty finding a suitable occupation and in settling down. His eyesight did not fit him for dentistry, a hearing deficiency ruled out a venture into law, and suitable office work in New York City was not obtainable. For brief periods Stanwix worked in Kansas and California, but nothing came of these experiences. Elizabeth Melville described her son as "possessed with a demon of *restlessness*" (JL 2:733). Whenever Stanwix stayed at East 26th Street, his father seemed to develop mysterious aches and pains and feel more pressure than usual. The family's primary concerns, however, were the father's health and mental condition. Melville suffered from back pains and frequent depressive periods. Elizabeth, who was "nervous" herself, did all she could for him, perhaps exacerbating matters with her unimaginative if caring approach. In the hectic months prior to the publication of *Clarel* in 1876, she asked relatives not to visit them because Herman was in a "frightfully nervous state." In an 1877 letter to Catherine Lansing, Elizabeth asked that she mention Herman by name in letters to the family. In a lengthy and friendly letter to a favorite brother-in-law, John Hoadley, Melville added a postscript, "N.B. I ain't crazy" (JL 2:747, 759, 761).

Melville was well aware that Elizabeth usually worried about his mental condition and that others in the family had at least occasional doubts about his balance or stability. He had his own doubts. During trying circumstances at home or at work, he likely felt once again the old fear of the twisted mind, of inherited insanity. Having begun work on *Clarel* not long after the death of Malcolm, Melville clearly thought about insanity, for several important characters in the poem show evidences of mental stress and unbalance. Bezanson refers to the "monomaniac sequence" of Celio, Mortmain, Agath, and Ungar.[7] In the long poem Mortmain appears unable to compromise and obsessed with finding the truth. He is very lonely and self-destructive. Ungar, regarded as a character with a sensibility like Melville's, is another searcher, an Ishmael of sorts, a tormented being. Such characters point toward Claggart in *Billy Budd*.

Casting a pall over life at 104 East 26th Street was the recurrent news of someone's death. Melville's brother Allan died of a collapsed lung in 1872, and later that year the family matron, Maria, died at eighty-one. His favorite sister Augusta and uncle Peter Gansevoort, a lifelong family friend, died in 1876. Evert Duyckinck died in 1878. Between 1884 and 1888 his brother Tom, sisters Frances and Helen, and brothers-in-law Hoadley and Griggs died.

The most distressing death was the loss of Stanwix in San Francisco in 1886. Stanwix was only thirty-five, the last son, and no more successful in life than Malcolm had been. His death brought back painful memories of Malcolm. Melville would feel his deep involvement in both deaths. As commentators have explained, he saw reflected in their failures his own failures and these in turn were related in his own mind to failures of his father over fifty years before. Robert Penn Warren in particular has convincingly examined Melville's relationships with his sons and Melville as a father. Melville was evidently a poor father and a factor in the suicide of Malcolm. But whether a poor father or, as another critic believes, an "unnatural one," Melville was at times, as Warren explains, an attentive father and on occasion an affectionate father.[8] In *Billy Budd, Sailor*, he tried to resolve the ironies and complexities of the father-son relationships that in actual life more often than not he handled ineptly.

Although the manuscript of *Billy Budd, Sailor* was left in semifinal form at Melville's death, the writing skills are impressive. They are not the techniques of a fatigued writer but of a firmly conscious and reflective one. The omniscient point of view is generally serious and meditative, but it is also flexible, allowing for portrayals of the near at hand and overall the concrete and speculative. The language and syntax tend to be rather formal and intricate, creating a sense of history and reflection, but they are also direct and graphic. In commenting on headnotes for the John Marr stories and *Billy Budd*, Sealts observes, "The narrator of *Billy Budd* . . . sounds very much like the authors of these earlier headnotes—which is to say, like Melville himself."[9] Melville's characteristic interest in exposition is evident in examples of life history and poetic analysis. These are often masterful, particularly the histories of Claggart and Vere. The accounts may lack the abundance of details found in expositions in previous works, but they are nonetheless intense, informative, and dramatic. The familiar technique of relying to some extent on real-life characters appears less apparent in the final novel, although Vere bears similarities to the author and Claggart, the naval lieutenant, and the shipmaster may be related in some respects to sailors and officers of Melville's past.

The society of Melville's last novel appears more complex than that of *The Confidence-Man* because it possesses both greater balance and variety. Life in the naval world is naturally strongly influenced by war, but it is influenced as well by peace and stability. Despite oppressive laws and conditions, sanity to some extent counterbalances insanity. As insanity is endemic in life, Captain Vere, a good man, develops over the years an obsession with the proper observance of laws. Yet even when most determined, he is generally a thoughtful, considerate man. Vere admires and loves Billy. Sailors on the Liverpool dock admire their black companion, and the shipmaster aboard the *Rights of Man* is described as a "respectable man" (p. 45). When the naval lieutenant drafts Billy for service aboard the *Bellipotent*, he is reminded by the shipmaster that "you are going to take away my peacemaker!"[10] The remark is not delivered ironically. Captain Vere by necessity must condemn Billy to death, but neither he nor his views of Billy are diminished by that death. The novel ends with accounts of admiration for Billy. Although Melville's final society is cruel and oppressive, some in it learn to live with dignity and integrity.

Three figures aboard the *Bellipotent* disclose some degree of mental aberration. Master-at-Arms Claggart, the unnamed surgeon, and Captain Vere reveal that Melville's knowledge of insanity had not diminished after *Clarel* (1876), although his interest in scientific explanations had apparently abated.[11] The remarkable portrayal of Claggart is superior in execution if not necessarily in conception to the portrayal of Bland. Claggart's monomania is nonetheless subtle. On the surface the master-at-arms appears prudential, efficient, and governed by rationality. Described as an intellectual man, Claggart is proud and respectable. At the same time, he looks at Billy with feelings of envy and sadness because of the young man's beauty and goodness and his realization that Billy is beyond him. Although there is allegedly nothing "sensual" in

Claggart's attitudes toward Billy, he nevertheless hides a yearning for him. Suspicious of Billy's motives, he makes "ogres of trifles" (p. 80). Claggart's repressions, impulses, and paranoid reactions indicate that his dominant monomania is conditioned by symptoms of moral insanity.

In portraying Claggart, Melville had in mind such literary models as Shakespeare's Iago and Milton's Satan and materials from other familiar sources—phrenology and philosophy. In *White-Jacket* Bland is described as "phrenologically . . . without a soul." In *Billy Budd*, Claggart's brow "was of the sort phrenologically associated with more than average intellect" (p. 64).[12] To clarify Claggart's monomaniac hatred, Melville drew from Plato's definition of natural depravity, "a depravity according to nature," only found in "certain phenomenal men" and intellectual ones at that. Relying on his own knowledge, Melville adds, "These men are madmen, and of the most dangerous sort, for their lunacy is not continuous, but occasional, evoked by some special object" (p. 76).

Ideas of Schopenhauer evidently contributed to the characterization. Melville may have first encountered Schopenhauer's ideas in 1871 in a volume of selections by different writers, edited by a friend of Lemuel Shaw; the man eventually went insane (JL 2:720). In February 1891, Melville borrowed a few Schopenhauer volumes from the New York Society Library and shortly thereafter purchased several books, including a three-volume set of *The World as Will and Idea*. Schopenhauer's pessimism and fatalism apparently appealed to Melville's skepticism and may account for the deterministic strain in Claggart. Schopenhauer's idea that the evil man suffering within himself seeks to assuage that suffering by observing it in others may be illustrated by Claggart's need to harm Billy.[13] If Melville found nothing new in Schopenhauer's interpretations of conscious and unconscious levels of the mind, Schopenhauer's analogy of the mind and a body of water—with the surface as consciousness and the depths as unconsciousness—may have appeared interesting. Melville likely agreed with the philosopher that "we can often give no account of the origin of our deepest thoughts. They are the birth of our mysterious inner life. Judgments, thoughts, purposes, rise from out that deep . . . and to our own surprise."[14] If the description of Claggart's eyes at the time he confronts Billy and makes his charges owes nothing to Schopenhauer, it is nonetheless pertinent: "Meanwhile the accuser's eyes, removing not as yet from the blue dilated ones, underwent a phenomenal change, their wonted rich violet color blurring into a muddy purple. Those lights of human intelligence, losing human expression, were gelidly protruding like the alien eyes of certain uncatalogued creatures of the deep. The first mesmeristic glance was one of serpent fascination; the last was as the paralyzing lurch of the torpedo fish" (p. 98).

The description is appropriately short because the focus in *Billy Budd* is much more concentrated than in *Moby-Dick* or *Pierre* and passages on the unconscious are much shorter than comparable passages in earlier works. But the quoted passage and eye imagery in particular brilliantly evoke a sense of irrational, unconscious forces emerging on the conscious level. Claggart's evil intentions, his monomaniac delusions about himself and Billy, have stirred up primitive forces in the collective unconscious. Lacking Pip's intuitive powers or Ahab's analytic strengths, Claggart cannot control or attempt to control the forces. One critic finds in the passage and throughout *Billy Budd* evidence of Melville's use of electrical concepts and images to illustrate dynamic forces in characters, including Claggart.[15]

Summoned to Captain Vere's cabin, Claggart approaches Billy with the "measured step and calm collected air of an asylum physician approaching in the public hall some patient beginning to show indications of a coming paroxysm" (p. 98). The allusion is both dramatic and pertinent, for the British frigate resembles an asylum. The *Bellipotent* contains compartments and halls, men who can be regarded as patients, and officers or attendants for them, and it operates according to rules and regulations. The only physician on the ship is of course the surgeon, who, unlike Surgeon Cuticle, is sane or appears to be sane. At least after Claggart's death he enters the cabin as a "self-poised character," a man of science. A moment later, however, the surgeon is "disturbed by the excited manner he had never before observed in the *Bellipotent*'s captain." When Vere exclaims that the angel of God, or Billy, must hang, at "these passionate interjections, mere incoherences to the listener as yet unapprised of the antecedents, the surgeon was profoundly discomposed." After the surgeon learns what has transpired and leaves the cabin, he is full of "disquietude and misgiving." Even in these difficult circumstances, however, the surgeon should be composed. He is after all an experienced medical officer responsible for the physical and mental well-being of all men and officers aboard ship. In the scene, he may be as psychologically vulnerable as the captain. Yet, ironically, the surgeon's main function is to raise questions about the captain's behavior and specifically about his sanity. "Was Captain Vere suddenly affected in his mind, or was it but a transient excitement, brought about by so strange and extraordinary a tragedy?" Although these are the author's words, they suggest the surgeon's attitude. But at that the surgeon does clearly wonder, "Was he unhinged?" (pp. 100, 101, 102).

The surgeon's emotional reactions and the remarkable scene in Captain Vere's cabin in Chapter 19 set the stage for the opening of Chapter 21: "Who in the rainbow can draw the line where the violet tint ends and the orange tint begins? Distinctly we see the difference of the colors, but where exactly does the one first blendingly enter into the other? So with sanity and insanity. In pronounced cases there is no question about them. But in some supposed cases, in various degrees supposedly less pronounced, to draw the exact line of demarcation few will undertake, though for a fee becoming considerate some professional experts will. There is nothing namable but that some men will, or undertake to, do it for pay" (p. 102).

Vere's case seems to be one of those "less pronounced"; that is, if he is temporarily "unhinged" or abnormal. Many considerations of the captain do not customarily raise the point. Supporters of the old "testament of acceptance" argument would likely see nothing more unexpected or unnatural in Vere's behavior than a temporary excitement or at most a possible confusion. They would regard his judgments as essentially sound. Supporters of the irony argument might find in his behavior something not only mysterious but mentally suspect as well.[16]

Captain Vere's position in the first cabin scene is clearly difficult. He must decide on the veracity of Claggart's charges, and he must prompt Billy to respond verbally. Yet Vere possesses little information on either man. He knows of Claggart's efficiency but feels a slight revulsion toward him. Amazed by Billy's inability to respond verbally to the charges, Vere is enlightened when he recalls a school incident in which a classmate was "struck by much the same startling impotence" (p. 99). After Billy reacts by striking Claggart, Vere remains calm and rational, carefully attending to the dead man and then assuming the role of disciplinarian. Only after the surgeon appears on the scene does Vere become emotional.

"A sailor of distinction," Captain Vere is highly regarded for outstanding abilities, extensive service, and brave wartime action: he has been decorated for gallantry. Vere is a thoroughly professional naval officer, an "austere devotee of military duty." Mindful of his men, he never tolerates an "infraction of discipline" (pp. 60, 115). Given the captain's background and experience, his emotional reactions in the cabin do not appear to be natural or appropriate. Further clarification of the scene appears necessary. After Claggart falls to the floor dead, Vere stands "impassive" in thought. After the surgeon examines the body, the captain catches the surgeon's arm "convulsively" and exclaims about the divine judgment on Ananias. The surgeon regards Vere's manner as "excited." A moment later, after standing in thought, Vere suddenly exclaims "vehemently." His remarks about the angel of God are regarded by the surgeon as "passionate" and incoherent to the uninformed (pp. 100, 101). Shortly thereafter, Vere, totally in control, makes his fateful decisions about the drumhead court and Billy Budd.

At the drumhead court-martial a few hours later, Captain Vere, motivated by a monklike sense of duty, appears in control once again, responding respectfully and when necessary at length to all questions raised by members of the court. When the marine officer asks Billy why Claggart would lie to him, "since you declare there was no malice between you" (p. 107), Vere explains that the only one who can answer rightly is dead and that the court must be concerned not with motives but with consequences. Vere is necessarily the pragmatist as he explains to the marine and the court that "what remains mysterious in this matter" is not for the military court but for "psychologic theologians." Having spoken as a witness, Vere speaks as "your coadjutor for the time" and admits that he too admires Billy, "a fellow creature innocent before God," but explains that the court must act on the basis not of scruples, nature, or conscience but of facts and "the law of the Mutiny Act" (pp. 108, 110, 111). Near the end of the trial, the captain explains again in reasoned tones that the court must decide to condemn Billy or to let him go; under the present circumstances there is no other alternative.

Although the captain's manner during the trial appears commendable, evidences of emotional strain appear. Even though the court members may lack the discernment of the surgeon, they are trained to be observant. On one occasion, the captain's voice "indicat[ed] a suppressed emotion not otherwise betrayed" (p. 106). A short time later, after Vere makes a complex statement about motives and the "blow's consequence" (p. 107), the court's reaction is that the captain had made a "prejudgment" about Billy's fate and that "served to augment a mental disturbance previously evident enough" (p. 108). The last point may refer to the earlier noted "suppressed emotion" or to something else; it is not clear. The members of the court may be overreacting to implications of Vere's explanations or they may be misinterpreting his mental state, but, as the term "mental disturbance" appears serious and not ironic, one inference is that the captain, customarily self-possessed, is under such a strain that occasionally his emotions and thinking are erratic. Another indication of this likelihood appears shortly after Billy is led away. The court members shift about in their chairs, exchange "looks of troubled indecision," and the captain himself stands "unconsciously with his back toward them, apparently in one of his absent *fits*" (p. 109, my italics).

Such a condition is probably not unusual for an officer who habitually betrays a "certain dreaminess of mood" (p. 61), presumably of thought. However, the frequency of such moods appears unusual. Three times in the first cabin scene involving Billy, Claggart, and later the surgeon, Vere stands impassively, motionless, and apparently in thought. In the last two instances he comes out of the reverie or abstracted state in a state of excitement. During these states or shortly after the last one, Vere makes remarkable decisions about Billy's life and the need for a drumhead court. The decisions and reasons for them provide the most significant evidence of the captain's temporary loss of emotional and mental balance. He is "the sudden victim of [a] . . . degree of aberration" (p. 102).

One critic contends that Captain Vere suffers from a form of "adjudicatory 'insanity.'" According to this interpretation, Vere intentionally makes a number of serious "procedural errors," including a failure to delay the case until the admiral can make the decisions, the improper use of summary procedures, and the assumption during the trial of different roles. Weisberg explains that the captain also manipulates the court members and the trial proceedings in such a way that the only sound verdict can be Billy's execution by hanging. Vere is motivated primarily by an obsessed jealousy of the great Admiral Nelson, who is a "sublime embodiment . . . of the heroic sailor-like mode." Believing that his own career and rank have been dwarfed by Nelson's example, Vere is determined to attack the image of Nelson through the embodiment aboard ship of Billy, who on a lower level represents comparable qualities of heroic courage and physical beauty. Vere must therefore destroy Billy. This approach is wide-ranging and original: it examines reasons for Vere's alleged obsessed jealousy of Admiral Nelson; similarities in ethical qualities, attitudes, and goals of Vere and Claggart; Vere's masterfully covert and self-serving actions during the trial in particular and at other times as well.[17] The opinion here, however, is that the novel contains no direct evidence that Vere is obsessed with envy of Admiral Nelson or that because of such envy or any other feeling or conviction Vere manipulates naval law and procedures or deceives the court in order to fulfill personal ambitions.

As Melville indicates in Chapter 21 and elsewhere in *Billy Budd*, distinctions between sanity and insanity are sometimes very difficult to determine. This general view is illustrated in the case of Captain Vere. As Melville states, Vere honestly believes that because of recent outbreaks in the British fleet at Spithead and Nore and because of circumstances aboard the *Bellipotent* (Claggart's death in particular), prompt action is necessary if a mutiny is to be averted. A "sense of the urgency of the case overruled in Captain Vere every other consideration" (p. 104). Melville makes clear also that Vere had to make his decisions in a sense "under fire"; forces beyond his control compel him to make controversial decisions.

For once, however, the superbly dedicated and efficient officer misreads the evidence. The surgeon and other officers are correct: Vere is not the one to make the decision; only the admiral can make it. Nor do the officers believe that shipboard conditions could lead to a mutiny. Vere made mistakes in judgment because of pressures and personal attitudes. The actions in his cabin—Billy's blow and Claggart's death—may not be traumatic but they are nonetheless very disturbing. Complicating the matter is Vere's admiration and love for Billy. Vere is probably not Billy's natural father, but as shown in cabin scenes in Chapters 19 and 21 his concern for Billy is strong and paternal. In the private, undramatized interview with Billy in Chapter 22 after the trial, Captain Vere is described as "old enough to have been Billy's father." In the statement, Vere "may in end have caught Billy to his heart" (p. 115), some critics see Vere's revelation of love for Billy. Lesser writes of the relationship: "No less instinctively than he had recoiled from Claggart's hostile assault, Billy submits to his sentence because he feels that Captain Vere has decreed it in love."[18] In the execution scene in Chapter 25, as Billy utters the words "God bless Captain Vere" and the "spontaneous echo . . . voluminously rebounded them," Captain Vere, "either through stoic self-control or a sort of momentary paralysis induced by emotional shock, stood erectly rigid" (pp. 123–24).

Despite his austere devotion to naval law, duty, and custom, Captain Vere is a vulnerable man. Brilliance and discipline fail him because the decisions about Billy and the drumhead court-martial are made on the mistaken assumption that "forms, measured forms" must always be the final standard of judgment in naval life. This assumption rules out, as the trial demonstrates, other standards of judgment such as individual conscience and religious codes, of which the captain is deeply aware. Vere rejects them and other nonmilitary standards because during the time of the action he is deluded on the point. In respect to naval law and customs or his interpretations of these, Vere may be as inflexible as he is discerning. In the Chapter 19 cabin scene, he temporarily loses sight of his own humanity and the value of Billy's life. For a brief period he becomes obsessed with the need to uphold the letter of naval law as he understands it, to remain true to the facts as he sees them. In losing sight of his own humanity, he mistakenly assumes that he is the only one who can act in the matter. Vere's failure is a cognitive one, a consequence or manifestation of his delusions. Without trying to rival Admiral Nelson or to encroach upon prerogatives of the commanding admiral, Captain Vere is convinced that the buck stops here, that he is the officer to make the decision. He may be misled after all by "the most secret of all passions, ambition" (p. 129).

Because of Captain Vere's complex mind and temperament, the extent and nature of his mental aberrations are not at all clear. Vere appears to be suffering from a mild form of monomania as indicated by his delusion and mental failures. The monomania is attended by symptoms of moral insanity most evident in periods of aloofness and irascibility.[19] Causes of Vere's condition, in the terminology of the day, are "moral causes," emotions or states of mind that include anxiety, passion, frustration, and distress, and also the factor of the environment. But the depths and subtleties of his condition remain obscure. The far reaches of Vere's psyche may be suggested by the different implications of such words as "dreamy," "austere," "irascible," "bookish," "fatherly," and "intrepid," which for a brief spell seem to hover on the side of abnormality.

As some critics have explained, Melville and Captain Vere share several qualities and interests: intellectual books, a predilection for speculative thought, a strong sense of pride and devotion to duty, and a degree of inflexibility.[20] They share also a psychological vulnerability. Yet, as indicated, by the time Melville began serious work on the *Billy Budd* manuscript, he had likely come to terms with the irascibility, moods, and depressions that had confounded relatives and friends since the early days of his marriage in the late 1840s. After Malcolm's death in 1867 and the completion of *Clarel* in 1876, he had likely placated ghosts of the twisted mind, fears of inherited insanity. "The years of his preoccupation with his own emotions were over. The writing of

Clarel had been a genuine turning point in his life."[21] Perhaps during that period or during his retirement and work on the manuscript, Melville had gained an understanding of his failures as a father, his strict demands and assumptions in New York City and at Arrowhead that he was the family head, in effect the captain, and everyone should do as he wanted. At one time or another Melville must have realized that in family affairs he was not often considerate of others and he was particularly severe in judgments of his four children. One rule in 1867 was that Malcolm should be home by 11:00 P.M. or he would be locked out. On 10 September, after an evening with friends, Malcolm returned home at 3:00 A.M. to be let in by his waiting mother. The next morning his father decided that Malcolm was not to be awakened, that getting to work late would constitute a form of punishment (JL 2: 688). It was that Wednesday evening, after the father returned from work, that Malcolm was found dead in his room.[22] In later years when the younger son Stanwix came home after one of his long mysterious absences, Melville may have believed afterward that he could have appeared more interested in his son and accounts of his experiences. But by the late 1880s, Melville likely believed that such matters were more or less behind him—as were doubts of friends or relatives about his mental stability.

In their discussion of Melville's additions in the "late pencil stage" to the *Billy Budd* manuscript, Hayford and Sealts explain that the additions stress Vere's excitability and the surgeon's doubts about Vere's sanity. But they believe that the intention of the additions and revisions remains unknown. "Which way—if either—Melville expected the reader to determine the question he had thus raised concerning Vere's possible 'aberration' is by no means clear" (p. 11). If Melville had lived long enough to add to the pencil stage, he might have clarified the way to go. But that is impossible to say. It seems likely that he would have deepened the characterization of Captain Vere and probed further into his complex mentality, but not necessarily to make "the exact line of demarcation" between sanity and insanity any clearer. Given Vere's inherent complexity, that might have been impossible anyway. But as the manuscript stands, the final days of Captain Vere's marvelously controlled life and brilliant career illustrate his fallibility; he does for a short time edge over the thin red line.

CONCLUSION

Herman Melville went his admired father one or two better. He did not succumb to mental illness or to despair, and he did survive. He managed to cope with many problems, including fears of the twisted mind. This is not to say that the son was noticeably more successful than the father. Of the ten works of fiction published before Melville's death in 1891, only the first novels, *Typee* and *Omoo*, sold reasonably well. Major novels like *Moby-Dick* and *Pierre* were regarded as failures by most readers and critics, and the last novel published during Melville's life, *The Confidence-Man* (1857), was probably forgotten by all but a few in 1890. In that year, according to syndicated newspaper columnist Edward Bok, "There are more people today who believe Herman Melville dead than there are those who know he is living." The journalist explained that "the famous writer of sea stories" could be seen any morning about nine walking along East Eighteenth Street in New York City. But the informed Bok mistakenly assumed that Melville still worked in the customs service, from which he had retired in late 1885. As Bok indicated, literary fame was indeed short-lived. Writing in 1919, art critic Frank J. Mather, Jr., explained that in 1890 the poet-critic Edmund Clarence Stedman arranged a dinner for Melville and "with difficulty got him to attend it. It was about the only public recognition he ever received."[1] Years later, beginning with the "Melville Revival" in the 1920s, the writer received recognition that placed him among the great authors in American literature.

Since the revival, Melville's novels and stories have been acclaimed for many things: characters like Fayaway, Ahab, and Billy Budd, remarkable scenes of whaling and South Sea island life, realistic accounts of city life, romantic tales of adventure, powerful indictments of failures of American society. The writings have been recognized also for Melville's understanding and portrayals of insanity.

An important source of the understanding was no doubt Melville's lifelong practice of earnest and highly assimilative reading. From works by Shakespeare, Milton, Byron, Coleridge, and others, Melville obtained noteworthy confirmation of what he had already learned from experience, and from Shakespeare's plays in particular he gained a greater sensitivity to depths and subtleties of insanity. A habitual reader of newspapers and magazines, Melville likely found in printed accounts of trials involving insanity or articles on mental disease and its treatment further evidence that in this country abnormality was a fact of everyday life. In mid-century monomania was not a household word or a frequent topic in newspapers, but the word and disease were becoming familiar. Melville learned of monomania from experience, literary classics, and probably journalistic accounts and reference and technical works. One proven source of factual information for Melville, the twenty-seven-volume *Penny Cyclopaedia*, contained an excellent and moderately technical article on the nature, causes, and treatment of insanity that he may have read.[2] Any of the numerous scientific books on the subject also available in the New York Society Library could have provided information for a writer with scientific interests and a commitment to realistic observations and hardheaded insights.

Crucial in the development of Melville's sensitivity to mental illness was the education he received in his father's family and at sea. Allan Melvill's raving and incoherence in January 1832, when Melville was twelve, left the son with impressions that he would never forget and with deep fears of "maniacal" behavior and apparently of insanity in any form. Melville's fears and confusion were nurtured by an overly attentive mother, known among relatives for her family concerns and "nervousness," and perhaps by a brilliant and emotional older brother, who in his late teens was bedridden for fifteen months for a minor injury. Family life was not without its benefits, however; family members got along together pretty well; Herman learned to accept changes and disappointments; he became adaptable and realistic. In the teenage years, work in a bank and his brother's fur store and on his uncle's farm apparently toughened him. The first lengthy journeys to Liverpool and Galena, Illinois, expanded Melville's awareness of life's possibilities and ironies, and his education continued in 1841–42 aboard his first whaler, the *Acushnet*, with a crew which included not only many competent seamen but an assortment of drifters, potential suicides, troublemakers, and deserters. In many months on two other whalers Melville completed the education in what he later described as "my Yale College and my Harvard" and then went beyond that in service aboard an American frigate.[3] He returned to this country in 1844, a skeptical young man with strong reflective tendencies, pent-up angers and frustrations, a sometimes easy, natural manner, and an array of lively views and opinions, some of them derived from observations of eccentric, strange, and abnormal people. The New York City years (1847 to 1850), married life, moderate success as a writer, and immersion in the social and intellectual scene smoothed rough edges and provided necessary intellectual stimulation and fulfillment.

The first signs in Melville's fiction of an interest in insanity appear in fairly mild and direct form in *Typee* and *Omoo* and with satiric bent in *Mardi*, which contains lively portrayals of monomaniacs. By 1849 the interest in mental illness may have grown into a preoccupation. In *Redburn* and *White-Jacket* major characters like Jackson, Bland, and Surgeon Cuticle, various minor ones, and arrays of unidentified poor and working figures show effects of moral insanity, monomania, or a combination of the two.

Perhaps because of Melville's concerns over his own stability the preoccupation developed in the 1850s into an exploration of abnormality as significant and as driven as his involvement with ideas or philosophy. To search for the psychological equivalents of white whales in *Moby-Dick* and Krakens in *Pierre*, Melville drew from familiarity with personal conflicts and depressions to describe depths of monomania and moral insanity in Ahab and Pierre, both deluded by self-images and fanatic ideas. The range of the writer's exploration is illustrated in several stories, *The Confidence-Man*, and *Billy Budd*, in which abnormal behavior and thought may be less profoundly evoked than in *Moby-Dick* and *Pierre* but presented in a more sharply focused manner.

Melville's contributions to American fiction include several based on his understanding and portrayal of mental abnormality. He was the first major American fiction writer to show that insanity was a natural and significant part of life, that it appeared in many forms, and that it could be found anywhere in an American village, on a Pacific island, aboard a ship, in a city, asylum, or home, and in characters as various as the ex–naval lieutenant in *Typee*, Isabel Banford and Mrs. Glendinning in *Pierre*, and Babo in "Benito Cereno." Melville may have also cleared the air a little through his satiric portrayals of phrenology and its weaknesses at a time when some reputable scientists appeared impressed by aspects of that form of character and psychological evaluation.

The writer's most significant contributions appear in descriptions of effects of mental illness or trauma on mental processes and on unconscious levels of mind and in portrayals of speech of disturbed characters. The pioneering researches of Henry A. Murray and others have explained the nature of Melville's understanding of the unconscious and his remarkable anticipation in fiction of several discoveries of Freud and Jung. In this respect Melville was ahead of American scientists of his own day. This study, indebted to Murray's discoveries, has limited discussion of Melville's knowledge of the unconscious to a few elements of the unconscious mind in Ahab and other driven characters. Melville painstakingly follows the course of Ahab's tortured monomania as delusions of self and whale drive everything out of his mind except the idea of destroying the whale. The involutions of Ahab's thought, controlled at times by irrational, unconscious forces, are brilliantly described and dramatized. Pierre's thinking and consciousness are followed more sequentially so that effects of Isabel's letter or Mrs. Glendinning's behavior on Pierre's mentality can be shown at the time. If conscious and unconscious levels of Pierre's mind are presented with greater clarity but perhaps with less power and depth than appear in portrayals of Ahab, Melville seems at times in *Pierre* to be expanding the boundaries of the unconscious, using remarkable metaphors of space to delineate the farthest reaches of the mind. Isabel's two-part story may be regarded as a detailed autobiography and also as a dramatic revelation of unconscious materials too frightening for Isabel to consider objectively and analytically even if she were capable of doing so. The dreadful old French couple and insane figures in the American asylum may represent in acceptable form the "dark side" of her psyche. Claggart, in turn, more observant and reflective than most, appears largely unaware of conflicts deep within his mind.

The speech of Melville's mentally disturbed characters may be no more revealing than speech of comparable Hawthorne or Poe characters, but Melville created many more such figures. Some do not use ordinary, everyday words. Ahab's speech is often Shakespearean, Gabriel's pronouncements have a formal biblical ring, and Surgeon Cuticle employs a pompous, formal language. Other characters speak in relatively commonplace ways. Jermin uses a sailor lingo, and the moody Titan blunt, ominous words. Bartleby's subdued, simple language and flutelike tone suggest something of his isolation and obsession with self. It is his lack of speech, his "great stillness," that best conveys a sense of his obsession and predicament. The blacksmith Perth reveals melancholy through silence. Pip, seldom silent, indicates his complexities through witty, playful, silly, philosophic talk. His words, riddles, and speech patterns come from American folklore and minstrelsy, Shakespeare's plays, and perhaps New England idiom. Pip's talk or speech reveals a tormented, racing mind and erratic emotions. Isabel Banford may be as insecure as Pip, but her moody, serious temperament makes for a rather formal, often intense language with long sentences and a rich variety of words. The flow of sentences and descriptions in her long story hides fears and bad memories as well as reveals them. Language may be her only connection to the real world.

In the psychological voyaging which began with *Typee* and ended with *Billy Budd*, Melville was more concerned with the nature of insanity than with its causes. Yet causes are always factors in the fiction. They appear representative of causes regarded as significant by American scientists of the time: harsh environment (including poverty and crime), family troubles, heredity, alcoholism, physical ailments, or wounds. Portrayals in the fiction of environment and the family, and their effects, are more than routine, however; they often clarify important contributing influences. Distinctive qualities of environment affect figures ranging from renegade Jimmy in *Typee* to Captain Vere. For family materials and insights, Melville drew from his own experiences. The absent father and family poverty account in part for Redburn's bitterness and defiance on the steamboat and anguish over memories of his father. Ishmael in bed with Queequeg recalls a troubling childhood experience involving his stepmother, a nightmare, and a strange consciousness. Family influences are pivotal in *Pierre*. The youth is disturbed by consequences of his father's bachelor excesses, his mother's demands, and his own family inheritance. He refers to the insanity that may await him because of his parents. Ahab, Perth the blacksmith, Goneril, and Colonel Moredock suffer in different ways because of failures or losses in the family.

The major techniques in Melville's fiction may well be those cited by

Leon Howard in 1940—allusiveness and suspense, which are essential in several areas, including characterization.[4] Techniques stressed in this study—language, first-person narrators, expository devices, and biographical models—appear familiar and useful also in characterization and description. Melville's rich, flexible language is with few exceptions appropriate: it is relatively straightforward in accounts of unstable sailors and natives in *Typee* and *Omoo*, complex and figurative in describing abnormal qualities in Bland, Ahab, or Pierre, and concise and exact in characterizations of Bartleby and Goneril. The aptness of abnormal speech has been noted. Most complications of Melville's first-person narrators lie outside the province of this study; many are worth consideration. Little has been done here with the indeterminate relationship of author and narrator, which appears deceptively simple in such works as *Typee*, *Omoo*, and *Billy Budd*. A few related points have been noted: the psychology of Redburn as youth and adult and of Ishmael the character. Melville's expository powers are superbly suited to portrayals of insanity because of the importance of such concrete matters as place and environment, life and class histories, and behavior and because of his general understanding of intangibles of the mind and his determination to understand and portray them. Whether expository materials dominate a single paragraph, several consecutive ones, or a chapter, the techniques of explanation, description, and analysis are essential in accounts of insanity. Biographical materials make for a more persuasive realism in most works, although in the later ones such materials are usually absorbed in the portrayal. Yet, paradoxically, in the last novel appear resemblances between Melville and his sons on the one hand and Captain Vere and Billy on the other.

Even though a difficult life made Melville skeptical and critical of people, he appeared sympathetic toward individuals deprived in some way. Handicapped or abnormal characters in his fiction come off pretty well unless they are actually unethical, harmful, or malicious. Melville shows little regard or sympathy for early disturbed captains like Vangs, Crash, Riga, or Claret, and he was fascinated more than anything else by the behavior of Jackson and Bland. For others like Rope Yarn, Pip, Elijah, Perth, Isabel, Turkey, Nippers, Jimmy Rose, Bartleby, Charlemont, China Aster, and Captain Vere there was probably warmth as well as sympathy because of his own experiences, family teachings, and a sense of moral rightness.

Melville wrote about such characters and insanity because it was his story to write. He kept returning to it in all of the novels except *Israel*

Potter because he had experienced the effects of mental disturbances and wrote about them to understand himself and others. His exploration of what must have been for him a major part of life does not reveal so much persistent scientific interests or abilities, although at times these are impressive, as the familiar gifts of imagination, keenness of mind, and integrity. At his best Melville portrayed things as he had experienced or observed them. "Events," he wrote in *Pierre*, "are brass."[5] Portraying things on that level may have been a late dream of his youth; it was at least one of his dreams or goals as a writer. In *Pierre* he was apparently too close to his own experiences, but in works like *Moby-Dick* and "Bartleby the Scrivener" he wrote about psychological aberrations with greater objectivity and recognition of his own principles. The bottom line for Melville may have been expressed in *Billy Budd, Sailor*: "Truth uncompromisingly told will always have its ragged edges."[6] Melville was deeply aware of the ragged edges and insidious encroachments of insanity, just as he was deeply aware of the great difficulties of writing about them and of convincing readers to believe what he had written. His perseverance somehow paid off. Melville's fiction illustrates the depth of his understanding of abnormality and the integrity, determination, and art with which he expressed that understanding.

NOTES

Introduction

1. Merrell R. Davis and William H. Gilman, eds., *The Letters of Herman Melville*, p. 83.

2. See Henry A. Murray, "In Nomine Diaboli," pp. 10–21; idem, ed., "Introduction," in Herman Melville, *Pierre, or the Ambiguities*; Morris Beja, "Bartleby and Schizophrenia," *Massachusetts Review* 19 (1978): 555–68; Nathaniel M. Floyd, "*Billy Budd*: A Psychological Autopsy," *American Imago* 34 (1977): 28–49; Leon Howard, *Herman Melville: A Biography*, pp. 163–72, passim. See also Edwin Haviland Miller, *Melville*.

3. Howard, *Herman Melville*, p. 127.

Chapter One. Family and Sea Experiences

1. Leon Howard, *Herman Melville*, p. 2. Hereafter, page references will be placed in the text. Gansevoort added an *e* to the family name to mislead creditors. This spelling was subsequently adopted.

2. T. Walter Herbert, Jr., *Moby-Dick and Calvinism: A World Dismantled*, pp. 58–60.

3. Herman Melville, *Pierre, or the Ambiguities*, p. 70.

4. William H. Gilman, *Melville's Early Life and Redburn*, pp. 59–60, 308–9.

5. Henry A. Murray, ed., "Explanatory Notes," in *Pierre, or the Ambiguities*, p. 454.

6. Susan Weiner and William J. Weiner, "Allan Melvill's Death: A Misdiagnosis," *Melville Society Extracts* 67 (September 1986): 9–11.

7. Jay Leyda, *The Melville Log: A Documentary Life of Herman Melville 1819–1891*, 1:51. Hereafter, page references will be placed in the text. Professor Leyda, in a 9 August 1984 letter to me, made the following corrections—incorporated above—of the *Log* passage for 10 January: mind to Mind, melancholy to melancholly, and immediately to *immediately*. I am indebted to Professor Leyda for this information.

8. Quoted by Gilman, *Melville's Early Life*, pp. 308–9.

9. Herman Melville, *Redburn: His First Voyage*, p. 36; *Pierre*, p. 70.

10. Weiner and Weiner, "Allan Melvill's Death," p. 11.

11. Robert Jean Campbell, M.D., *Psychiatric Dictionary*, p. 155.

12. Isaac Ray, *A Treatise on the Medical Jurisprudence of Insanity*, p. 297. In Noah Webster, *An American Dictionary of the English Language*, the word *delirium* is defined as "a state in which the ideas of a person are wild, irregular and unconnected, or do not correspond with the truth or with external objects; a roving or wandering of the mind; disorder of the intellect" (p. 232).

13. Ray, *Treatise*, pp. 300–301; Herman Melville, *Moby-Dick or the Whale*, p. 314.

14. Miller, *Melville*, pp. 96, 97.

15. Several physicians attended Gansevoort Melville during his final illness. The available sources have been checked by Jay Leyda. I have quoted ("a state of nervous derangement . . .") from a letter cited by Professor Leyda (p. 213). This 4 May letter and a 14 May letter ("suffering from a functional . . ." in the notes) to Secretary of State Buchanan are in Dispatch No. 45, 18 May 1846, National Archives, Washington, D.C. See also 12 May letter from Dr. Ed D. Moore.

16. I wish to thank Professor Leyda for bringing this letter, in the Gansevoort-Lansing Collection at the New York Public Library, to my attention.

17. Michael Paul Rogin, *Subversive Genealogy: The Politics and Art of Herman Melville*, pp. 175–76.

18. Jay Leyda, ed., *The Complete Stories of Herman Melville*, p. xxviii.

19. Gilman, *Melville's Early Life*, p. 187. "That the conditions [Melville] . . . describes actually existed is corroborated from numerous sources." See p. 136.

20. Howard P. Vincent, *The Tailoring of Melville's White-Jacket*, pp. 124, 136–37.

21. Herman Melville, *White-Jacket, or the World in a Man-of-War*, p. 74.

22. "Medical & Surgical Journal of the Frigate *United States*, 1842–1844," n.p.; Willard Thorp, "Historical Note," p. 411.

23. Campbell, *Psychiatric Dictionary*, pp. 148, 58; "Medical & Surgical Journal," n.p.; James Cowles Prichard, *A Treatise on Insanity and other Disorders Affecting the Mind*, p. 171.

Chapter Two. Scientific Background

1. Recent information on Melville's education in New York and Albany schools can be found in John Runden, "Columbia Grammar School: An Overlooked Year in the Lives of Gansevoort and Herman Melville," *Melville Society Extracts* 46 (1981): 1–3; and David K. Titus, "Herman Melville at the Albany Academy," *Melville Society Extracts* 42 (1980): 1, 4–10; Tyrus

Hillway, "Melville's Education in Science," *Texas Studies in Literature and Language* 16 (1974): 411–25; Gilman, *Melville's Early Life*, p. 103.

2. Herman Melville, *Omoo: A Narrative of Adventures in the South Seas*, p. 36.

3. Herman Melville, *Redburn, His First Voyage*, p. 86. For a description of the Newgate Calendar, see Elizabeth S. Foster, "Explanatory Notes," in Herman Melville, *The Confidence-Man: His Masquerade*, p. 342.

4. Wilson L. Heflin, "New Light on Herman Melville's Cruise in the *Charles and Henry*," *Historic Nantucket* 22 (1974): 11–17.

5. Merton M. Sealts, Jr., "A Second Supplementary Note to *Melville's Reading* (1966)," *Harvard Library Bulletin* 27 (1979): 331.

6. Melville, *White-Jacket*, pp. 167–68.

7. John Mason Good, *The Book of Nature*, pp. 429–48; Hillway, "Melville's Education," p. 417.

8. Wilson L. Heflin kindly informed me in a letter dated 25 July 1981 that he was reasonably certain that the Upham book, #100 in the Family Library, was aboard the ship during Melville's tour of duty. *Alphabetical and Analytical Catalogue of the New York Society Library with the Charter, By-Laws, &c., of the Institution*, p. xlviii; Howard, *Herman Melville*, pp. 172–73.

9. Quoted by Howard, *Herman Melville*, p. 172; Thomas C. Upham, *Outlines of Imperfect and Disordered Mental Action*, pp. 193–224.

10. Upham, *Outlines*, pp. 345, 356–65.

11. Merton M. Sealts, Jr., *Melville's Reading: Revised and Enlarged Edition*, pp. 38, 24.

12. Ibid., pp. 38–39.

13. Charles Knight, ed., *The Penny Cyclopaedia of the Society for the Diffusion of Useful Knowledge*.

14. Vincent, *Tailoring*, p. 131; Kendra H. Gaines, "A Consideration of an Additional Source for Melville's *Moby-Dick*," *Extracts: An occasional newsletter* 29 (1977): 6–12; and Walter E. Bezanson, "Historical Note," in Herman Melville, *Israel Potter: His Fifty Years of Exile*, p. 234.

15. James Cowles Prichard, *A Treatise on Insanity and Other Disorders Affecting the Mind*. *A Treatise* is apparently an outgrowth of an article on insanity in *The Cyclopaedia of Practical Medicine*, pp. 10–33. See Prichard, *Treatise*, pp. v–vi.

16. See the library listings in the *Alphabetical Catalogue* and also in the *Supplement* (1850) for works by Ray, Prichard, Pinel, Esquirol, Conolly, Burroughs, Heinroth, Upham, and also Amariah Brigham, Earle Pliny, John Gait, Benjamin Rush, and William Sweetser. Vincent, *Tailoring*, p. 131, explains that after Melville read *Cyclopaedia* articles related to gunshot wounds he likely turned to authorities cited for more information.

17. Knight, ed., *Penny Cyclopaedia*, p. 484.

18. Norman Dain, *Concepts of Insanity in the United States, 1789–1865*, p. 73.

19. Knight, ed., *Penny Cyclopaedia*, p. 484. See also Henry Nash Smith, "The Madness of Ahab," in *Democracy and the Novel: Popular Resistance to Classic American Writers*, p. 38. I have relied in these pages and in Chapter 5 on ideas and materials in pp. 38–48 of Smith's study. See also Smith's earlier version, "The Madness of Ahab," *Yale Review* 66 (Autumn 1976): 14–32.

20. Knight, ed., *Penny Cyclopaedia*, p. 484.

21. Prichard, *Treatise*, pp. 5, 6, and Ray, *Treatise*, pp. 186–87.

22. Prichard, *Treatise*, pp. 17–22; see also Ray, *Treatise*, pp. 186–87.

23. Knight, ed., *Penny Cyclopaedia*, p. 484.

24. Ibid., p. 485.

Chapter Three. Beginnings: *Typee, Omoo,* and *Mardi*

1. Leon Howard, "Historical Note," in Herman Melville, *Typee: A Peep at Polynesian Life*, pp. 278–79. Hereafter, references to this edition will appear in the text. Gordon Roper, "Historical Note," in Herman Melville, *Omoo: A Narrative of Adventures in the South Seas*, p. 325. Hereafter, all references to this edition will appear in the text.

2. See, for example, Miller, *Melville*, pp. 120–21; Miller regards Tommo's predicament and the relationship of author and narrator in Freudian terms.

3. See Sealts, Jr., *Melville's Reading*, p. 88, about Melville's newspaper reading; *New York Herald*, 1 January 1845, 23, 24, 25 May 1845; Dain, *Concepts of Insanity*, pp. 157, 248, n. 29, 266; *Herald*, 18, 24, 28 September, 13 October 1846. See C. W. Crozier and A. R. M'Kee, *Life and Trial of Dr. Abner Baker, Jr. (A Monomaniac)*, for an account of the trial, of events before and after, and the address of a judge during the trial on kinds of insanity, pp. 49–90. There is no evidence that Melville read the book.

4. Merrell R. Davis, *Melville's Mardi: A Chartless Voyage*, p. 112, n. 8, discovered the Robinson lecture. However, Davis incorrectly identifies the book: it was *Matthias and His Impostures*, not *The Life of Matthias*, and only a short paragraph in one lecture on 1 April was devoted to Matthias and his book, not three lectures as indicated; New-York Historical Society, Reference library letters, no dates, 1989; Sealts, *Melville's Reading*, p. 217, no. 491a. *Littel's Living Age*, 7 March 1846, had an article on insanity.

5. *Albany Argus*, 27 March 1846; *New York Herald*, 25–30 March 1846; *Albany Argus*, 27 July 1846; Dain, *Concepts of Insanity*, p. 157.

6. Herman Melville, *The Piazza Tales and Other Prose Pieces, 1839–1860*, pp. 460, 191–204; see Merrell R. Davis and William H. Gilman, eds., *The Letters of Herman Melville*, pp. 7–16; Warner Berthoff, *The Example of Melville*, pp. 92–93.

7. Howard, *Herman Melville*, p. 54.

8. Prichard, *Treatise*, p. 24.

9. For interesting views of Tommo's melancholy, see T. Walter Herbert, Jr., *Marquesan Encounters: Melville and the Meaning of Civilization*, pp. 162–65. Miller, however, regards Tommo on Nukuheva as generally in an infantile or childhood state (pp. 122–31).

10. Howard, *Herman Melville*, p. 55; Roper, "Historical Note," pp. 320–21; Harrison Hayford and Walter Blair, "Explanatory Notes," in Herman Melville, *Omoo*, p. 357.

11. Hayford and Blair, "Explanatory Notes," p. 360.

12. Howard, *Herman Melville*, p. 55; Hayford and Blair, "Explanatory Notes," p. 357.

13. Hayford and Blair, "Explanatory Notes," pp. 428–29, does not refer to Captain Crash or a model for him.

14. Elizabeth S. Foster, "Historical Note," in Herman Melville, *Mardi and a Voyage Thither*, p. 658. Hereafter, all references to this edition will appear in the text.

15. Sealts, *Melville's Reading*, p. 182.

16. Tyrus Hillway, "Melville's Use of Two Pseudo-Sciences," *Modern Language Notes* 64 (March 1949): 145–50; Dain, *Concepts of Insanity*, pp. 61–63. See also Ray, *Treatise*, pp. x–xii.

17. Sealts, *Melville's Reading*, p. 193; Melville, *Pierre or the Ambiguities*, p. 79.

18. Davis, *Melville's Mardi*, p. 112.

Chapter Four. Insane Figures in *Redburn* and *White-Jacket*

1. Foster, "Historical Note," p. 665.

2. Hershel Parker, "Historical Note," in Herman Melville, *Redburn: His First Voyage*, p. 318. Hereafter, all references to this edition will be placed in the text.

3. Leyda, ed., *Complete Stories*, p. xxviii.

4. Parker, "Historical Note," p. 321.

5. Brian Saunders, "Facing the Fire at Home: Redburn's 'Inland Imagination,'" *Studies in the Novel* 17 (Winter 1985): 350–70, believes that in describing Redburn's childhood Melville is revealing elements of the unconscious. See, for example, pp. 358–60.

6. Gilman, *Melville's Early Life*, p. 131.

7. Knight, ed., *Penny Cyclopaedia*; Ray, *Treatise*, pp. 416–23; Amariah Brigham, *An Inquiry Concerning the Diseases and Functions of the Brain, The Spinal Cord & The Nerves*, pp. 260–66.

8. Prichard, *Treatise*, pp. 21–22.

9. Isaac Ray, "The Causes of Insanity," in his *Contributions to Mental Pathology*, p. 45; Brigham, *Inquiry*, pp. 289, 290; Prichard, *Treatise*, p. 175.

10. See Ray, *Treatise*, pp. 173–74.

11. Ibid.

12. Isaac Ray, "Objections to Moral Insanity Considered," in his *Contributions to Mental Pathology*, p. 100.

13. Prichard, *Treatise*, p. 19.

14. Thorp, "Historical Note," pp. 410, 411. Hereafter, all references to this edition will be placed in the text.

15. Vincent, *Tailoring*, pp. 124–27, 136–38; Thorp, "Historical Note," pp. 410–11; *Medical and Surgical Journal*.

16. Campbell, *Psychiatric Dictionary*, distinguishes between delirium tremens and mania-a-potu, which "is characterized by extreme excitement ('alcoholic fury') with aggressive . . . even homicidal reactions. Persecutory ideas are common" (pp. 333–34).

17. Vincent, *Tailoring*, pp. 136–37.

18. Prichard, *Treatise*, p. 27.

19. Vincent, *Tailoring*, pp. 124–27.

20. Quen, "Introduction," p. ix; Dain, *Concepts of Insanity*, p. 71; Campbell, *Psychiatric Dictionary*, p. 393; Winfred Overholser, ed., "Editor's Introduction," in Ray, *Treatise*. J. W. Fay, *American Psychology before William James*, points out that Ray's book provides a discussion of one aspect of modern psychology that "constitutes a vigorous refutation of the statement that there was no psychology in America prior to 1883" (p. 135). See also Gregory Zilboorg, M.D., and George W. Henry, M.D., *A History of Medical Psychology*, pp. 417–19.

Chapter Five. The World Is Mad: *Moby-Dick*

1. Herman Melville, *Journal of a Visit to London and the Continent By Herman Melville 1849–1850*, p. 4.

2. Sanford E. Marovitz, "More Chartless Voyaging: Melville and Adler at Sea," pp. 376, 377.

3. Davis and Gilman, eds., *Letters*, pp. 115, 118, 122, 123.

4. Leyda, *Melville Log*, 1:403. Longfellow wrote in his journal on 17 April 1853 of a visit by Adler. "He has overworked his brain; and has a monomania. . . . Crowds look him [*sic*] strangely in the street, and voices under his window at night cry, 'Go home! Go home'" (1:468). Howard, *Herman Melville*, p. 208, explains that in 1853 Adler "had developed such a severe case of agoraphobia that he was to be confined in the Bloomingdale Asylum in October." Agoraphobia has been defined in this century as "the dread of open spaces. The patient becomes panic-stricken, sometimes at the thought of, but more often at the impending visit to an open space." The patient generally prefers to remain indoors and near "a kind, helpful,

guiding influence." Campbell, *Psychiatric Dictionary*, p. 19. For George J. Adler's opinions, see his *Letters of a Lunatic, or a Brief Exposition of My University Life, During the Years 1853–1854*, pp. 5–10.

5. Augustus Kinsley Gardner, M.D., *Old Wine in New Bottles: or, Spare Hours of a Student in Paris*.

6. Howard, *Herman Melville*, p. 110.

7. Samuel W. Francis, "Augustus Kinsley Gardner, M.D.," in *Biographical Sketches of Distinguished Living New York Physicians*, pp. 124–27; Howard, *Herman Melville*, p. 7.

8. Leonard W. Levy, *The Law of the Commonwealth and Chief Justice Shaw*, pp. 211–18; H.A.B. (H. Amariah Brigham), "Medical Jurisprudence of Insanity," *American Journal of Insanity* 1 (June, 1845): 258–74. For a different view of Shaw's understanding, see Quen, "Introduction," p. x. For Isaac Ray's understanding, see ibid. For Ray's 1861 discussion of the "uncontrollable impulse" or "irresistible impulse," see "Objections to Moral Insanity Considered" in ibid., pp. 102–3.

9. Brigham, "Medical Jurisprudence," pp. 268–69. The second sentence is quoted by Smith, "The Madness of Ahab," p. 38. Smith also discusses the McNaghten decision and Brigham's 1848 views on pp. 38–39 and refers to an October 1844 article by Brigham on p. 175.

10. Brigham, "Medical Jurisprudence," p. 269.

11. See ibid.; Thomas M. McDade, comp., *The Annals of Murder: A Bibliography of Books and Pamphlets on American Murders from Colonial Times to 1900*, pp. 246–47.

12. Herman Melville, "Hawthorne and His Mosses," in *The Piazza Tales and Other Prose Pieces 1839–1860*, pp. 243, 244.

13. Ibid., p. 244.

14. Davis and Gilman, *Letters*, p. 128.

15. Howard, *Herman Melville*, p. 173.

16. Davis and Gilman, *Letters*, p. 121.

17. Melville, *Moby-Dick*, p. 4. Hereafter, all page references to this edition will appear in the text.

18. Prichard, *Treatise*, p. 28.

19. Ibid., p. 12.

20. James Prichard, *On the Different Forms of Insanity in Relation to Jurisprudence*, p. 69.

21. Ray, *Treatise*, p. 164.

22. Prichard, *Treatise*, p. 115.

23. A check of primary works by Ray and the Englishman Prichard discloses little comment on speech as such in discussions of insane patients. See, for example, Prichard's discussion in *A Treatise* of representative cases of moral insanity. Speech is seldom referred to and is not analyzed.

24. *Webster's Third New International Dictionary, . . . Unabridged*, p. 1055.

25. Melville, *Moby-Dick*, p. 12; Campbell, *Psychiatric Dictionary*, p. 295.

26. Smith, "The Madness of Ahab," p. 174, explains ideas expressed by Armin Staats, "Melville—*Moby-Dick*," p. 123; Prichard, *Treatise*, p. 12; "Insanity," in Knight, ed., *Penny Cyclopaedia*, p. 484.

27. For a detailed discussion in Freudian terms of the counterpane, try-works, and other episodes involving Ishmael, see Harold Hellenbrand, "Behind Closed Doors: Ishmael's Dreams & Hypnagogic Trances in *Moby-Dick*," *American Transcendental Quarterly* 61 (October 1986):47–71.

28. Nathalia Wright, *Melville's Use of the Bible*.

29. Smith, "The Madness of Ahab," p. 40.

30. Ray, *Treatise*, p. 135. Edward F. Edinger, *Melville's Moby Dick: A Jungian Commentary*, provides a Jungian interpretation of the "torn body . . . soul" image: "The body bleeds into the soul; that is, the collective unconscious with its archetypal images streams into consciousness. Instead of relating to these images meaningfully, however, Ahab becomes identified with them, succumbs to inflation, and thus to madness" (p. 56).

31. Prichard, *Treatise*, pp. 26, 31.

32. To my knowledge Ray, Prichard, Brigham, Conolly, and Esquirol were not engaged in the mid 1800s in attempts to understand the nature of the unconscious, although European scientists, notably German, had been active by studying that area for some time. See Henri F. Ellenberger, *The Discovery of the Unconscious: The History and Evolution of Dynamic Psychiatry*, pp. 205–10, passim.

33. Melville, *Pierre*, p. 167; see Murray, "In Nomine Diaboli," pp. 6–7, 8.

34. Smith, "The Madness of Ahab," p. 47, discusses interpretations by Paul Brodtkorb, Jr., *Ishmael's White World: A Phenomenological Reading of Moby-Dick*; and by Robert Zoellner, *The Salt-Sea Mastodon: A Reading of Moby-Dick*, p. 127.

35. Charles Feidelson, Jr., ed., Herman Melville, *Moby-Dick, or the Whale*, p. 271.

36. Brodtkorb, *Ishmael's White World*, p. 63; Zoellner, *Salt-Sea Mastodon*, pp. 98–101.

37. See Ray, *Treatise*, pp. 162–66; Prichard, *Treatise*, pp. 36–44.

38. Howard, *Herman Melville*, pp. 60, 166, 171–72. Millicent Bell, "Pierre Bayle and *Moby Dick*," *PMLA* 66 (September 1951):626–48, explains that Melville's conception of Ahab owes something to Bayle's essay on Zoroaster. This figure's unusual powers and views of good and evil would suggest something of the will. Wilson Heflin kindly informed me of this in a 25 July 1981 letter.

39. Upham, *Outlines*, p. 384.

40. Ibid., pp. 396–97.

Chapter Six. The Mad Family: *Pierre*

1. Amy Elizabeth Puett, "Melville's Wife: A Study of Elizabeth Shaw Melville," pp. 76, 77.

2. Howard, *Herman Melville*, pp. 180–83.

3. Brian Higgins and Hershel Parker, "Reading *Pierre*," p. 223.

4. Leon Howard and Hershel Parker, "Historical Note," in Herman Melville, *Pierre: or the Ambiguities*, pp. 370–72. Hereafter, all references to this edition will appear in the text.

5. Davis and Gilman, eds., *Letters*, p. 143.

6. Higgins and Parker, "Reading *Pierre*," p. 223.

7. Ibid., p. 223.

8. Davis and Gilman, eds., *Letters*, p. 146.

9. Leyda, *Melville Log*, 1:441. Hereafter, all references to this edition will appear in the text.

10. Brian Higgins and Hershel Parker, "Introduction," In *Critical Essays on Herman Melville's Pierre; or, the Ambiguities*, p. 12; Howard and Parker, "Historical Note," p. 231.

11. Higgins and Parker, "Introduction," p. 14.

12. Ibid.

13. Murray, ed., *Pierre*, pp. xxi–xxii.

14. For a statement of the opinion that Allan Melvill had an affair and fathered an illegitimate daughter, see Amy Puett Emmers, "Melville's Closet Skeleton: A New Letter about the Illegitimacy Incident in *Pierre*," pp. 339–43; and Henry A. Murray, Harvey Myerson, and Eugene Taylor, "Allan Melvill's By-Blow," *Melville Society Extracts* 61 (February 1985):1–6.

15. Rogin, *Subversive Genealogy*, p. 165.

16. Murray, ed., *Pierre*, pp. lxv, 461.

17. Richard Chase, *Herman Melville: A Critical Study*, pp. 118–19, regards the houses in mythical and Freudian terms.

18. Howell and Tenney, *Bicentennial History of Albany*, pp. 349–52; Albany Public Library, Ref. Dept., James R. Hobin; materials, 11 August 1989; Lansingburgh Public Library, Ref. Dept., Mrs. Warren Broderick, telephone conversation, 15 August 1989; Galena Public Library, Historical Collections, H. Scott Wolfe, letter and materials, 7 February 1989; Berkshire Athenaeum, Local History and Literature Services, Ruth T. Degenhardt, letter and materials, 13 December 1988; David J. Rothman, *The Discovery of the Asylum*, provided helpful information on the development of asylums, poor houses, etc., in New York City, pp. 197–98, 283, 291–92; A. E. Costello, *History of the New York Police from the Earliest Period to the Present*, pp. 64, 65; John Hardy, comp., *Manual of the Corporation of the City of New York*, map, pp. 88–89; Rothman, *Discovery*, pp. 144, 148–49.

19. Knight, ed., *Penny Cyclopaedia*, pp. 485–86; Dain, *Concepts of Insanity*, pp. 95–96.

20. Murray, ed., *Pierre*, pp. xxv–xxvi, xxxvii; Ray, *Treatise*; Brigham, *Inquiry*; Pritchard, *Treatise*; John Conolly, M.D., *An Inquiry Concerning the Indications of Insanity*; Frederich Rauch, *Psychology: or, a View of the Human Soul: Including Anthropology*. An excellent study of Pierre's mental processes and unconscious level is provided by Brian Higgins and Hershel Parker, "The Flawed Grandeur of Melville's *Pierre*," pp. 162–96, 168–75. For a general comment on the depth of Melville's examination of the unconscious, see Edwin S. Shneidman, "Some Psychological Reflections on Herman Melville," *Melville Society Extracts* 64 (November 1985): 7–9.

21. Ellenberger, *Discovery*, pp. 205–10.

22. Murray, ed., *Pierre*, p. 489. For clarifications of Jung's views of the unconscious, I have relied upon Ellenberger, *Discovery*, pp. 705–13; Edinger, *Melville's Moby-Dick*, pp. 49–72; and Patrick Mullahy, *Oedipus Myth and Complex: A Review of Psychoanalytic Theory*, pp. 145–53. In "The Iconography of Madness," Joan Magretta explains that Melville and Dostoevsky had similar views toward nineteenth-century models of madness, the nature of the unconscious, and failures of reason and science to explain madness. See Chapter 3, *Pierre*, and *The Idiot*, pp. 65–103.

23. Murray, ed., *Pierre*, p. 499.

24. Ibid., p. 467; Campbell, *Psychiatric Dictionary*, pp. 5, 295, 686.

25. Prichard, *Treatise*, pp. 405, 452–55. See also Ellenberger, *Discovery*, p. 123; Shepard, "Pierre's Psyche and Melville's Art," p. 90.

Chapter Seven. City and Sea Madness: Stories

1. Leyda, *Melville Log*, 1:455–63. Hereafter, all references to this edition will be placed in the text.

2. Merton M. Sealts, Jr., "Historical Note," in Herman Melville, *The Piazza Tales and Other Prose Pieces: 1839–1860*, p. 476.

3. Ibid., p. 483; quotes from Henry A. Murray in "Bartleby and I," *Melville Annual 1965, a Symposium: "Bartleby the Scrivener,"* pp. 22–23.

4. Puett, "Melville's Wife," p. 93.

5. Herman Melville, *The Piazza Tales and Other Prose Pieces 1839–1860*, p. 342. Hereafter, all references to this edition will be placed in the text.

6. William B. Dillingham, *Melville's Short Fiction: 1853–1856*, pp. 61–66.

7. Ibid., p. 171.

8. Prichard, *Treatise*, p. 33.

9. Rogin, *Subversive Genealogy*, pp. 193, 194.

10. See Richard Harter Fogle, *Melville's Shorter Tales*, pp. 18–19.

11. Ray, "Objections," p. 108.

12. Nathalia Wright, "Melville and 'Old Burton,' with 'Bartleby' as an Anatomy of Melancholy," *Tennessee Studies in Literature* 15 (1970): 7. For a modern view that Bartleby's immobility, need for privacy, and the protection of walls and "anorexic politics" identify him as an agoraphobic, see Gillian Brown, "The Empire of Agoraphobia," *Representations* 20 (1987): 134–37, 150. See also Howard, *Herman Melville*, p. 208.

13. I have relied on Dillingham's discussion of four points of view (*Melville's Short Fiction*, pp. 242–47).

14. Campbell, *Psychiatric Dictionary*, p. 658.

15. Ibid., p. 295.

16. Dillingham, *Melville's Short Fiction*, p. 258. See Perry, pp. 407–15.

17. Prichard, *Treatise*, pp. 405–10, 31–32; Ellenberger, *Discovery*, pp. 122–23; See also Campbell, *Psychiatric Dictionary*, pp. 658, 96.

18. See M. M. Vanderhaar, "A Re-examination of 'Benito Cereno,'" *American Literature* 40 (May 1968): 179–91; Max Putzel, "The Source and the Symbols of Melville's 'Benito Cereno,'" *American Literature* 34 (May 1962): 191–206; Marvin Fisher, *Going Under: Melville's Short Fiction and the American 1850's*, pp. 108–9.

19. Dillingham, *Melville's Short Fiction*, pp. 264, 265.

Chapter Eight. Insanity out West: *The Confidence-Man*

1. Herman Melville, *The Confidence-Man: His Masquerade*, p. 9. Hereafter, all references to this edition will be placed in the text.

2. Leyda, *Melville Log*, 2:498. Hereafter, all references to this edition will be placed in the text.

3. Howard, *Herman Melville*, p. 221.

4. Watson Branch, et al., "Historical Note," in Herman Melville, *The Confidence-Man: His Masquerade*, p. 276; Howard, *Herman Melville*, p. 225.

5. Branch, "Historical Note," pp. 277–78.

6. Ibid., p. 277.

7. Sealts, *Melville's Reading*, p. 88; *Pittsfield Sun*, 17 February 1853, 12 June 1851, 16 October 1851; *New York Herald*, 28 September 1855.

8. Rogin, *Subversive Genealogy*, p. 249; Miller, *Melville*, pp. 280–81.

9. H. Bruce Franklin, ed., Herman Melville, *The Confidence-Man: His Masquerade*, p. 5, n. 17.

10. *The Columbia Encyclopedia in One Volume*, p. 865.

11. See Tom Quirk, "Literary Models," Chapter 4 in his *Melville's Confidence-Man: From Knave to Knight*, pp. 75–103.

12. Franklin, *The Confidence-Man*, p. 83, n. 3.

13. Quirk believes that society then would regard the husband as mad, not the wife (*Melville's Confidence-Man*, pp. 13–14).

14. Franklin, *The Confidence-Man*, pp. 82–83.

15. Campbell, *Psychiatric Dictionary*, p. 656.

16. Prichard, *Treatise*, pp. 31–32, 171. See Ray, *Treatise*, pp. 121–22.

17. Quirk, *Melville's Confidence-Man*, p. 114.

18. Hayford, "Poe," pp. 207–18.

19. Ibid.

20. Branch, "Historical Note," p. 276.

21. See Audrey C. Peterson, "Brain Fever in Nineteenth-Century Literature: Fact and Fiction," *Victorian Studies* (September–June 1975–76):447. Peterson refers to an incident in *The Confidence-Man* involving brain fever (p. 461).

22. Franklin, *The Confidence-Man*, p. 213, n. 22.

Chapter Nine. "Who . . . can draw the line?": *Billy Budd, Sailor*

1. Branch, "Historical Note," pp. 318–20.

2. Stanton Garner, "Surviving the Gilded Age: Herman Melville in the Customs Service," *Essays in Arts and Sciences* 15 (June 1986):3–4. According to Hardy, comp., *Manual*, 245 inspectors and 110 night inspectors were employed in the Surveyor's Department in 1870 (p. 213).

3. Garner, "Surviving," pp. 6–9.

4. Walter D. Kring and Jonathan S. Carey, "Two Discoveries Concerning Herman Melville," pp. 11–16.

5. Robert Milder, "Commentary," in *The Endless, Winding Way in Melville: New Charts by Kring and Carey*, ed. Yannella and Parker, p. 46; Puett, "Melville's Wife," p. 162.

6. Leyda, *Melville Log*, 2:725. Hereafter, all references to this edition will be placed in the text.

7. Walter E. Bezanson, ed., "The Characters: A Critical Index," in Herman Melville, *Clarel: A Poem and Pilgrimage in the Holy Land*, p. 530.

8. Miller, *Melville*, p. 318; Robert Penn Warren "Introduction," in his *Selected Poems of Herman Melville*, pp. 60–63, 79, 81–83.

9. Merton M. Sealts, Jr., "Innocence and Infamy: *Billy Budd, Sailor*," p. 412.

10. Herman Melville, *Billy Budd, Sailor (An Inside Narrative)*, pp. 45, 47. Hereafter, all references to this edition will be placed in the text.

11. In the 1870s and 1880s in America, the ideas and practices of Brigham, Conolly, Prichard, Ray, and others cited in this study were still regarded as influential. For comment on Brigham, see Richard Hunter and Ida Macalpine, *Three Hundred Years of Psychiatry: 1535–1860*, pp. 821–23, 940. For comment on Conolly, see ibid., pp. 805–6, 1030–34. For com-

ment on Prichard, see ibid., pp. 836–39; and Vieda Skultans, "Moral Insanity," in *Madness and Morals: Ideas on Insanity in the Nineteenth Century*, pp. 6–8. For comment on Ray, see Hunter and Macalpine, *Three Hundred Years*, pp. 974–75; and Franz G. Alexander, M.D., and Sheldon T. Selesnick, M.D., *The History of Psychiatry: An Evaluation of Psychiatric Thought and Practice from Prehistoric Times to the Present*, pp. 349–50.

12. Melville, *White-Jacket*, p. 188.

13. Olive L. Fite, "Billy Budd, Claggart, and Schopenhauer," *Nineteenth-Century Fiction* 23 (December 1968):341–42.

14. Arthur Schopenhauer, *The World as Will and Idea*, 2:328.

15. Harold Aspiz, "The 'Lurch of the Torpedo-Fish': Electrical Concepts in *Billy Budd*," *ESQ* 26 (1980):127–36.

16. See, for example, Wendell Glick, "Expediency and Absolute Morality in *Billy Budd*," *PMLA* 68 (March 1953):103–10; and Phil Withim, "*Billy Budd*: Testament of Resistance," *Modern Language Quarterly* 20 (June 1959):115–27.

17. Richard H. Weisberg, "The Creative Use of Statutes for Subjective Ends: The Case of *Billy Budd, Sailor*," pp. 146, 147–59, 161.

18. Quoted by Harrison Hayford and Merton Sealts, eds., *Billy Budd, Sailor*, p. 188, n. 288.

19. For the view that Vere's "mental disturbance" is caused by the conflict between his "primitive instincts" or "instinctive being" and his "imperial conscience" or "spellbound intellect," see William B. Dillingham, "Keeping True: *Billy Budd, Sailor*," in his *Melville's Later Novels*, pp. 375–76. The mental disturbance is an intensification of the customary spellbound condition.

20. See William Braswell, "Melville's *Billy Budd* as 'An Inside Narrative,'" *American Literature* 29 (May 1957):133–46; and Sealts, "Innocence and Infamy," pp. 415–16.

21. Howard, *Herman Melville*, p. 322.

22. Peter L. Hays and Richard Dilworth Rust, "'Something Healing': Fathers and Sons in *Billy Budd*," *Nineteenth-Century Fiction* 34 (1979): 330.

Conclusion

1. Leyda, *Melville Log*, 2:827, 831.

2. Knight, ed., *Penny Cyclopaedia*, pp. 484–88.

3. Melville, *Moby-Dick*, p. 112.

4. Leon Howard, "Melville's Struggle with the Angel," *Modern Language Quarterly* 1 (June 1940):195–206.

5. Melville, *Pierre*, ed. Hayford et al., p. 289.

6. Melville, *Billy Budd, Sailor*, p. 128.

BIBLIOGRAPHY

Adler, George J. *Letters of a Lunatic, or a Brief Exposition of My University Life, During the Years 1853–1854.* New York: Printed for the author, 1854.

Alexander, Franz G., M.D., and Sheldon T. Selesnick, M.D. *The History of Psychiatry: An Evaluation of Psychiatric Thought and Practice from Prehistoric Times to the Present.* New York: Harper and Row, 1966.

Alphabetical and Analytical Catalogue of the New York Society Library with the Charter, By-Laws, &c., of the Institution. "Supplement to the Alphabetical Catalogue. Books Added Since the Volume was Put to Press." R. Craighead, Printer, 1850.

Anderson, Charles Roberts. *Melville in the South Seas.* 1939. Repr. New York: Dover, 1966.

Aspiz, Harold. "The 'Lurch of the Torpedo-Fish': Electrical Concepts in *Billy Budd.*" *ESQ: A Journal of the American Renaissance* 26 (Fall 1980): 127–36.

Beja, Morris. "Bartleby and Schizophrenia." *Massachusetts Review* 19 (1978): 555–68.

Bell, Millicent. "Pierre Bayle and *Moby Dick.*" *PMLA* 66 (September 1951): 626–48.

Berthoff, Warner. *The Example of Melville.* Princeton: Princeton University Press, 1962.

Bezanson, Walter E. "Historical Note." In Herman Melville, *Israel Potter: His Fifty Years of Exile.* Ed. Hayford, Parker, and Tanselle. Evanston and Chicago: Northwestern University Press and the Newberry Library, 1982.

———. "Introduction." "The Characters: A Critical Index." In Herman Melville, *Clarel: A Poem and Pilgrimage in the Holy Land.* New York: Hendricks House, 1960.

Branch, Watson, et al. "Historical Note." In Herman Melville, *The Confidence-Man: His Masquerade.* Ed. Hayford, Parker, and Tanselle. Evanston and Chicago: Northwestern University Press and the Newberry Library, 1984.

Braswell, William. "Melville's *Billy Budd* as 'An Inside Narrative.'" *American Literature* 29 (May 1957): 133–46.

Brigham, Amariah, M.D. *An Inquiry Concerning the Diseases and Functions of the Brain, The Spinal Cord & The Nerves*. New York: George Adlard, 1840.

———. "Medical Jurisprudence of Insanity." *American Journal of Insanity* 1 (January 1845): 258–74.

Brodtkorb, Paul, Jr. *Ishmael's White World: A Phenomenological Reading of Moby-Dick*. New Haven: Yale University Press, 1965.

Brown, Gillian. "The Empire of Agoraphobia." *Representations* 20 (Fall 1987): 134–57.

Bryant, John, ed. *A Companion to Melville Studies*. New York: Greenwood Press, 1986.

Campbell, Robert Jean, M.D. *Psychiatric Dictionary*. 5th ed. New York: Oxford University Press, 1981.

Chase, Richard. *Herman Melville: A Critical Study*. New York: Macmillan, 1949.

Columbia Encyclopedia in One Volume. 2nd ed. Ed. Bridgwater and Sherwood. New York: Columbia University Press, 1950.

Conolly, John, M.D. *An Inquiry Concerning the Indications of Insanity*. London: John Taylor, 1830.

Costello, A. E. *History of the New York Police from the Earliest Period to the Present*. Published by the author, 1885.

Crozier, C. W., and A. R. M'Kee. *Life and Trial of Dr. Abner Baker, Jr. (A Monomaniac)*. Louisville, Ky.: Prentise and Weissinger, Printers, 1846.

Dain, Norman. *Concepts of Insanity in the United States, 1789–1865*. New Brunswick: Rutgers University Press, 1964.

Davis, Merrell R. *Melville's Mardi: A Chartless Voyage*. New Haven: Yale University Press, 1952.

Davis, Merrell R., and William H. Gilman, eds. *The Letters of Herman Melville*. New Haven: Yale University Press, 1960.

Degenhardt, Ruth T. Letter to author. 13 December 1988.

Dillingham, William B. *Melville's Later Novels*. Athens: University of Georgia Press, 1986.

———. *Melville's Short Fiction: 1853–1856*. Athens: University of Georgia Press, 1977.

Edinger, Edward F. *Melville's Moby-Dick: A Jungian Commentary*. New Directions, 1978.

Ellenberger, Henri F. *The Discovery of the Unconscious: The History and Evolution of Dynamic Psychiatry*. New York: Basic Books, 1970.

Emmers, Amy Puett. "Melville's Closet Skeleton: A New Letter about the Illegitimacy Incident in *Pierre*." In *Studies in the American Renaissance 1977*. Ed. Joel Myerson. Boston: Twayne, 1978.

Esquirol, E. *Mental Maladies: A Treatise on Insanity*. Trans. E. K. Hunt, M.D. Philadelphia: Lea and Blanchard, 1845.

Fay, Jay W. *American Psychology before William James*. New York: Octagon Books, 1966.

Feidelson, Charles, Jr., ed. Herman Melville, *Moby-Dick, or the Whale*. Indianapolis: Bobbs-Merrill Company, 1964.

Fisher, Marvin. *Going Under: Melville's Short Fiction and the American 1850's*. Baton Rouge: Louisiana State University Press, 1977.

Fite, Olive L. "Billy Budd, Claggart, and Schopenhauer." *Nineteenth-Century Fiction* 23 (December 1968): 336–43.

Floyd, Nathaniel M. "*Billy Budd*: A Psychological Autopsy." *American Imago* 34 (1977): 28–49.

Fogle, Richard Harter. *Melville's Shorter Tales*. Norman: University of Oklahoma Press, 1960.

Forbes, John, M.D., Alexander Tweedie, M.D., and John Conolly, M.D., eds. *The Cyclopaedia of Practical Medicine*. Vol. 2. London: Sherwood, Gilbert and Piper, 1833.

Foster, Elizabeth S., ed. "Explanatory Notes." In Herman Melville, *The Confidence-Man: His Masquerade*. New York: Hendricks House, 1954.

———. "Historical Note." In Herman Melville, *Mardi and a Voyage Thither*. Ed. Hayford, Parker, and Tanselle. Evanston and Chicago: Northwestern University Press and the Newberry Library, 1970.

Francis, Samuel W. *Biographical Sketches of Distinguished Living New York Physicians*. New York: George P. Putnam and Son, 1867.

Franklin, H. Bruce, ed. Herman Melville, *The Confidence-Man: His Masquerade*. With an Introduction and Annotation. Indianapolis: Bobbs-Merrill Company, 1967.

Gaines, Kendra H. "A Consideration of an Additional Source for Melville's *Moby-Dick*." *Extracts: an occasional newsletter* 29 (January 1977): 6–12.

Gardner, Augustus Kinsley, M.D. *Old Wine in New Bottles: or, Spare Hours of a Student in Paris*. New York: C. S. Francis and Company, 1848.

Garner, Stanton. "Surviving the Gilded Age: Herman Melville in the Customs Service." *Essays in Arts and Sciences* 15 (June 1986): 1–13.

Gilman, William H. *Melville's Early Life and Redburn*. New York: New York University Press, 1951.

Glick, Wendell. "Expediency and Absolute Morality in *Billy Budd*." *PMLA* 68 (March 1953): 103–10.

Good, John Mason. *The Book of Nature*. Hartford: Belknap and Hamersley, 1839.

Hardy, John, comp. *Manual of the Corporation of the City of New York*. New York, 1871.

Hartley, David. *Observations on Man: His Frame, His Duty, and His Expectations*. Introduction by T. L. Huguelet. 1749. Repr. Gainsville: Scholars' Facsimiles and Reprints, 1966.

Hawthorne, Nathaniel. *The House of the Seven Gables*. Columbus: Ohio State University Press, 1965.

―――. *Mosses from an Old Manse*. Columbus: Ohio State University Press, 1974.

―――. *The Scarlet Letter*. Columbus: Ohio State University Press, 1962.

―――. *Twice-Told Tales*. Columbus: Ohio State University Press, 1974.

Hayford, Harrison. "Poe in *The Confidence-Man*." *Nineteenth-Century Fiction* 14 (December 1959):207–18.

Hayford, Harrison, and Walter Blair. "Editors' Introduction" and "Explanatory Notes." In Herman Melville, *Omoo: A Narrative of Adventures in the South Seas*. New York: Hendricks House, 1969.

Hayford, Harrison, and Merton M. Sealts, Jr., eds. *Billy Budd, Sailor (An Inside Narrative)*. "Notes and Commentary." Chicago: University of Chicago Press, 1962.

Hays, Peter L., and Richard Dilworth Rust. "'Something Healing': Fathers and Sons in *Billy Budd*." *Nineteenth-Century Fiction* 34 (December 1979):326–36.

Heflin, Wilson L. Letter to author. 25 July 1981.

―――. "New Light on Herman Melville's Cruise in the *Charles and Henry*." *Historic Nantucket* 22 (October 1974):6–27.

Hellenbrand, Harold. "Behind Closed Doors: Ishmael's Dreams and Hypnagogic Trances in *Moby-Dick*." *American Transcendental Quarterly* 61 (October 1986):47–71.

Herbert, T. Walter, Jr. *Marquesan Encounters: Melville and the Meaning of Civilization*. Cambridge: Harvard University Press, 1980.

―――. *Moby-Dick and Calvinism: A World Dismantled*. New Brunswick: Rutgers University Press, 1977.

Higgins, Brian, and Hershel Parker. "The Flawed Grandeur of Melville's *Pierre*." In *New Perspectives on Melville*. Ed. Faith Pullin. Kent, Ohio: Kent State University Press, 1978.

―――. "Introduction." In *Critical Essays on Herman Melville's Pierre: or, the Ambiguities*. Boston: G. K. Hall, 1983.

―――. "Reading *Pierre*." In *A Companion to Melville Studies*. Ed. John Bryant. New York: Greenwood Press, 1986.

Hillway, Tyrus. "Melville's Education in Science." *Texas Studies in Literature and Language* 16 (Fall 1974):411–25.

―――. "Melville's Use of Two Pseudo-Sciences." *Modern Language Notes* 64 (March 1949):145–50.

Hillway, Tyrus, and Luther S. Mansfield, eds., *Moby-Dick Centennial Essays*. Dallas: Southern Methodist University Press, 1953.

Howard, Leon. *Herman Melville: A Biography*. Berkeley: University of California Press, 1951.

―――. "Historical Note." In Herman Melville, *Typee: A Peep at Polynesian*

Life. Ed. Hayford, Parker, and Tanselle. Evanston and Chicago:
Northwestern University Press and the Newberry Library, 1968.

———. "Melville's Struggle with the Angel." *Modern Language Quarterly* 1
(June 1940): 195–206.

Howard, Leon, and Hershel Parker. "Historical Note." In Herman
Melville, *Pierre or the Ambiguities*. Ed. Hayford, Parker, and Tanselle.
Evanston and Chicago: Northwestern University Press and the Newberry
Library, 1971.

Howell, George R., and Jonathan Tenney. *Bicentennial History of Albany*.
New York: W. W. Munsell, 1886.

Hunter, Richard, and Ida Macalpine. *Three Hundred Years of Psychiatry:
1535–1860*. London: Oxford University Press, 1963.

Inge, M. Thomas, ed. *Bartleby the Inscrutable: A Collection of Commentary on
Herman Melville's Tale "Bartleby the Scrivener."* Hamden, Conn.: Archon
Books, 1979.

Kenney, Alice P. *The Gansevoorts of Albany: Dutch Patricians in the Upper
Hudson Valley*. Syracuse: Syracuse University Press, 1969.

Knight, Charles, ed. *The Penny Cyclopaedia of the Society for the Diffusion of
Useful Knowledge*. 29 vols., including supplement. London: Charles
Knight, 1833–1843.

Kring, Walter D., and Jonathan S. Carey. "Two Discoveries Concerning
Herman Melville." In *The Endless, Winding Way in Melville: New Charts
by Kring and Carey*. Ed. Yannella and Parker. Glassboro, N.J.: Melville
Society, 1981.

Lee, Dwight, A. "Melville and George J. Adler." *American Notes & Queries*
12 (May/June 1974): 138–41.

Levy, Leonard W. *The Law of the Commonwealth and Chief Justice Shaw*.
Cambridge: Harvard University Press, 1957.

Leyda, Jay. Letter to author. 9 August 1984.

———. *The Melville Log: A Documentary Life of Herman Melville 1819–1891*.
2 vols. New York: Gordian Press, 1969.

———, ed. "Introduction" and "Notes." In *The Complete Stories of Herman
Melville*. New York: Random House, 1949.

McDade, Thomas M., comp. *The Annals of Murder: A Bibliography of Books
and Pamphlets on American Murders from Colonial Times to 1900*. Norman:
University of Oklahoma Press, 1961.

Magretta, Joan. "The Iconography of Madness: A Study in Melville and
Dostoevsky." Ph.D. dissertation, University of Michigan, 1976.

Marovitz, Sanford E. "More Chartless Voyaging: Melville and Adler at
Sea." In *Studies in the American Renaissance 1986*. Ed. Joel Myerson.
Charlottesville: University Press of Virginia, 1986.

"Medical & Surgical Journal of the Frigate *United States*, 1842–1844."
Vols. 1, 2. Princeton: Princeton University Library, n.d.

Melville, Herman. *Billy Budd, Sailor (An Inside Narrative)*. Ed. Hayford and Sealts. Chicago: University of Chicago Press, 1962.

———. *Clarel: A Poem and Pilgrimage in the Holy Land*. Ed. Bezanson. New York: Hendricks House, 1960.

———. *The Confidence-Man: His Masquerade*. Ed. Hayford, Parker, and Tanselle. Evanston and Chicago: Northwestern University Press and the Newberry Library, 1984.

———. *Israel Potter: His Fifty Years of Exile*. Ed. Hayford, Parker, and Tanselle. Evanston and Chicago: Northwestern University Press and the Newberry Library, 1982.

———. *Journal of a Visit to Europe and the Levant October 11, 1856–May 6, 1857*. Ed. Howard C. Horsford. Princeton: Princeton University Press, 1955.

———. *Journal of a Visit to London and the Continent By Herman Melville 1849–1850*. Ed. Eleanor Melville Metcalf. Cambridge: Harvard University Press, 1948.

———. *Mardi and a Voyage Thither*. Ed. Hayford, Parker, and Tanselle. Evanston and Chicago: Northwestern University Press and the Newberry Library, 1970.

———. *Moby-Dick: or the Whale*. Ed. Hayford, Parker, and Tanselle. Evanston and Chicago: Northwestern University Press and the Newberry Library, 1988.

———. *Omoo: A Narrative of Adventures in the South Seas*. Ed. Hayford, Parker, and Tanselle. Evanston and Chicago: Northwestern University Press and the Newberry Library, 1968.

———. *The Piazza Tales and Other Prose Pieces, 1839–1860*. Ed. Hayford, Parker, and Tanselle. Evanston and Chicago: Northwestern University Press and the Newberry Library, 1987.

———. *Pierre, or the Ambiguities*. Ed. Hayford, Parker, and Tanselle. Evanston and Chicago: Northwestern University Press and the Newberry Library, 1971.

———. *Redburn: His First Voyage*. Ed. Hayford, Parker, and Tanselle. Evanston and Chicago: Northwestern University Press and the Newberry Library, 1969.

———. *Typee: A Peep at Polynesian Life*. Ed. Hayford, Parker, and Tanselle. Evanston and Chicago: Northwestern University Press and the Newberry Library, 1968.

———. *White-Jacket: or the World in a Man-of-War*. Ed. Hayford, Parker, and Tanselle. Evanston and Chicago: Northwestern University Press and the Newberry Library, 1970.

Metcalf, Eleanor Melville. *Herman Melville: Cycle and Epicycle*. Cambridge: Harvard University Press, 1953.

Milder, Robert. "Commentary." In *The Endless, Winding Way in Melville:*

New Charts by Kring and Carey. Ed. Yannella and Parker. Glassboro: Melville Society, 1981.

Miller, Edwin Haviland. *Melville*. New York: George Braziller, 1975.

Mullahy, Patrick. *Oedipus Myth and Complex: A Review of Psychoanalytic Theory*. Introduction by Erich Fromm. New York: Hermitage Press, 1948.

Murray, Henry A. "Bartleby and I." In *Melville Annual 1965, a Symposium: "Bartleby the Scrivener."* Ed. Vincent. Kent, Ohio: Kent State University Press, 1966.

———. "In Nomine Diaboli." In *Moby-Dick: Centennial Essays*. Ed. Hillway and Mansfield. Dallas: Southern Methodist University Press, 1953.

———, ed. "Introduction" and "Explanatory Notes." In Herman Melville, *Pierre, or the Ambiguities*. New York: Hendricks House, 1962.

Murray, Henry A., Harvey Myerson, and Eugene Taylor. "Allan Melvill's By-Blow." *Melville Society Extracts* 61 (February 1985): 1–6.

Myerson, Joel. *Studies in the American Renaissance*. Charlottesville: University Press of Virginia, 1977, 1978, 1986.

National Archives. Dispatch No. 15, 1846. Washington, D.C.

New-York Historical Society letters and materials, 1989 (no date or month given).

Novak, Stephen E. Letter to author. 5 September 1985.

Overholser, Winfred, ed. "Editor's Introduction." In Isaac Ray, *A Treatise on the Medical Jurisprudence on Insanity*. Cambridge: Harvard University Press, 1962.

Parker, Hershel. "Historical Note." In Herman Melville, *Redburn: His First Voyage*. Ed. Hayford, Parker, and Tanselle. Evanston and Chicago: Northwestern University Press and the Newberry Library, 1969.

———, ed. Herman Melville, *The Confidence-Man: His Masquerade*. New York: W. W. Norton, 1971.

Perry, Dennis R. "'Ah, Humanity': Compulsive Neuroses in Melville's 'Bartleby.'" *Studies in Short Fiction* 24 (Fall 1987): 407–15.

Peterson, Audrey C. "Brain Fever in Nineteenth-Century Literature: Fact and Fiction." *Victorian Studies* 19 (1975–76): 445–64.

Pinel, Philippe. *A Treatise on Insanity*. Trans. D. D. Davis. Sheffield: Printed by W. Todd, for Cadell and Davis, London, 1806.

Prichard, James Cowles. *A Treatise on Insanity and Other Disorders Affecting the Mind*. London: Sherwood, Gilbert and Piper, 1835.

———. *On the Different Forms of Insanity in Relation to Jurisprudence*. London: Hippolyte Bailliere, 1842.

———. "Insanity." In *The Cyclopaedia of Practical Medicine*. Ed. Forbes, Tweedie, and Conolly. London: Sherwood, Gilbert and Piper, 1833.

Puett, Amy Elizabeth. "Melville's Wife: A Study of Elisabeth Shaw

Melville." Ph.D. dissertation, Northwestern University, 1969.

Pullin, Faith, ed. *New Perspectives on Melville*. Kent, Ohio: Kent State University Press, 1978.

Putzel, Max. "The Source and the Symbols of Melville's 'Benito Cereno.'" *American Literature* 34 (May 1962): 191–206.

Quen, Jacques M., M.D. "Introduction." In Isaac Ray, *Contributions to Mental Pathology*, 1873. Repr. Delmar, N.Y., 1973.

Quirk, Tom. *Melville's Confidence Man: From Knave to Knight*. Columbia: University of Missouri Press, 1982.

Rauch, Frederich H. *Psychology, or, a View of the Human Soul: Including Anthropology*. 1841. Repr. Delmar, N.Y.: Scholars' Facsimiles and Reprints, 1975.

Ray, Isaac. *Contributions to Mental Pathology*, 1873. Introduction by Jacques M. Quen, M.D. Repr. Delmar, N.Y.: Scholars' Facsimiles and Reprints, 1973.

———. *A Treatise on the Medical Jurisprudence of Insanity*. Boston: Charles C. Little and James Brown, 1838.

Rogin, Michael Paul. *Subversive Genealogy: The Politics and Art of Herman Melville*. New York: Alfred A. Knopf, 1983.

Roper, Gordon. "Historical Note." In Herman Melville, *Omoo: A Narrative of Adventures in the South Seas*. Ed. Hayford, Parker, and Tanselle. Evanston and Chicago: Northwestern University Press and the Newberry Library, 1968.

Rothman, David J. *The Discovery of the Asylum: Social Order and Disorder in the New Republic*. Boston: Little, Brown and Company, 1971.

Runden, John P. "Columbia Grammar School: An Overlooked Year in the Lives of Gansevoort and Herman Melville." *Melville Society Extracts* 46 (May 1981): 1–3.

Saunders, Brian. "Facing the Fire at Home: Redburn's 'Inland Imagination.'" *Studies in the Novel* 17 (Winter 1985): 350–70.

Schopenhauer, Arthur. *The World as Will and Idea*. 3 vols. Trans. R. B. Haldane and J. Kemp. London: Routledge and Kegan Paul, 1883.

Sealts, Merton M., Jr. "Historical Note." In Herman Melville, *The Piazza Tales and Other Prose Pieces: 1839–1860*. Ed. Hayford, Parker, and Tanselle. Evanston and Chicago: Northwestern University Press and the Newberry Library, 1987.

———. "Innocence and Infamy: *Billy Budd, Sailor*." In *A Companion to Melville Studies*. Ed. John Bryant. New York: Greenwood Press, 1986.

———. *Melville's Reading: Revised and Enlarged Edition*. Columbia: University of South Carolina Press, 1988.

———. "A Second Supplementary Note to *Melville's Reading* (1966)." *Harvard Library Bulletin* 27 (1979): 330–35.

Shepard, Gerald W. "Pierre's Psyche and Melville's Art." *ESQ: A Journal of the American Renaissance* 30 (Summer 1984):83–98.

Shneidman, Edwin S. "Some Psychological Reflections on Herman Melville." *Melville Society Extracts* 64 (November 1985):7–9.

Skultans, Vieda. *Madness and Morals: Ideas on Insanity in the Nineteenth Century*. London and Boston: Routledge and Kegan Paul, 1975.

Smith, Henry Nash. "The Madness of Ahab." *Yale Review* 66 (Autumn 1976):14–32.

———. "The Madness of Ahab." In *Democracy and the Novel: Popular Resistance to Classic American Writers*. New York: Oxford University Press, 1978.

Staats, Armin. "Melville—*Moby-Dick*." In *Der Amerikanische Roman Von den Anfängen bis zur Gegenwart*. Ed. Hans-Joachim Lang. Dusseldorf, 1972.

Stark, John. "Melville, Lemual Shaw, and 'Bartleby.'" In *Bartleby the Inscrutable: A Collection of Commentary on Herman Melville's Tale 'Bartleby the Scrivener.'* Ed. M. Thomas Inge. Hamden, Conn.: Archon Books, 1979.

State Hospital, Medical Records Department. Letter to author. 17 October 1985. Harrisburg, Pa.

Stone, William L. *Matthias and His Impostures*. New York: Harper and Brothers, 1835.

Thorp, Willard. "Historical Note." In Herman Melville, *White-Jacket: or the World in a Man-of-War*. Ed. Hayford, Parker, and Tanselle. Evanston and Chicago: Northwestern University Press and the Newberry Library, 1970.

Titus, David K. "Herman Melville at the Albany Academy." *Melville Society Extracts* 42 (May 1980):4–10.

Upham, Thomas C. *Outlines of Imperfect and Disordered Mental Action*. New York: Harper and Brothers, 1840.

Vanderhaar, M. M. "A Re-examination of 'Benito Cereno.'" *American Literature* 40 (May 1968):179–91.

Vincent, Howard P. *The Tailoring of Melville's White-Jacket*. Evanston: Northwestern University Press, 1970.

Warren, Robert Penn, ed. "Introduction." In his *Selected Poems of Herman Melville*. New York: Random House, 1970.

Webster's Third New International Dictionary of the English Language Unabridged. Springfield: Mass.: Merriam-Webster, 1981.

Webster, Noah. *An American Dictionary of the English Language*. New York: Harper and Brothers, 1846.

Weiner, Susan, and William J. Weiner. "Allan Melvill's Death: A Misdiagnosis." *Melville Society Extracts* 67 (September 1986):9–11.

Weisberg, Richard H. "The Creative Use of Statutes for Subjective Ends: The Case of *Billy Budd, Sailor*." In *The Failure of the Word: The*

Protagonist as Lawyer in Modern Fiction. New Haven: Yale University Press, 1984.

Withim, Phil. "*Billy Budd*: Testament of Resistance." *Modern Language Quarterly* 20 (June 1959): 115–27.

Wolfe, H. Scott. Letter to author. 7 February 1989.

Wright, Nathalia. "Melville and 'Old Burton,' with 'Bartleby' as an Anatomy of Melancholy." *Tennessee Studies in Literature* 15 (1970): 1–13.

———. *Melville's Use of the Bible*. Durham, N.C.: Duke University Press, 1949.

Yannella, Donald, and Hershel Parker, eds. *The Endless, Winding Way in Melville: New Charts by Kring and Carey*. Glassboro: Melville Society, 1981.

Zilboorg, Gregory, M.D., and collab. George W. Henry, M.D. *A History of Medical Psychology*. New York: W. W. Norton, 1941.

Zoellner, Robert. *The Salt-Sea Mastodon: A Reading of Moby-Dick*. Berkeley: University of California Press, 1973.

INDEX

Abulia (aboulia), definition of, 91

Acushnet, 9, 12, 18, 21, 56, 76; and Captain Pease, 9; and Melville's education, 138

Adler, George J., 50–51, 56, 57, 148 n.4; and Bloomingdale Asylum, 83

Admiral Nelson (*Billy Budd, Sailor*), 132–133, 134

Agoraphobia, 51, 153 n.12; definition of, 148 n.4

Ahab (*Moby-Dick*), 58, 67–73; compared to "Bartleby the Scrivener's," Bartleby, 104; compared to "Benito Cereno's" Babo, 108; and delirium, 4; and insanity, xi, 19, 30, 56; Melville's conception of, 150 n.38; and monomania, 16, 54; and Perth, 59–60

Albany Argus, 20

Albany Microscope, 20

Albion, 94

Alcoholism, 22, 24, 38–39, 46, 60, 140

American Journal of Insanity, 103

Anatomy of Melancholy (Burton), 104

Arcturion, 29

Arrowhead (family farm), 55, 57, 74, 75, 77, 83, 94; and *Pierre*, 78–79; as possible site for a state hospital, 111; and sale to Allan Melville, 123

Asthenia, 10, 106

Asylums, 7, 51, 82–83, 111–112, 114, 129, 139, 151 n.18

Babo ("Benito Cereno"), xi, 104, 106, 107–108; as viewed by Captain Delano, 107

Bartleby ("Bartleby the Scrivener"), xi–xii, 100–101, 102–104, 153 n.12; and Melville's friend, Fly, 100

"Bartleby the Scrivener," 38, 97; and Bartleby, 100–101, 102–104; and insanity, 100; and Nippers, 101, 102, 104; and Turkey, 38, 101–102, 104

Battle-Pieces, 123, 124

Bayle, Pierre, as influence on Melville, 72

Bellipotent, 127, 133; resemblance to an asylum, 129

"The Bell-Tower," 124

Bembo (*Omoo*), 9, 25–26

"Benito Cereno," 97, 104–108; and Atuful, 104; and Babo, 104, 106, 107–108; and Captain Delano, 105–107, 108; and Don Benito Cereno, 104, 105–107, 108; and Francesco, 104; and Lecbe, 104; and the *San Dominick*, 104, 105, 108

Bentley, Richard, 33, 77–78

Berthoff, Warner, 21

Billson, James, 124

Billy Budd (*Billy Budd, Sailor*), xii, 127–129, 130, 131–132, 133–134; and the drumhead court, 131–132

Billy Budd, Sailor, xiii, 122–135;

Billy Budd, Sailor (*continued*)
and Admiral Nelson, 132–133, 134; and the *Bellipotent*, 127, 129; and Billy Budd, 127–129, 130, 131–132, 133–134; and Captain Vere, 127, 129–134; and Claggart, 127–129, 130–131, 133; and father-son relationships, 126; and the *Rights of Man*, 127; and the Surgeon, 129–130, 131; use of asylums, 114
Bloomingdale Asylum, 7, 51, 83
Bok, Edward, 136
Boston Anthenaeum, 32
Boston Post, 94
Brain fever, in *The Confidence-Man*, 120–121, 154 n.21
Brainwashing, and Benito Cereno, 107
Brigham, Amariah, 14, 28, 38, 40, 48; study of unconscious mind, 86; views of insanity, 84
Brown, Oliver P., 37
Burroughs, W. C., 14
Butler, John, 84
Byron, George Gordon, 54, 137

Calenture, 121
Captain Delano ("Benito Cereno"), 105–107, 108
Captain Riga (*Redburn*), 35–36, 38, 40, 48; as compared to Oliver P. Brown, 37
Captain Vere (*Billy Budd, Sailor*), xiii, 127, 129–134, 155 n.19
Carlyle, Thomas, xii, 54, 72
Carus, Carl, 86; layers of the unconscious, 87, 89
Catalepsy, 107
Cervantes, Miguel, 114
Charlemont (*The Confidence-Man*), 109, 118–119

Charles and Henry, 9, 12
China Aster (*The Confidence-Man*), 109, 112, 118, 119–120
Claggart (*Billy Budd, Sailor*), xi, xiii, 127–129, 130–131; death of, 133
Clarel, 124, 134–135; characters affected by instability, 125–126
Class history, 41, 141
"Cock-A-Doodle-Doo!," 97; and monomania, 98
Coleridge, Samuel Taylor, xii, 54, 137
The Confidence-Man, xiii, 109–121; and Charlemont, 109, 118–119; and Charles Noble, 116–117; and China Aster, 109, 112, 118, 119–120; and Colonel Moredock, 109, 117; and the *Fidèle*, 109, 110; and Goneril, 109, 114–115; and the Harpe brothers, 113; and the herb-doctor, 115–116; as influenced by Melville's family life, 112; and Johnny Ringman, 109; reviews of, 122; and the "soldier of fortune," 116; and terms identifying abnormality in, 109; and the Titan, 109; use of asylums, 114; and Winsome, 116–118; and the wooden-legged man, 114
Conolly, James, 14, 48; study of unconscious mind, 86
Consciousness, 128–129; and Arthur Schopenhauer, 128
Constitution, 9, 10
The Contemporary Review, 124

Dana, Richard Henry, Jr., 54
Debility, definition of, 9–10; modern term for, 106
Delirium, 4, 28, 35; definition of, 144 n.12
Delirium Tremens, 12, 35, 39

Delirium tremens, 38–39, 46, 148 n.16; as identified in the *Pittsfield Sun*, 112

Depravity, definition of, 128

Depression, 65–66; and Herman Melville, 56, 125; and Maria Melvill, 5

Dickens, Charles, 40

Dillingham, William B., 107, 108, 155 n.19

Dolly, 18, 22

Don Benito Cereno ("Benito Cereno"), 105–107, 108; and insanity, 104

Duyckinck, Evert, death of, 126; friendship with Melville, 74; library of, 13; *Literary World*, xi, 52, 56–57; Melville letter to, 20, 34, 51, 56–57

Elijah (*Moby-Dick*), 58, 60–61, 73; speech of, 63–64

"The Encantadas," 97, 98–100; and Dog-King, 99; and Oberlus, 99–100

Epilepsy, 10, 116

Esquirol, E., 14, 16, 48, 49, 70

Essays on Physiognomy (Lavater), 29

Fictional worlds, xiii

Fidèle, 109; passengers of, 110–111, 113–114

Fly, Eli James Murdock, 8, 76, 83, 100, 112–113

Foster, Elizabeth, 27

Freud, Sigmund, and analyses, xii; and the unconscious mind, 139

Gabriel (*Moby-Dick*), 61–62; and delirium, 4; and insanity, 56; and monomania, 16, 60; speech of, 64

Gansevoort, Herman, 3

Gansevoort, Maria, 7, 33

Gansevoort, Peter, 3, 5, 11, 100; death of, 126; and loan to Allan Melvill, 119; and payment of *Clarel* publication, 124

Gansevoort, Stanwix, 7

Gardner, Augustus Kinsley, 52, 148 n.5, 149 n.7

Gibberish, definition of, 64

Gilman, William H., 37

Glendinning, Mr. (*Pierre*), 79, 80; as compared to China Aster (*The Confidence-Man*), 120

Glendinning, Mrs. Mary (*Pierre*), xii, 79, 80; and Maria Melvill, 81

Goethe, Johann Wolfgang von, 86

Goneril (*The Confidence-Man*), 109, 114–115

Good, John Mason, 12; and brain fever, 120–121

Gothic romances, 54, 78

Graham's Magazine, 94

Greene, Toby, 9

Hallucination, 63, 67

Harpers (publishers), 74, 77, 78, 95

Harper's Family Library, 12–13

Harper's Monthly Magazine, 97

Hartley, David, 13, 28

"Hawthorne and His Mosses," 54

Hawthorne, Nathaniel, and Agatha Robertson story, 95; effects of environment on characters, 40; friendship with Melville, 7, 54, 56, 57, 122; and *The House of the Seven Gables*, 86; influence on Melville's pieces, 35, 55, 75–76, 79; and *Pierre*, 78, 94; and *The Scarlet Letter*, 86; and speech of characters, 139–140; and the unconscious mind, 70, 86

Hawthorne, Sophia, 77

Hayford, Harrison, 24, 25, 118, 135

Heflin, Wilson, 72, 145 n.8

Heinroth, Johann, 14

Higgins, Brian, and Hershel Parker, 75–76, 86

Highlander, 37, 38, 39, 44

Hoadley, John, 28, 124, 125; death of, 126

Hoffman, Charles Fenno, xi, 34

Holmes, Oliver Wendell, 111

The House of the Seven Gables (Hawthorne), 86

Howard, Leon, xiii, 1–2; and Augustus Kinsley Gardner, 52; and Melville, 56, 111; and Melville's techniques, 140–141; on *Omoo*, 24; and *Omoo*'s Bembo, 9; on *Typee*, 18, 22, 25.

"Hume's on Suicide," 120

"Hyperborean regions," 91

Hypobulia, 91

Hypochondriasis (Hypochondria), 106, 107; as viewed by Prichard, 116

Illusion, 67

Insanity, xi–xiii, 51, 56, 60, 76; and Abner Rogers, 16, 52–53; and "adjudicatory 'insanity'" and *Billy Budd*'s Vere, 132; and Allan Melvill, 2; and the *American Journal of Insanity*, 103; and "Bartleby the Scrivener's" Bartleby, 103; and "Benito Cereno," 104; and *Billy Budd, Sailor*, 127; causes of, 141; and *The Confidence-Man*'s Goneril, 114–115, Harpe brothers, 113, and Moredock, 117; definitions of in *The Confidence-Man*, 120; and delirium, 4; and "The Encantadas," 99; and *Fidèle* passengers, 110–111; and Gan-

sevoort Melvill, 7; and Henry Melvill, 7, 56; and mammalian insanity, 58; and *Mardi*, 27–28; and the medical and surgical journal of the frigate *United States*, 9; Melville's initial fictional interest in, 138–139; and Melville's short stories, 97; and *Moby-Dick*, 57; and *Moby-Dick*'s Gabriel, 64; and *Omoo*, 24–27; and phrenology, 28; and physiognomy, 28–29; and *Pierre*'s Isabel, 82–83, Mr. Glendinning, 80, and Pierre, 85, 91, 92; and the *Pittsfield Sun*, 112; and *Redburn*, 34, 35, 39, 40; and speech, 63–65; synonyms for, 69; texts on, 12–15; and *Typee*, 19; as viewed by Augustus Kinsley Gardner, 52; as viewed by scientists, 84; and *White-Jacket*, 45, 46, 48

Irving, Washington, 35

Isabel Banford (*Pierre*), 79–80, 81–83, 84–85, 88, 89; and "Benito Cereno" character, 105

Ishmael (*Moby-Dick*), 57, 66–67, 71–73; as compared to *Pierre*'s Isabel, 82; and depression, 65–66; and Elijah, 60–61; on human madness, 69

Israel Potter, 14, 25, 97, 111; and lack of insanity in, 141–142

Jackson (*Redburn*), 19, 34, 35–36, 37, 39–40, 44, 48, 63; as compared to *The Confidence-Man*'s Goneril, 115

Jackson, Robert, 37

Jeroboam, 58, 61–62, 64

Jimmy (*Typee*), 19, 22, 25

"Jimmy Rose," 97

Johnson, Surgeon William, of the *United States*, 46–47

Julia, 23, 24, 25, 27

Jung, Carl, and the collective unconscious, 71, 90, 150n.30; and the personal unconscious, 89, 139

Kemble, Frances, 115
Kleim, Andrew, murder trial of, 20
Krakens, 75, 77, 79, 138

Language, and Melville's characters, 139–140
Lansing, Catherine, 125
Lansingburgh Academy, 11
Lansingburgh Democratic Press, 20
Leviathan, 26
Levy, Leonard W., 53
Leyda, Jay, 143n.7; on Gansevoort Melville, 144n.15; on the twisted mind, 7
Life history, and characterization, 21, 22, 39–40, 42, 141
"The Lightning-Rod Man," 97, 98
Literary World, xi, 52, 57
Littell's Living Age, 146n.4
Long Ghost, Dr. (*Omoo*), 12, 23; and Captain Crash, 26, 27
Lucy (*Pierre*), 79–80, 88–99; and Mrs. A.M.A., 82
Lucy Ann, 9, 12, 24; and *Omoo's* Bembo, 9, 25

McLane, Ambassador, on Gansevoort Melville, 6
McLean Asylum, 83
McNaghten rules, 52–53
Mania, 4, 15; and epilepsy, 10; and hypochondriac mania, 116; and moral mania, 38
Mania-a-potu, 46, 148n.16
Mardi, xiii, 27–31; and Azzageddi, 30; and Babbalanja, 30; character influences in, 27; and Dox-

odox, 30; and Hivohitee, 30–31; influences for, 12, 13; and insanity, 27; and Jarl, 29; and King Peepi, 31; and Media, 29, 30; and Mohi, 30; and monomania, 29; and Oh Oh, 30; and phrenology and physiognomy, 28; reviews of, 32–33; and Samoa, 28; and Taji, 29–30; and Yillah, 29

Master-at-Arms Bland (*White-Jacket*), 9, 19, 47–48; compared to *Billy Budd's* Claggart, 128; and insanity, 44, 46; as a literary model, 43

Mather, Frank J., Jr., 136
Melancholy, 12, 35, 47, 53; and "Bartleby the Scrivener" characters, 104; and Pierre, 89; and Redburn, 40; and *Typee's* Tommo, 147n.9
Melvill, Allan, 1–5, 11, 151n.14; character resemblance in *The Confidence-Man,* 118–120; death of, 2–3, 7; insanity, 2, 137; resembling *Pierre's* Mr. Glendinning, 79, 80
Melvill, Henry, 7, 56
Melvill, Maj. Thomas, 7
Melvill, Maria, 1, 2, 4–5, 8, 79, 81, 94; concern for Herman's health, 96; death of, 124; and depression, 5, 7
Melvill, Priscilla, 7, 79; and *Pierre's* Isabel, 81
Melvill, Robert, 54, 76
Melvill, Thomas, 3, 8, 76, 80; death of, 126; visit by Melville and Fly, 112
Melville, Allan, 100; death of, 126
Melville, Augusta, 76–77; death of, 126; thoughts on Herman, 124
Melville, Elizabeth Shaw, 27, 33, 54, 55–56, 79, 96; and death of

Melville, Elizabeth Shaw (*continued*)
Malcolm, 124; letter to Catherine
Lansing, 125; memoirs by, 111,
125

Melville, Frances, 126

Melville, Gansevoort, 1, 100,
144 n.15; death of, 6; illness of,
6; political career of, 5–6

Melville, Helen, 76–77, 96; death
of, 126

Melville, Herman, and asylum
awareness, 83; compared to *Billy
Budd*'s Vere, 134; and depression,
56, 125; as district inspector,
123–124, 154 n.2; and doubts of
sanity, 96, 125; education of, 8,
11–12, 144 n.1; and family, 1–8,
17–18, 32–34, 54, 55–56, 74–
77, 79, 95–96, 100–111, 122–
124, 125, 137–138; and family
religion, 2; and fears of the
"twisted mind," 7–8, 56; and fictional techniques, 140–141; and
finances, 55, 77–78, 96, 111–112,
123, 124; and Galena, Illinois,
trip, 8, 83; and George J. Adler,
50–51; and historical periods,
xii; influence of Pittsfield on, 76;
marriage of, 13; and Nathaniel
Hawthorne, 7, 54–55, 56, 57,
75, 95, 122; recognized works of,
136–137; sciatica attack of, 111;
and the sea, 8, 9, 12, 37, 43–44,
50, 52, passim; and Shakespeare's characters, 54; and
study of unconscious mind,
86–87; and teenage jobs, 8

Melville, Kate, 96

Melville, Lucy, 7

Melville, Malcolm, 33, 52, 96,
134–135; death of, 124

Melville, Stanwix, 77, 96, 125, 135;
death of, 126

Milton, John, xii, 54, 114, 137;
Satan and *Billy Budd*'s Claggart,
128

Misanthropic monomania, 100

Moby-Dick, xiii, 35, 50–73; and
Ahab, 54, 56, 58, 59–60, 67–73;
and alcoholism, 38; and Bildad,
58–59; and Captain Mayhew,
64; compared to *The Confidence-
Man,* 109; and Elijah, 58, 60–61,
63–64, 73; fictional world of, 58;
and Gabriel, 56, 60, 61–62, 64;
Hawthorne's admiration for, 75;
insane speech in, 63–64; and
Ishmael, 57, 58–59, 60–61, 62,
63, 65, 66–67; and madness,
57–58; and monomania, 16,
60–63; and moral insanity, 63,
66, 68; and the *Penny Cyclopaedia,* 14; and the *Pequod,* 57;
and Perth, 38, 59; and Pip, 60,
62–63, 64–65; and Queequeg,
65, 66; and Radney, 59; reviews
of, 78; Shakespeare's influence
on, 72; and Starbuck, 68; and
Steelkit, 59; and Stiggs, 59; and
study of unconscious mind, 70–
72, 87; Upham's influence on,
72–73; and the white whale, 58

Monomania, 13, 15, 16, 19–20, 35,
49, 53, 54; and Abner Rogers,
16; and Ahab, 59–60, 66, 68–
70, 71–72, 73; and "Bartleby the
Scrivener's" Bartleby, 104; and
"Benito Cereno's" Babo, 107,
108; and *Billy Budd*'s Claggart,
127–128, and Vere, 134; charac-
teristics of, 104; and *Clarel* characters, 125–126; and "Cock-
A-Doodle-Doo!," 98; and *The
Confidence-Man*'s Goneril, 115,
Moredock, 117, and wooden-
legged man, 114; and "The

Encantadas," 99; and "The Encantadas'" Oberlus, 99; and epilepsy, 10; and Gabriel, 61–62; and George J. Adler, 51; and hypochondria, 116; and *Mardi,* 29–30; Melville's awareness of, 137; in *Moby-Dick,* 16; and *Moby-Dick's* Perth, 59, and Radney, 59; and *Omoo's* characters, 25; and *Pierre's* Isabel, 83, 84, and Mary Glendinning, 81; and Pierre's trance, 92–93; and Pip, 62–63, 64–65; and poverty, 42–43; and *Redburn's* Jackson, 39; and *Typee's* characters, 21; and the *United States,* 9; in *White-Jacket,* 16; and *White-Jacket's* Cuticle, 47

Moon-calf (as a colloquial term), 109, 113

Moral insanity, 13, 15–16, 22, 25, 31, 35, 48–49, 66; and Abner Rogers, 53; and "Bartleby the Scrivener's" Bartleby, 104, Nippers, 102, and Turkey, 101–102; and Benito Cereno, 107; and *Billy Budd's* Claggart, 128, and Vere, 134; and *The Confidence-Man's* Goneril, 115, "soldier of fortune," 116, Winsome, 118, and wooden-legged man, 114; definition of, 15; and "The Encantadas," 99; and hypobulia, 91; and hypochondria, 116; and "Jimmy Rose's" Jimmy, 97–98; and Master-at-Arms Bland, 48; and *Moby-Dick's* Ahab, 68, Elijah, 61, Ishmael, 66, 67, Perth, 60, and Pip, 62; and the *Pequod* crew, 59; and *Pierre's* Isabel, 83, 84, and Mrs. Glendinning, 81; and poverty, 42–43; and *Redburn's* Jackson, 39; and speech of patients, 149 n.23; and the *United*

States, 9; and *White-Jacket's* Cuticle, 47, and Scriggs, 45

Moredock, Colonel (*The Confidence-Man*), 109, 117

Morewood, Sara, 74, 77

Murray, Henry A., 81–82, 86, 90; and the "Hyperborean regions," 91; and the unconscious mind, 87, 139

Neversink, 9, 24, 38, 44, 45, 106; compared to the *Fidèle,* 110

Newgate Calendar, 12, 43, 145 n.3

New York Custom-House, 123–124, 125, 137

New York Herald, 19–20, 112

New York Society Library, 12, 13, 28, 54, 72, 137; and Schopenhauer volumes, 128

Nippers ("Bartleby the Scrivener"), 101, 102, 104

Nourse, Dr. Amos, 77

Nukuheva, 17, 19, 22, 23, 24, 27

Observations on Man (Hartley), 13

Omoo, xii–xiii, 23–27; and alcoholism, 38; and Bembo, 25–26; and Bungs, 24; and Captain Crash, 26–27; character portrayal in, 37; and Chips, 24; compared with "The Encantadas," 99; and Dr. Long Ghost, 12, 23, 26, 27; fictional world of, 23; insanity in, 19, 24–25, 31; and Jermin, 24, 38; and Kory-Kory, 27; and Mad Jack, 24; and Queen Pomaree, 25; and Rope Yarn (Ropey), 25; and Salem, 24; and Sydney Ben, 26; and Tanee, 25; and Varvy, 24

Pease, Captain, of the *Acushnet,* 9, 19, 21

Penny Cyclopaedia, and delirium tre- mens, 38; as Melville's resource on insanity, xii, 14–15, 84, 137; on monomania, 16; and moral insanity, 15, 66; and *Redburn*, 35, 37, 48

Pequod, compared to the *Fidèle*, 110; the crew and monomania, 68–69; and *Moby-Dick*'s Captain Mayhew, 64, Ishmael, 66–67, and Pip, 62–63; as a "tranced ship," 57–58

Perth (*Moby-Dick*), and mono- mania, 59–60

Phrenology, 12, 13, 28, 139; and portrayal of Claggart, 128

Physiognomy, 12, 28; and *Pierre*, 87

The Piazza Tales, 122

Pierre (*Pierre*), xi–xii, 19, 30, 79–80, 81, 85, 86–93; and the Apostles, 90, 91; and Delly, 89, 90; and the Enceladus vision, 91–92; and hypobulia, 91; and insanity, 85; and Isabel, 81–83, 84–85, 88, 89, 90; and Lucy, 88–89, 90; and unconscious mind, 86, 87

Pierre, 74–93; causes of insanity, 84–85; compared to *The Confi- dence-Man*, 109; and Delly, 89, 90; effect on Melville's family, 81; and Glen Stanly, 7; and insanity, 14; and Isabel, 79–80, 81–83, 84–85, 88, 89; and Lucy, 79–80, 82, 88–89; and mental instabil- ity, 6–7; and Mr. Glendinning, 79, 80; and Mrs. Glendinning, 79, 80, 81; and physiognomy, 29; and Pierre, 79–80, 81, 85, 86–93; and poetic analysis, 85–86; reviews of, 94–96; and Saddle Meadows, 79, 81; and the

unconscious mind, 70, 86–87; use of asylums, 114

Pinel, Ph., 14, 15

Pip (*Moby-Dick*), and monomania, 60, 62–63; speech of, 64–65

Pittsfield Sun, 112

Plato, 27; and depravity, 128

Poe, Edgar Allen, 35, 70, 94; and *The Confidence-Man*'s Winsome, 118; and speech of characters, 139–140

Poor House Lunatic Asylum, 52

Poverty, in *Redburn*, 41–42

President, 10

Prichard, James C., 40, 61; and awareness of conditions, 107; and description of trance, 92; and hallucinations, 63; on mono- mania, 16, 39, 47, 60, 70; and moral insanity, 15, 22, 39; study of unconscious mind, 86; and *A Treatise on Insanity and Other Dis- orders Affecting the Mind*, 14, 15, 66, 145 n.15, 149 n.23; views of hypochondria, 116; views of in- sanity, 14, 48–49, 84

Psychiatric Dictionary, on delirium, 4

Putnam's, 96–97, 111

Quen, Jacques M., 53

Rabelais, François, 27, 32

Rauch, Frederich, 86

Ray, Isaac, 40, 69; and the Abner Rogers' trial, 53; on Allan Mel- vill, 4; and the *American Journal of Insanity*, 103; and delirium tre- mens, 38; on monomania, 16, 70; on moral insanity, 15, 42; on phrenology, 28; study of uncon- scious mind, 86; and *A Treatise on Medical Jurisprudence of In-*

sanity, 4, 48, 53, 144 n.12; views of insanity, 14, 48–49, 84

Redburn, Wellingborough (*Redburn*), 36–37, 40, 41; and Jackson, 39

Redburn, xii, xiii, 3, 33–43, 147 n.5; and alcoholism, 38; and Captain Riga, 35–36, 37, 38–40, 48; compared to *White-Jacket*, 44; and Greenlander, 37; and the *Highlander*, 8; and insanity, 19, 31, 76, 79; and Irishman Blunt, 37; and Jackson, 34, 35–36, 37, 39–40, 63; and Max the Dutchman, 37; and the *Penny Cyclopaedia*, 14; royalties from, 55; and the *St. Lawrence*, 12; and Wellingborough Redburn, 36–37, 39, 40, 41

Rights of Man, 127

Robertson, Agatha, 95

Robinson, Professor Edward, 20

Roderick Random (Smollett), 47

Rogers, Abner, 16; and murder trial of, 16, 52–53

Russell, W. Clark, 124

Salt, H. S., 124

San Dominick, 104, 105, 108

The Scarlet Letter (Hawthorne), 86

Schizophrenia, 103

Schopenhauer, Arthur, 86; and character contribution, 128

Sealts, Merton M., Jr., on *Billy Budd*, 126, 135; review of *Pierre*, 95

Shakespeare, William, xii, 27, 32, 54, 55, 76, 78; and *The Confidence-Man*'s Goneril, 115; Iago and *Billy Budd*'s Claggart, 128; influence in *The Confidence-Man*, 114; influence on Ahab's charac-

ter, 72; and Melville's sensitivities to insanity, 137

Shaw, Lemuel, 3, 7, 16, 52–53, 55, 95, 122

Simms, William Gilmore, 95

Slavery, and "Benito Cereno's" Babo, 108

Smith, Henry Nash, 15, 66

Somnambulism, 20; and Benito Cereno, 107

Southampton, 50, 52

Southern Quarterly Review, 95

Springfield Republican, 112

St. Lawrence, 8, 12, 37, 43

Staats, Armin, 66

Stedman, Edmund Clarence, 136

Stone, William L., 20, 146 n.4

Suicide and suicidal ideation, 25, 38; as identified in the *Pittsfield Sun*, 112; and *Mardi*'s Taji, 30; and *Moby-Dick*'s Stiggs, 59; and *Pierre*'s Isabel, 84

Surgeon Cuticle (*White-Jacket*), compared to *Mardi*'s Doxodox, 30; compared to *Moby-Dick*'s Ahab, 70; and insane speech of, 63; and insanity, 19, 44; as a literary model, 43; and monomania, 16

Thin red line (of insanity), 19, 24, 117; and *Billy Budd*'s Vere, 135

Tic Douloureux ("Tic Doloreux and Neuralgia"), 112; definition of, 115

Tirrell, Albert J., murder trial of, 20

Tommo (*Typee*), 21, 22–23, 146 n.2, 147 n.9

Torpor, and Benito Cereno, 107

Trance, 91–93; hypnagogic, 67; Pierre's hallucinatory, 92

A Treatise on Insanity and Other Disorders Affecting the Mind (Prichard), 14, 15, 66, 145 n.15, 149 n.23

A Treatise on the Medical Jurisprudence of Insanity (Ray), 144 n.12

Turkey ("Bartleby the Scrivener"), 38, 101–102, 104

"Twisted mind," 76; and Melville's fear of, 56, 125, 134, 136

Typee, xii–xiii, 13, 17–23; and alcoholism, 38; and "The Bell-Tower," 124; and Captain Vangs, 19, 21; characterization in, 19, 37; compared to "The Encantadas," 99; compared to *Mardi*, 27; compared to *Redburn*, 37; and the English harbor pilot, 19, 21–22; fictional world of, 18–19; and Jimmy, 19, 22; and Karky, 19, 21, 23; and Mow-Mow, 19–21; and *Omoo* characters compare, 25; and Toby, 22, 23; and Tommo, 21, 22–23

Unconscious mind, 86–87, 90, 128–129, 139, 150 n.32, 152 n.20, 152 n.22; and Carl Jung, 89, 90, 150 n.30

United States, crew of, 10, 43–44; and delirium tremens, 38; Melville's time aboard, 9, 12, 17, 47; and Upham's book, 19, 72; and William Johnson, 46–47

Upham, Thomas, *Outlines of Imperfect and Disordered Mental Action*, 12–13, 19, 72–73

Vincent, Howard P., 9, 47

Warren, Robert Penn, 126

Weiner and Weiner, on Allan Melvill, 4

White-Jacket, 33, 35, 39, 43–49; and alcoholism, 46; and *Book of Nature*, 12; and Claret, 38, 46; fictional world of, xiii; and Jack Chase, 44; and Landless, 45; and Mad Jack, 38, 46; and Master-at-Arms Bland, 43, 44, 46, 47–48; and Nord, 44; and Quoin, 46; royalties from, 55; and Scriggs, 45, 46; and Surgeon Cuticle, 43, 44, 46–47; and the *United States*, 10; use of asylums, 114; use of *Penny Cyclopaedia* for, 14; and White Jacket, 44; and Williams, 44

Winsome (*The Confidence-Man*), 116–118

Withdrawal states, and Benito Cereno, 107

Woodward, S. B., 28

The World as Will and Idea (Schopenhauer), 128

Young Men's Association, 11

Zanoni, 75